THE HOW-TO-DO-IT
ENCYCLOPEDIA
OF PAINTING &
WALLCOVERING

BY BOB PERCIVAL

TAB **TAB BOOKS Inc.**
BLUE RIDGE SUMMIT, PA. 17214

FIRST EDITION

FIRST PRINTING

Library of Congress Cataloging in Publication Data

Percival, Bob.
  The how-to-do-it encyclopedia of painting and wallcovering.

  Includes index.
  1. House painting—Dictionaries. 2. Wall coverings—Dictionaries. 3. Do-it-yourself work—Dictionaries. I. Title.
TT320.P53 1982   698   82-5934
ISBN 0-8306-2460-0   AACR2
ISBN 0-8306-1460-5 (pbk.)

Contents

Introduction

Tom Sawyer knew how to paint. He had other people do it for him. Chances are you won't be so lucky.

House painting—both interior and exterior—and hanging wallcoverings are two major periodic repairs that face you as a homeowner. There are two reasons to paint or hang wallcoverings: the first is to keep your house looking its best. Beauty is not the only reason, though, for smoothing a skin of paint or paper over your dwelling. The new skin will also protect your walls, ceilings, and floors from the environment.

Each year the paint and coatings industry offers easier to use and more durable paint products. If Tom were painting his aunt's fence today, he probably would choose a coating other than whitewash. Perhaps he would settle on an oil-base stain or paint. He might even try one of the new latex stains. Each has a place on your paint dealer's shelves. It is often more difficult to select the proper coating for a job than it is to apply the coating.

Once you have decided to paint or hang a wallcovering you will ask yourself these questions:

—Should I choose a dark or light color?
—How about a mildewcide?
—Should I roll the paint or brush it on?
—Do I want a glossy, flat, or semigloss surface?
—What about spraying?
—How much paint will I need for the job?
—What if my paint peels unexpectedly after only one year?
—How do I clean up after the job?
—Can I paper the bathroom?
—Where should I begin?

The salesman at your local paint store will be able to answer some of these questions. Once you get the material home, though, you are on your own.

You will never get the job done if you are running down to the paint store every five minutes to ask questions. Pretend that this book is a salesman. Pick a topic that you have a question about, say, blistering.

Flip through Part 1 (it is arranged alphabetically by topic) until you reach *blistering*. Below the title you will find an illustrated and concise text explaining what blistering is, its common causes, and preventative measures.

Let's pick another topic—oil-base paints. Again, flip through Part 1 until you find *oil-base paint*. The illustrations and topic headings will help you through this explanation of oil-base paint.

There are more than 300 entries in this book covering topics such as painting interiors, painting exteriors, masonry, preparation, brushes, cleanup, hanging wallcovering, and strippable wallcoverings. Each entry will guide you step by step through the completion of even the most difficult job. At the end of some entries you will see more italicized references. These key words will steer you toward other related topics.

After you have used this book for a couple of painting and wallcovering jobs, you will be better than Tom Sawyer in every phase of painting except one—getting someone to help you. Only Tom can help with that one.

PART 1
PAINTING

ABRASION RESISTANCE

The ability of paint to withstand repeated rubbing without peeling or discoloring. Flat interior and exterior paints have little abrasion resistance. *Enamels, varnishes,* and *porch and floor paints* are designed for use on high traffic areas such as woodwork, floors, and doors. As a general rule, the glossier a paint, the higher its abrasion resistance.

See *Durability; Hardness; Paint, Choosing;* and *Toughness*.

ABRASIVES

Materials used for grinding, polishing, and shining softer substances. The most familiar application of abrasives is the rough side of sandpaper. Emery, sand, garnet, and Carborundum abrasives are glued to paper or cloth and used to sand wood or metals. Longer lasting synthetic abrasives such as silicon carbide and aluminum oxide are also available.

See *Sanding*.

ACOUSTIC PAINT

Usually a flat finish paint designed to cover acoustic materials without reducing the sound-absorbing qualities of their surfaces. When painting over acoustic surfaces like tiles, be careful not to fill in the holes. A good way to prevent this is to thin the paint slightly and use either a short nap roller or a lightly loaded brush.

ACRYLATE RESINS

A group of thermoplastic resins commonly used in transparent coatings. These resins are most often found marketed under the tradenames Lucite and Plexiglas.

See *Synthetic Resins*.

ACRYLIC RESINS

Transparent plastic substances used in such high quality plastics as Plexiglas. When added to paints such as *acrylic enamel* and *varnish*, they add long life and *flexibility* to the paint.

These resins are resistant to water and alkali and prevent further oxidation of the surfaces to which they are applied.

See *Enamel, Latex Paint, Oil-Base Paint,* and *Synthetic Resins.*

ACRYLIC VARNISH

Made with preoxidized resins that prevent further oxidation. They are useful on exterior wood that has been stained or left natural, when you want the personality of the wood to show through. Applied with a brush, acrylic varnishes afford good resistance to water and *alkali* but must be recoated every one or two years. These varnishes are especially useful on metals such as copper screens.

See *Acrylic Resins,* and *Varnishes.*

ADHESION

The ability of paint to stick to the surface to which it is applied. To increase adhesion and thereby reduce *peeling, cracking,* and *blistering,* prepare all surfaces carefully. Remove any grease, dirt, or loose paint before applying new coatings. A bonding agent like Bondo can be added to the paint in especially troublesome areas.

Follow the directions on the bonding agent carefully. The incorrect addition of this material will alter the characteristics of your paint. *Epoxy,* or two-component *paints,* have the highest bonding power of any coatings. They are virtually permanent once they have been applied. When painting over slick surfaces such as semigloss or glossy paints, sand the surface to provide a *tooth* for the topcoating.

See *Binders, Intercoat Adhesion,* and *Intercoat Peeling.*

AGGLOMERATION

A term used to describe the congealing of the pigment into lumps. A paint that has not been thoroughly mixed will often show signs of agglomeration. Paint that has set for an extended period of time on warehouse and paint store shelves will suffer this defect. In most cases, a thorough shaking on the mixer at the paint store should break up the lumps and suspend the pigments in the paint.

AIR-DRY

A coating should be allowed to dry by air. Some coatings—the enamel on your automobile, for example—require baking to cure properly. Coatings that air-dry will cure correctly when allowed to stand in contact with the atmosphere at temperatures ranging from 45 to 85 degrees Fahrenheit. The lower the *relative humidity* and the higher the temperature, the quicker these coatings will dry.

AIRLESS SPRAYERS

Paint spraying machines that force the paint through a nozzle and onto a surface without the use of air. There are two types of airless spray guns: electric and hydraulic. Originally created for industrial and professional use, airless spray equipment is now available for almost any home fix-up job. Check with your local rental store or paint dealer to see what is available for the job you have in mind.

Electric Airless Sprayers. These sprayers operate on current from ac outlets. Paint is fed to the nozzle from a cup attached at the hand piece. Electric airless sprayers are useful for small jobs such as painting a single room or refinishing furniture. See the illustration. They will handle most latex paints and the thinner oil-base coatings like shellac and varnish. Heavy oil-base paints like primers and topcoatings may require excessive thinning for use in an electric airless unit.

Airless Sprayers. Electric sprayers operate on 115-volt household current. They spray most of the thin paints and work best on small jobs (courtesy Wagner Spray Tech Corporation, Minneapolis, MN).

Hydraulic Airless Sprayers. Unlike an electric unit, this sprayer uses a compressor separate from the nozzle to force paint through a hose to the spray head and out of the nozzle tip. Hydraulic sprayers are more elaborate and able to handle higher volumes of heavier paint than small electric units. They are usually used only for exterior jobs. Oil-base primers and topcoatings can be sprayed—unthinned— through hydraulic airless units in addition to the lighter coatings mentioned earlier.

Hydraulic spraying can be dangerous. The pump of an airless spray can develop up to 3,000 pounds per square inch of pressure at the nozzle tip. The sprayed paint often reaches speeds approaching 200 miles per hour. This is enough force to inject paint through your skin. Wear long sleeves and a respirator when operating any spray gun.

If you or a helper are injured by being sprayed at close range with the gun, seek medical treatment immediately. The staff at a hospital emergency room will know how to treat paint poisoning more effectively and quickly than your family doctor.

Despite the apparent danger of airless spraying, this method can substantially reduce the time required to paint your home. Once your house has been prepared, a brush and roller job of several days may be reduced to a single day by spraying. The finish will be smoother than a conventional paint job.

See *Spraying Paint.*

ALKALI

A soluble salt or mixture of soluble salts. High alkali content in concrete blocks and masonry

Alkali. Alkali problems are caused when the alkaline materials in masonry products attack a paint.

5

present problems for painters. When painted over with the improper paint, the salts mix with the paint and form a crude soap that is not weatherproof. As the alkali-affected paint washes off, it causes *chalking, peeling,* and *flaking.* See the illustration. Alkali-induced damage may result in paint pigments turning green or yellow. Alkali readily attacks oil-base paints, but application of latex or rubber-base paints to alkali-prone areas will often combat the problem.

Alkali problems can be prevented if you allow new masonry or cinder block walls to age six months to a year before you apply the first coat of paint or sealer. It may be necessary to masonry walls with a light coat of *muriatic acid* to battle the alkaline condition. Alkali formation is often the result of water seepage, and this should be investigated. If water is leaking in through a below-grade wall or down the inside of a cinder block wall through a leaky roof, no amount of painting or combination of coatings will cure the problem. If the alkali problem is outside, a waterproof topcoating should be applied to prevent water from reaching the alkali-forming chemicals.

See *Efflorescence, Masonry, Moisture,* and *Preparation.*

ALKYD PAINTS

Many of today's oil-base paints are concocted from a combination of modified *linseed* or *soybean oils* and alkyd resins, which are thermoplastic or thermosetting *synthetic resins* that produce a fast-drying, tough paint film. Alkyd resins are used in many types of paint. The more common ones are glossy interior and exterior trim paints, porch and floor paints, varnishes, interior and exterior primers, and interior and exterior flat finishes. Each of these alkyd paints will be discussed in further detail later in this book.

All alkyd paints, except the new latex ones, require paint *thinner, mineral spirits,* or *solvent* for thinning and cleanup. Unlike other oil-based paints, alkyds often dry in less than eight hours. Unlike traditional oil-base paints, alkyds are odorless. Alkyds should be used only in well-ventilated areas.

Many people pass over the oil-base alkyds in favor of latex paints. Occasionally this misdirected emphasis on paint that is easy to clean and apply will result in an inferior job. Alkyd paints are preferred as a topcoating over paints of unknown type. Alkyd paint is the least likely to react with an unknown undercoating, and almost any paint will adhere to an alkyd primer. Alkyd paints can be brushed, rolled, or sprayed on like other paints.

Exterior Alkyds. Alkyd flat *exterior paints* adhere to and cover all surfaces well except unprimed masonry or metal. For these special cases, you will need to prime the metal or masonry with a suitable primer before applying an alkyd topcoating. Most paint salesmen will recommend a latex for masonry, although special alkyd paints can be bought for application to masonry.

Some alkyd flat exterior paints have a regulated, self-cleaning property known as *chalking.* The chalking chemicals produce a powder that lifts off dirt. The dirt can then be carried away by rain or a garden hose. For this reason, chalking paints come in white or light pastel shades and should not be applied to siding that is above a brick or masonry wall. Alkyd paints are the only ones that will stick to a chalking surface. Because alkyd paints produce a paint film that is impervious to water, they should not be used on areas subject to *blistering* caused by moisture seeping from within the wall. They will, however, cure many paint problems related to water penetrating the topcoating from the outside.

A new exterior alkyd latex paint combines the best properties of latex paint (easy cleanup, quick drying, and breathability) and alkyd paint (long lasting, tough finishes) into one paint. Some of these will outlast older exterior paints and may need repainting only every 8 to 10 years. Ask your paint dealer for more detailed information.

Interior Alkyds. Like exterior alkyds, interior alkyd paints are durable. They come in a wide range of finishes from glossy to flat and will wash more easily than latex coatings.

Interior alkyd paints will not adhere to bare masonry or plaster and should not be used on untreated drywall. On untreated plaster such as a patch, alkyd paints will flatten out and leave a blemish in your paint job. On untreated drywall, alkyd paint will raise a nap on the wall's paper covering, foiling all your best efforts at creating a smooth paint job. If you inadvertently apply an alkyd to bare drywall, the raised nap can be corrected by applying a latex primer and then repainting with an alkyd finish coat. Most interior alkyd paints will dry sufficiently for a second coat within 8 to 10 hours.

Dripless alkyd paints are so thick that they will not drip from brushes or rollers and are especially suited for painting ceilings and difficult to reach places. They cannot, however, be sprayed. Dripless alkyds are more expensive than latex or regular alkyds, and more paint is required to cover a given area.

Primers. Alkyd *primers* are best suited for use on raw wood. The oil in alkyd primers helps draw the paint into the pore space of the surface, and the oil acts as a mild preservative. Alkyd primers should not be used on drywall or new masonry. Like interior alkyd paint, alkyd primers will raise a nap on drywall. The oils in the primers will aggravate any alkali problems present in masonry.

Trim Paints. Alkyd trim paints are shinier than their latex counterparts. These paints are extremely tough and will stand up under heavy traffic and repeated washing. They are most often used on doors, jambs, window sashes, and handrails.

Like most trim paints, alkyds come in a variety of colors and finishes—glossy, semigloss, eggshell, and flat. The shiny finishes are preferred because they are easier to clean and resist water.

Varnishes. Alkyd varnishes provide a tough, durable finish for surfaces where you want the natural color and grain of the wood to show through. They are not as durable as regular alkyd paints. You may have to refinish varnished surfaces every two or three years. The warm, hand-rubbed appearance of these finishes often make the extra maintenance worthwhile.

ALLIGATORING

A paint failure that resembles the hide of an alligator. See the illustration. Alligatoring is usually an advanced stage of *checking*, which is often caused by allowing insufficient drying time between coats of paint or by thinning paint excessively. Applying an incompatible paint such as a flat latex over a semigloss alkyd will also encourage alligatoring. This problem is often found on old houses where an excessive buildup of paint prevents the paint film from expanding and contracting with the underlying wood.

Serious alligatoring allows water to penetrate to the wood; this promotes decay. All old paint must be removed by *scraping, sanding,* or using a paint remover. The bare wood should be allowed to dry thoroughly. Then paint it with a primer. Allow for drying again, and then apply a topcoat.

Alligatoring. A common cause of alligatoring is excessive paint buildup.

ALUMINUM PAINT

A metal-base paint. It is a mixture of powdered aluminum suspended in oil or an alkyd resin. Aluminum paint produces a shiny metallic finish of very durable quality and is especially suited to barn roofs, metal sheds, and guttering.

Some aluminum paints come as self-priming metal coatings in which the primer and topcoatings are mixed into one solution and applied with one application. Non-self-priming metal paints should be applied only to properly primed metal. Metal-based paints are most effectively applied with a brush and are cleaned with solvents for oil-base paints.

These paints are not recommended for sidewalls of a house. The paint traps moisture in the wood, promoting decay.

See *Metals*.

AMALGAMATORS

Special solvents designed to repair scratches in varnish finishes without revarnishing. The chemical action of the liquid softens the varnish, and it settles to a smooth surface. The varnish will reharden in a few days. If the patch is shinier than the surrounding varnish, it can be rubbed lightly with fine steel wool. This will dull the patch so that it matches the *sheen* of the surrounding area. Amalgamators will not work on badly damaged varnish surfaces where there is not enough varnish to flow together and form a patch.

See *Varnishes*.

AMBER

A brown or yellow-brown translucent color, associated with the fossil resin of the same name. In painting, amber is a common color used to tint paint. It is available as a universal colorant.

See *Colors.*

ANGULAR SHEEN

The shine visible on flat paints when viewed from an extreme angle. Viewing a wall in this manner will often make you aware of problems that may not be evident from a head-on view. An example is flat interior paint that has been applied over an improperly primed plaster patch. The patch will appear as a flat, or low sheen, area on the wall. If not treated by re-priming and re-topcoating, the patch may show up as a stain mark within a year.

ANTIFOAM

The paint will not bubble or foam during vigorous shaking. Antifouling chemicals are added to paints, especially latex-base paints, to prevent foaming. Excessive foaming may cause *bubbles* to form in a paint as it dries. Allow all paints to stand 30 minutes between stirring and application.

ANTIFOULING PAINT

Used on boat hulls to prevent marine animals and plants from attaching themselves to the boat. Older antifouling paints contain mercury or copper-base oxides as repellents. These materials may cause a greater rate of deterioration on iron and steel hulls. The best antifouling paints contain tin-base repellents.

Antifouling paints also come in two hardnesses—soft and racing. If your boat is docked for long periods and operated at low speeds, soft paint will offer the best protection. If your boat is operated frequently and at high speeds, consider using a racing paint. This paint dries harder and smoother than conventional antifouling paint.

See *Marine Paint.*

APPLICATORS

Painting devices that differ from brushes, rollers, and sprays. A dauber applicator is a piece of flat plastic or metal, ranging in size from a matchbook to a large book, to which a handle has been attached. Various foam rubber or nylon pile fabrics are secured to the flat side of the device. The fabric is then dipped into paint and smoothed onto a surface. Some pad applicators resemble standard brushes, except that a tapered pad replaces the bristles.

Dauber applications work well on smooth surfaces, but often leave skips or *holidays* on rough-textured finishes such as stucco or masonry. Although they were originally made to paint outside shakes and weatherboarding, pad applicators are becoming popular for interior work.

Applicators are perhaps easier to use than brushes. They are lighter than brushes. One pass over an area is usually sufficient to lay down a smooth coating of paint (Fig. 1). The paint film thickness from a pad applicator tends to be deeper than that left by a brush or roller, and without the brush marks associated with these traditional tools. The absorbent nature of the pad prevents drips and runs. Some of the newer pad applicators have a set of wheels along one edge to make painting a straight line easy (Fig. 2).

When buying a pad applicator, choose one with a replaceable pad. Jobs like painting exterior weatherboarding chew up a pad quickly. Buying several complete applicators for one job will be expensive. You will be better off buying a good brush that will last several jobs.

A pad applicator designed to coat shingles or shakes has a short ruglike pile of nylon bristles. This pile lays over a soft foam rubber pad. The pile can conform to the grooves in shingles and shakes. To paint with the pad, dip it in a tray of paint. Beginning at the top of a

Fig. 1

Applicators. Small pad applicators can be used when painting window trim.

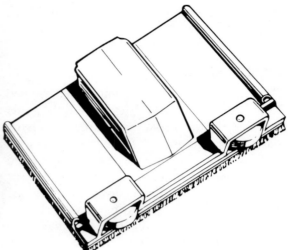

Fig. 2

Applicators. The wheels on this pad applicator make cutting in a corner a snap (courtesy Shur-Line).

shingle or shake, pull the pad along the entire length of the surface while applying medium pressure. Horizontal grooves can be painted by pulling the pad from left to right, or vice versa. The bottom edge of the shake or shingle can be painted with the edge of the pad.

To clean a pad applicator, remove as much excess paint as possible by squeezing the pad against newspaper. Remove the pad and wash it in the appropriate thinner. Several washes may be necessary. For the last wash, use a solution of detergent and water. Rinse in clear water, squeeze out excess water, and allow it to dry. Wrap the pad in brown paper or return it to the original wrapper. Store so there is no pressure on the pad, or it may become deformed.

See *Mitten Applicator.*

B

BALUSTRADE

A row of balusters topped by a rail. A balustrade is most common along staircases and balconies. Most balustrades inside the home are colored with a *stain* and top-coated with a *varnish*. Unless balustrades are in bad shape, it usually takes no more than a light sanding and a fresh coat of varnish to make them look great.

If your balustrades have been painted or you want to paint a newly built one, sand the surfaces thoroughly. The sanding will raise a tooth for the next coat of paint on varnished and painted surfaces. On new wood, sanding will smooth out rough spots and make the surface more uniform for painting.

Because balustrades usually get more than their share of wear and tear, use gloss or semigloss enamel for a topcoating. A compatible *primer* will make the job look its best and last the longest.

BAR FINISH

Bar tops present a special finishing problem because alcohol attacks most varnishes and lacquers. A natural wood look can be achieved with *polyurethane varnish*, which is extremely resistant to alcohol once it has thoroughly dried.

When refinishing a bar, you should usually plan to recoat the entire surface. A fresh coat of varnish applied over a small area will leave a patch shinier than the surrounding worn areas.

BARN PAINTS

Like your house, barns and other farm outbuildings last longer and look their best when properly maintained. Painting is a big part of this maintenance. Although exterior house paints can be used on barns, there are a couple of attractive alternatives.

11

Barn paints are similar to exterior house paints, although their vehicular composition may be slightly different. They usually contain red iron oxide as a pigment. The most important trait of barn paint is its ability to produce a uniform appearance on rough and poorly prepared surfaces. Barn paints are available in other colors like white, black, and green.

Penetrating stains are an attractive alternative to barn paints for farm buildings. The oils in stains penetrate to preserve the wood. They also eliminate *flaking, cracking,* and *peeling* problems associated with surface coatings. Stains also hide the imperfections of rough wood. Stains cannot be applied over old paint unless the paint has almost totally weathered away. Stains are easy to spray and come in many colors.

Galvanized steel is used extensively on barn roofs and siding. Most galvanized steels contain inhibitors that interfere with the adhesions of paint. The easiest way to remove these inhibiting agents is to allow the steel to weather for six months or more. Prime with a material designed for the metal; zinc dust and zinc oxide powders are best in an oil-base vehicle. Rust should be removed on old steel by sanding or wire brushing for best results. To insure proper *intercoat adhesion*, apply a topcoating compatible with the primer or, better yet, select a topcoating and match a primer to it. Metal can be rolled, brushed, or sprayed. Spraying is fastest, rolling puts on the most material, and brushing provides the most thorough coverage.

When ordering barn coatings, hedge your estimate on the amount of material needed to the long side. The weathered state of most barn siding is a thirsty surface that soaks up excessive amounts of the coating materials.

The exteriors of barns are painted using the same basic rules applicable to painting the outside of your house. Thoroughly prepare the surfaces by scraping loose paint. Don't worry too much about achieving a smooth surface; just make sure it is clean and sound. Begin at the highest point and work down. Save the trim for last.

Barn roofs are usually of galvanized steel, and they should be primed and top-coated with a metal-base paint like aluminum. Metal paints can be applied with rollers or brushes. They should be stirred occasionally to keep metal powders uniformly suspended.

The interior walls of farm service buildings must withstand almost constant rubbing by animals and frequent washing to remove manure and dirt. A durable paint is required. Two-component catalyzed enamels, epoxies, polyesters, and urethanes are the most durable and washable, although they are expensive.

To reduce the price of your paint job, you may want to paint with these two-component materials up to a line about 6 feet above the floor. Then paint the remainder of the walls, ceilings, or rafters with a latex or oil-base wood paint. Spraying will be the easiest way to paint areas with exposed trusses, floor joists, and other complicated construction supports.

Do not use lead-base paint on farm buildings. Animals may lick the paint or eat paint flakes that have fallen to the ground.

BASEBOARDS

Wood moldings that cover the bottom edge of interior walls, hiding the gap between wall and floor. Because of their location, baseboards demand a hard durable finish. Most manufacturers recommend the use of a latex or alkyd semigloss enamel for this job. A 2-inch-tapered sash tool, like you use for windows and doorjambs, will also work on baseboards. When painting baseboards with the same paint you used on other trim, save the baseboards for last so that drips and scuff marks can be covered. Don't move around too much while the baseboards are drying, as dust and lint will settle on them.

Some painters like to mask the floor off with masking tape to make the job easier. This is a good idea when two or more coats are to be applied. Wall-to-wall carpeting can present a problem, because the pile is often secured under the baseboard and cannot be pulled back. An inexpensive plastic or metal paint guard will solve the problem. The guard is worked into the crack between trim and floor, and then paint is brushed on the baseboard above it. Check the back of the guard frequently for paint. Do not use cardboard for a guard, as it will absorb paint and quickly become useless.

When varnishing or shellacking over previously finished baseboard, the undercoating should be roughened with a fine grade sandpaper before refinishing; 400 grit normally does the trick.

See *Trim*.

BATCH

The amount of paint made or colored at one time. Paint manufacturers usually turn out batches in excess of 6,000 gallons. Since all the paint made in one batch will have the same color, try to get all the paint necessary for one job from the same batch. The batch number will be printed on the carton or can of paint. It should be the same for all paint of the same color.

If you must paint with paint from two different batches, you can eliminate changes in shade by *boxing* the paint for one job before starting. You can stop painting with one batch at a natural dividing line—such as a corner—and begin the new wall with paint from the new batch.

See *Colors* and *Paint, Choosing*.

BEADING

A *cutting-in* technique in which a small bead of paint is drawn out of a brush so that it settles into the joint between two walls of different color. See the illustration. This technique is easy to master with a little practice and will eliminate the need to mask straight edges along walls and ceilings.

The best brushes for beading are sash tools with chiseled or beveled bristles. Grasp the brush with your thumb on one side of the metal band holding the bristles to the handle and with three or four fingers gripping the opposite side. Load the brush and press the bristles against the surface about an inch away from the corner. With a smooth, steady motion, draw the bead of paint up to the corner and

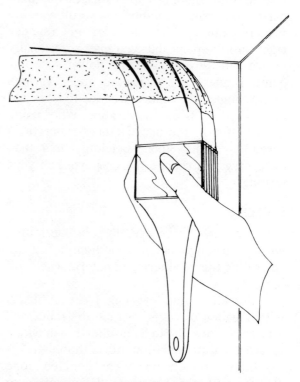

Beading. This beading technique for cutting-in eliminates the need to mask off the corner where two colors meet.

continue until the paint begins to thin out. Draw the brush away from the corner before lifting it free from the surface. You will end up with an arch that begins away from the corner, contacts the corner for 6 to 12 inches, and then curves away. Start the next stroke so that the paint overlaps about an inch of the previous stroke's end.

When painting around window panes, a bead of paint should flow 1/16 to 1/8 inch onto the glass. This extra paint acts as a moisture barrier and effectively seals the crack where glass, glazing, and wood meet.

See *Brushing Techniques* and *Cutting-In*.

BINDERS

One of the nonvolatile (nonevaporative) chemicals in paint. Binding agents stick the pigment particles in paint together and to the surface you are painting. Manufacturers mix a binder right into the paint, but you may occasionally desire a little extra holding power for your paint. Binders are marketed under various brand names. The binder is added to latex and oil-base paints before application. When using binders, follow the manufacturer's directions carefully. Adding more bonding agent than necessary will change the properties of your coating.

BLEACH

Bleaches have three uses in painting: killing *mildew*, making stained wood lighter, and accelerating the weathering of natural wood siding.

For killing mildew, mix 1 cup of bleach with 1 gallon of water. Scrape the mildewed area to remove all old paint, then brush with a bleach and water solution. Allow thorough drying before repainting. Wear goggles, long sleeves, and rubber gloves to keep bleach out of your eyes and off your skin. Under no cir-

cumstances should bleach be mixed with ammonia, as this mixture produces a poisonous gas.

When you want to lighten dark wood or a stain job, undiluted laundry bleach will do the trick. Only raw wood can be bleached. Any paint or varnish will prevent the bleach from penetrating to the wood.

Apply bleach with a rag or stiff brush. Wear protective clothing and flush all spatters immediately with water. Straight bleach is quick acting and can cause substantial problems if applied carelessly. When wood is slightly darker than you want, rinse off the bleach with water. The small amount of bleach left on the surface will finish the job. Allow bleached wood to dry thoroughly, then sand to remove raised grain. Apply varnish or shellac over bleached wood to seal out moisture.

There are a number of bleaching products that will produce a weathered look on your house's siding. Most of these materials produce a silver-gray finish similar to siding on houses along seacoasts. Unfortunately, bleached siding is not as durable as stained or painted siding. Instead of bleaching, try one of the "weathered look" stains. These materials produce a weathered effect and preserve your siding.

See *Mildew, Mildewcide*, and *Stains*.

BLEEDING

A common paint problem produced when the color of a substrate material leaks through the topcoating. Bleeding can be caused by rusting nails, wood knots, moisture, natural pigments in cedar or redwood, and previously applied stains.

Your topcoating will still look sharp a week after painting over any of these problems. The staining material will soon bleed through to the surface, discoloring your topcoating. The best method for combating bleeding is to seal the offending material beneath an impervious coating. Many manufacturers make stain sealers such as "Lok Tite." Some are latex and work well for resinous problems like wood knots; others are oil-base and work well on water-related stains.

Choosing a paint will also have an effect on bleeding. Most latex paints accelerate rust bleed-through. Oil-base paints may draw the pigments of previously applied stains to the surface. For specifics on bleed-through problems, consult your paint dealer and the sections in this book covering individual staining problems.

See *Copper Stains, Knots in Wood, Moisture, Nails, Sealer,* and *Staining Through.*

BLISTERING

Usually the first sign that you have a paint-related problem. Blisters form when pressure under the paint forces the paint skin off its substrate. See the illustration. These bubble-forming pressures are caused by the evaporation of water or solvents beneath the skin of impermeable paint.

The exact cause of a blistering problem can be diagnosed by cutting a blister open. If you see bare wood under the blister, it is probably a water vapor problem. If the blister is glossy and you find dry paint under the bulge, it is probably a solvent problem.

Water vapor or moisture problems are caused by excessive wetness in the wood or masonry behind the paint. Most moisture blisters involve several layers of paint.

Moisture may enter walls through faulty *caulking* around windows and doors, leaks between trim and wall surfaces, defects in gutters or downspouts, and leaky roofs or chimney flashings. Moisture may also seep into outside walls from high humidity within the

Blistering. Blistering paint is usually an indication that there is moisture in the wall. The source of the moisture should be corrected before repainting.

home. Inspect your house around the affected area. Repair any problem you find before correcting the blisters. If you don't the bubbles will certainly reappear.

Solvent or temperature blisters are formed when the solvent in an oil-base paint is trapped beneath a dry paint film. Solvent blisters usually involve only the most recent layer of paint and frequently occur on new or unseasoned wood.

Temperature blisters usually appear a day or two after painting a dark color over a lighter one in direct sunlight. The outer surface of the new paint dries before the inside surface, and the trapped solvent vapor raises blisters. Do yourself, and your house, a big favor and paint in the shade.

Occasionally small blisters may disappear completely, but larger ones will leave a rough spot on your finish. This roughness may lead to further *peeling* or *cracking* of your paint.

To correct blistering, Scrape off all loose paint down to the bare wood. Allow two or three days for drying before sanding smooth. Treat the exposed wood with a *wood preservative* or *primer*. Allow the new paint to dry thoroughly and then repaint with a topcoating. Some latex topcoatings "breathe" in that they let water vapor out while blocking the entrance of water droplets. This type of paint may be all that is needed to correct blistering problems.

If blistering reoccurs, the problem is not in your paint. It is in the wall. You may have to install vents or louvers to eliminate the moisture causing the blistering problem.

See *Preparation* and *Sanding*.

BLOCK FILLER

Unpainted masonry, especially cinder block walls, are laced with tiny holes. These holes can be filled with a paintlike block filler before painting to save both time and money. Why? These holes are just large enough to show if not filled with paint, yet they are too small to be easily filled. Filling them would require many gallons of extra paint and the additional time required to apply them. To eliminate this problem, many paint manufacturers have developed block filling preparations.

Commercial block fillers come in powder or liquid form. Both of these masonry primers contain solids which fill in and smooth out rough concrete surfaces. Block fillers should be applied with a stiff brush, like those used for

whitewashing, or with a medium length roller. In addition to providing a relatively smooth surface over which other paints can be applied, block fillers also make the wall slightly more watertight. Your paint dealer will match a block filler to the finish coat you wish to use.

You can make your own block filler using cement and water. Mix a slurry. Brush it onto a damp wall with a stiff brush. Because the filler works best when cured, keep the filler damp two or three days before allowing it to thoroughly dry. Top-coat with an alkali-resistant paint.

See: *Brick* and *Masonry*.

BLOOM

The discoloration of a new paint film from exposure to smoke, oil, or dust while still tacky. Avoid bloom by painting on calm, warm days so that fresh paint will dry quickly.

BLUSHING

A clouding of a paint film due to condensation, most commonly in the form of dew, during the drying period. It happens more often with oil-base paint than latex. Blushing can be avoided by quitting painting several hours before dark. Light rain also causes blushing. Stop painting long before threatening weather arrives.

BODY

The common term used to describe the viscosity or consistency of various coatings. Shellacs and stains have very little body and are considered thin. Dripless interior paints are quite heavy. Some dripless paints are thick to the point of supporting a stirring stick inserted vertically into the paint. Caution should be used when thinning paints, because the manufacturer has tried to match the body of the paint to the job it is to perform. Excessive thinning may result in *cracking* or *alligatoring*.

BOILED OIL

Oil that has been heat-treated so that it dries more quickly. These types of oils are used in many types of *oil-base paints*, especially exterior finishes.

See *Drying Oils*.

BOXING

To insure uniformity of color among large batches of paint, the paint should be poured back and forth from one container to another. Boxing is the best way of mixing paints from two different batches so that you achieve a uniform color.

To box paint, use two containers larger than the amount of paint you wish to mix. When mixing 4 gallons of paint, you'll need two 5 gallon buckets. Begin by pouring 2 gallons of paint into each bucket. Pour the contents of one bucket into the other. Pour back and forth until the paint is smooth and no color streaks remain. Pour mixed paint back into individual cans and seal until ready for use.

BREATHER FILM

Many of the new latex exterior paints have a property known as breathability. In short, a paint that produces a breather film creates a paint skin which allows moisture vapor within the wall to pass out while preventing water droplets in the form of rain or dew from penetrating to the wood. Choose a breather type paint for areas where moisture-induced *blistering* has been a problem. Your paint dealer will know which breather type paints are suited to your climate.

See *Moisture*.

BRICK

Painting brickwork presents many of the problems associated with cinder block or masonry walls. The motar around bricks can cause *alkali* deterioration of certain types of paint, and the bricks themselves are capable of soaking up excessive amounts of paint.

Although bare brick walls stand up well to weather, clear brick sealers are available for extra protection from the elements. These clear sealers are usually tinted a translucent blue to aid in application. They prevent water from reaching the bricks, thereby reducing the amount of chipping, alkali, and *efflorescence* present on the brickwork. These clear sealers can be brushed, rolled, or sprayed on to preserve the natural beauty of a wall or, in some instances, to ready it for paint.

Before painting or sealing a brick wall, the surface must be properly prepared. All loose mortar and brick should be chiseled from the wall. Holes left by the removal of loose mortar should be dusted, wet, and remortared. When the new mortar has dried, treat patches with a weak *muriatic acid* solution. A mixture of 10 parts water to 1 part acid, applied with a stiff brush, should do the trick. Wear goggles, rubber gloves, and protective clothing when working with any caustic substance. The acid is neutralized by swabbing the area with a solution of 1 part ammonia to 2 parts water. Rinse the wall thoroughly with water and allow it to dry before priming or sealing.

Brick can be primed with portland masonry paint (not really necessary) and a clear or opaque sealer, or another suitable primer. If you intend to paint the brickwork, choose a latex or rubber-base primer. Oil-base paints are attacked by alkali. When the sealer or primer is dry, apply a topcoating with a brush, roller, or sprayer.

See *Masonry* and *Sealer*.

BRIDGING

A term used to describe the ability of a particular paint to fill in and smooth out small holes and cracks in a surface. It is a highly desirable trait in exterior paints because a smooth coating allows water to run off instead of collecting on the surface. Bridging the profusion of tiny holes in cinder block is the main purpose of *block fillers*. Some coatings are designed to have as little bridging as possible. Paints for screens, acoustic tile, and stains have this characteristic.

BRUSHABILITY

A term used by painters to describe how easily a paint spreads. The brushability of a paint is dependent on several things. The most important is the weather. Latex paints tend to be difficult to handle in hot weather. They often become sticky and hard to work out of the brush. Oil-base paints tend to be difficult to handle in colder weather when the oil in them becomes too viscous to flow properly.

Another important determinant for a paint's brushability is the quality of the tools being used to apply the paint. Old worn-out brushes are more difficult to work with than new tools. See the illustration.

Quality of the paint and its age are important aspects of brushability. The older the paint and the cheaper its quality, the more difficult you can expect it to handle.

See *Brushes and Brushing Techniques*.

BRUSHES

Devices composed of bristles set into a handle and used for painting. There are almost as many brushes as there are types of paint. Choosing a brush for your home fix-up needs can be as confusing as choosing a paint.

Good paintbrushes are like a good wine; they get better with age. A good brush will break in and take shape with continued use,

Brushability. Hot weather, latex paint, and a worn-out brush equal bad brushability.

while an inferior brush will deteriorate rapidly from the time you bring it home. The bristles will splay and get paint on everything but what you intend to paint.

Choosing a Brush

A good brush will smooth out paint, carry more paint per dip (without dripping), put the paint where you want it, last longer, and clean easier than a cheap brush. Although it costs more, a good brush properly cared for will paint your house several times over. A poor brush may not make it through the first coat. Still, even the best brushes won't spread a paint for which they were not designed.

Just as important as matching paint to the surface you wish to cover is matching a brush to your paint. Latex paints require synthetic bristles, as natural (china hair or hog bristle) fibers absorb water and loose resilience. They also fuzz out and prevent sharp clean lines when cutting in. Oil-base and alkyd paint, especially glossy trim paint, require finely tapered natural fibers. High quality synthetic bristle brushes will work in flat and semigloss oil-base paints. Enamel, varnish, and lacquer should be applied with flat varnish brushes (natural fibers). Never use synthetic brushes in shellac; even the highest quality nylon bristles will become a mess in minutes.

Natural fiber brushes are increasingly hard to find and tend to be expensive when you do find them. They are being replaced by nylon, which means better, smoother paint spreading, less cost, and easy cleanup. Although nylon brushes are designed mainly for latex paints, they work well in oil-base and alkyd paints. The most important parts of any brush, be it synthetic or natural fiber, are the bristles.

Bristle length is important. As a rule of thumb, bristles should be 50 percent longer than the width of the brush, except in the extra wide (5 inches or more) and extra narrow (1½ inches or less) brushes. For example, a 3-inch brush should have 4 to 4½-inch bristles. Narrow brushes usually have longer bristles, because shorter bristles inhibit proper spreading of the paint. Wider brushes have shorter bristles that won't flop out of control.

Cheap bristles tend to be silky fine in order to make up for the inferior product. When wet with paint, these weak bristles tend to cross and flop all over your work. You'll end up smearing on paint with the base (near the ferrule) of the bristles instead of the last inch of tip, as you would with a good brush (Fig. 1).

Flexibility of the bristles also plays an important part in a smooth paint job. Good bristles bend like a fishing rod, more at the tip and less at the base. Bend the bristles along the breadth of the brush and check for this bend. If the bristles bend excessively after leaving the ferrule, return the brush to the display and try another brand.

Bristle shape is the final factor in a brush's performance. Bristles should taper from a thick base in the ferrule to a flagged or exploded tip (Fig. 2). Hog bristles do this naturally, and the better nylon bristles try to emulate this shape. The flagged ends smooth paint onto the surface as it flows out of the thicker bristles near the heel. Beware of the bristles that are cut off flat on the ends.

The handle of your brush is almost as important as the bristles. The smaller brushes, sash and trim tools, come in rounded handles that resemble a pencil or pen. The wider brushes have handles that bulge in the middle in what is known as a beaver tail.

Choose a brush of the correct size and shape for your job. Make sure it is compatible with the paint you plan to use. Don't use a brush wider than the surface to be covered,

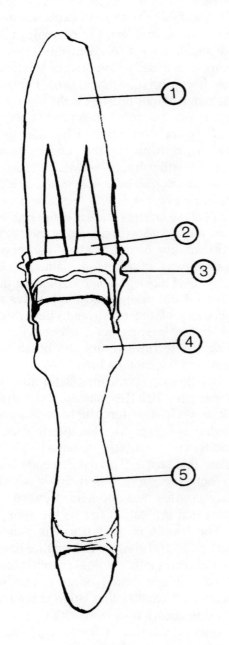

because all brushes tend to flare or widen when pressure is applied. Ask your paint dealer for help when selecting a bristle material for your paint.

Nothing frustrates a weekend painter quicker than a brush that loses bristles, won't spread paint evenly, and feels awkward in your hand. When you go to the paint store, perform these simple tests to insure that the brush you buy is worth the money.

—Hold the brush as if you were painting. How does it feel? If it feels clumsy, it will only get worse when loaded with paint.

—The ferrule, or the metal band holding the bristles into the handle, should be tight, perferably nailed with at least two nails in each side of the handle. Most good brushes use either aluminum or stainless steel ferrules. These materials are a must if you will be using latex paint.

—The handle should be smooth and coated with a moisture-resistant coating.

—The bristles should flare out evenly when pressed against your hand. They should spring back to their original shape when tension is released.

—When two brushes are the same width, the one with the longest, thickest bristles will hold more paint. Make sure the bristles are tapered or have an exploded or flagged tip.

—Pull the bristles apart and check the plug holding the bristles into the ferrule. The

Fig. 1

Brushes. The major parts of a brush include: (1) bristles, (2) plug, (3) ferrule, (4) heel, and (5) handle.

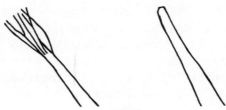

Fig. 2

Brushes. Good brushes have bristles with exploded (left) or tapered (right) tips. Avoid those with flat, cutoff tips.

plug should be less than half the thickness of the brush's heel.

—Slap the bristles against your hand and check for loose bristles. Pull on the bristles to insure against the brush shedding into your paint job.

Types of Brushes

Unless you plan on painting masonry or using lacquer or shellac, you will need only three types of brushes for painting: a wall brush, a sash tool, and a trim brush (Fig. 3).

Wall brushes range anywhere from 3 to 6 inches in width with a square tip and a beaver tail handle. These general purpose brushes work well on flat surfaces for cutting in around roller work or for brushing large walls, ceilings, and floors. The 4-inch-wide wall brush is

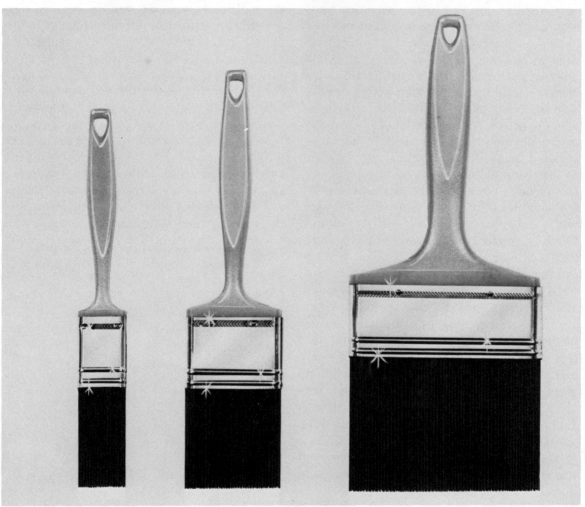

Fig. 3

Brushes. For most painting jobs you will need only three brush sizes: sash tool (left), trim brush (center) and a wall brush (right) (courtesy Wooster Brush Company).

about right for most home painters, and the beaver tail handle will afford a firm grip while balancing the heavy paint load in the bristles. Grip the brush as if you are shaking hands with it. Switch from hand to hand as necessary during the job.

Sash tools come in three shapes: square, oval, and beveled. These tools are used for the fine work around windows, baseboards, and other tight places. A 1 to 1½-inch-wide brush is about right for most purposes. Although sash tools are relatively inexpensive, you may not want to buy one of each shape. Most people find that the beveled tool is best for all-around work because the angled tip prevents excessive spreading of the bristles. By altering the angle of attack, various width strokes can be made. Beveled brushes usually come with a rounded handle and should be gripped lightly, as if writing, during use.

Trim brushes fill in the gap between sash tools and wall brushes. Usually 2 or 2½-inch-wide trim brushes work well on doors, cabinets, and for cutting in around roller work. Select nylon bristles for this brush so that you can use the brush in either latex or oil-base paints. A brush with chiseled bristle tips will allow precise edges and lines when cutting in.

Two special brushes you might consider buying are a masonry brush and a natural fiber trim brush. The masonry brush resembles a scrub brush more than a paintbrush, but its stout bristles work paint into the porous surfaces of concrete and cinder block effectively. Enamels, shellac, and varnish should be applied with a natural fiber varnish brush. If you try to use a nylon bristle brush, you will end up with a brush that sticks to itself and does not spread the coating.

Cleaning Brushes

There is no better way to get your in-vestment out of a brush than by properly cleaning it after every use. Without proper cleaning, paint builds up in the heel of the brush until the working length of the bristles is too short for effective application. Cleaning your brushes immediately after each use will also give you a chance to wash your hands before handling furniture.

If you only need to store your brush through lunch, you can wrap it in plastic to prevent the paint from drying out. Press the plastic against the bristles so air is sealed out. The plastic slips off easily when you return to the job.

For overnight storage you can keep the brushes in the thinner matched to the paint: water for latex paint and paint thinner for oil-base paint. Suspend the brushes in the solvent without agitation. Make sure the solvent reaches the ferrule. Do not allow a brush to rest on its tip, or it will take on a curved shape. A good method of suspension is to drill a hole through the heel of the brush, insert a stiff

Fig. 4
Brushes. One of the main advantages of latex paint is that it can be cleaned under running water.

wire, and then hang the brush in the can. Fill it with water or paint thinner and cover with a rag. In the morning wipe the brush with newspaper to remove the excess solvent, and you are ready to go.

To clean latex paint out of a brush, follow these easy steps:

—Rinse out paint under warm tap water.

—Mix a bowl or can of soap and water and agitate the brush in this solution. Work soapy water into the heel of the brush with fingers.

—Rinse in warm water until no more color shows (Fig. 4).

—Shake out excess water. Spin it with a paint spinner or tap it on the heel of a shoe. When tapping, do not dent the ferrule, or your brush will leak down the handle.

—Run a comb, fork, or wire brush through the bristles, stroking from heel to tip. Hang up to dry.

When dry, wrap in brown paper or return to original cardboard wrapper (Fig. 5).

To clean oil-base paint from brushes:

Fig. 6
Brushes. Old paint can be removed from a brush by stroking from the ferrule to bristle tips with a wire brush.

—Agitate the brush in a small quantity of paint thinner, kerosene, or commercial brush cleaner. Pour used thinner into a *gag bucket.*

—Repeat step one until no more than a trace of pigment remains in the cleaning fluid.

—Make the final cleaning in turpentine. Following the last cleaning, you can dip the brush in soapy water. (Be careful with bristle brushes—do not leave them in the water bath too long and do not use warm water.)

—Hang up the brush until it is dry. Then comb it and wrap it in brown paper or the original wrapper.

Lacquer base finishes require cleaning in an expensive lacquer thinner or multisolvent brush cleaner. Shellac is easily cleaned with ammonia and water.

Stiff, sticky bristles in an improperly cleaned high quality brush can be worked out,

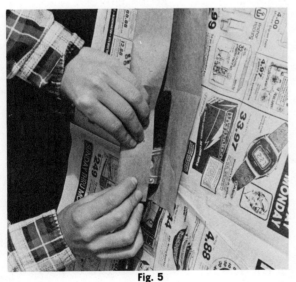
Fig. 5
Brushes. Wrap a clean brush in brown paper or its original wrapper for storage.

but not without effort. Cheap brushes are not worth cleaning. Soak the brush in a commercial paint remover until the paint softens to jelly. Remove old paint with a brush comb or wire brush (Fig. 6). Rinse in paint thinner and brush again. Repeat the paint remover/thinner process if necessary. When satisfied with the job, wash in soapy water. Rinse it in clear water, comb the bristles, dry, and wrap for storage.

See *Brushing Techniques, Cleanup, Solvents*, and *Thinners*.

BRUSHING TECHNIQUES

Few homes can be painted without the aid of a paintbrush. There are many corners, nooks, crannies, and trim pieces that are not accessible with a roller or spray gun. Many coatings just will not go on properly with anything but a paintbrush. Knowing the basic brushing techniques is essential to any home painting job.

Rolling and spraying are gaining in popularity because of their speed; yet many people still prefer the texture of a good brush job. Although brushing allows better coating penetration on wood and masonry than rolling or spraying, brushing usually takes from two to four times longer than the speedier methods. By using the brushing techniques in this section, you can do your brush work as quickly and thoroughly as possible.

Brushing Terms

Before discussing brushing techniques, here are some definitions for basic brushing terms. Laying on is the term used to describe the process of applying the bulk of a brush's paint to a new surface. The idea is to get the paint off the brush and onto the wall before it has a chance to drip or run on your work.

Brushing out is the stroke you use to smooth out the paint. Medium pressure strokes that bend the bristles are best for brushing out most paints.

Tipping off is going lightly over the fresh paint with the tips of your brush bristles *leveling* the paint. The end of the stroke should finish in a wet area, feathering the paint to prevent *lap marks*.

Feathering means lifting the brush during the follow-through of your tipping off stroke. This action spreads the paint to a thin coating and blends it into a dry area. This gradual thinning out will prevent lap marks between areas that cannot be painted consecutively, for example, when working from a ladder. Thin spots and *holidays* occur most often along the feathered edges of a painted section.

Lap marks are usually formed when the edge of a section of paint is allowed to dry before new paint is applied. They are more common in oil-base and glossy paints than flat latex wall paints. Lap marks show up as dark seams between two areas of paint. They can be avoided by carefully feathering all edges and ending an area of paint at a natural divider such as a corner or window.

You can make brushing easier and eliminate wasted motion by following these general rules. Before dipping your brush into paint, prime it by wetting it with thinner when using oil-base paints or water when using latex paints. Shake out excess thinner; then dip your brush into the paint. This simple precautionary measure will also make *cleanup* at the end of the job much easier.

Agitate the brush in the paint on the first dip. Work paint thoroughly into the bristles. Try not to get more than one-half the bristle length coated with paint. This will prevent excess paint from collecting in the heel of your brush. Too much paint in the heel of a brush is the major reason for drips and runs, and this buildup is difficult to clean out.

Most professional painters prefer to paint out of a wide-mouth pail known as a paint pot. The curled lip around paint cans is difficult to work around. To carry the most paint to the wall with each dip, slap the bristles once against the inside of the paint pot. Give the brush a half twist while carrying the brush to the wall. If you find that paint is dripping, you can scrap more paint off the brush along the inside of the pot. Do not scrape brushes against the lip of your pail, as you may curl the outside bristles.

Lay the load on the dry wall. Brush it out, working from dry to wet areas, and then tip it off. Use long, even strokes and keep steady pressure on the brush. End each brush stroke with a lifting motion. Try to paint with the grain of the wood whenever possible. Use quick light strokes to touch up any minor drips or skips.

Brush strokes begin with the brush angled low to the surface and increase to perpendicular as the brush moves through the middle of the stroke. At the end of the stroke, which should wind up in the previously applied paint, draw the brush away from the surface while completing the motion. The new and old paint will flow together and hide any brush marks.

The area you can cover and the speed at which you cover it will be determined in large part by the paint's characteristics and weather conditions. Hot dry weather and quick-drying paints will limit your work area to small (3 foot by 3 foot) sections. With slow-drying paint applied in cool, damp weather, you can work larger patches (6 foot by 6 foot). The edges of new paint should be feathered to prevent lap marks.

Try to keep your body positioned before an unpainted section of wall while painting. This allows you to lean against the wall for support without getting paint on your clothes

and hands. This position also enables you to spot any drips or runs, because they usually fall into unpainted areas.

Interior Brushwork

When painting an interior wall with a brush, begin in the upper right-hand corner (if you are right-handed) or upper left-hand corner (if you are left-handed). Keep your brush at about a 45-degree angle against the wall when smoothing out paint. When tipping off, make arc-shaped strokes. Avoid uniform horizontal or vertical strokes, because the resulting texture will be unpleasant after drying.

Cutting in corners and around trim is necessary before rolling open wall areas. Lay your brush's tip into the corner and pull out

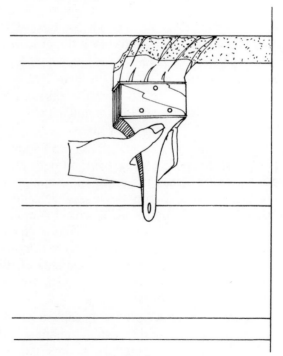

Fig. 1

Brushing Techniques. One method of painting weatherboard is to coat the bottom edge of two or three boards and then return to the flat of the boards.

25

perpendicular to the corner. Make four or five of these strokes, then go back and smooth the paint with a stroke parallel to the corner. Again, end the stroke by feathering into wet paint.

Exterior Brushwork

There are two basic techniques for putting paint on exterior weatherboarding. The first is painting the underside edge of 2 or 3 feet of two or three consecutive weatherboards. Then smooth paint onto the flat surfaces of these weatherboards. This method works well on slow drying paints (Fig. 1).

The second method works well with quick-drying paints. Load your brush and paint along the bottom edge of one weatherboard, then daub paint in three or four places on the weatherboard (Fig. 2). Smooth out the paint, move down the board, and repeat the process.

On butted side joints in weatherboarding, make a vertical stroke along the seam and then work over with light horizontal strokes. Try not to allow excess paint to remain in the joint, or the paint will crack as it dries.

On relatively small cracks and joints, cross brushing will work paint into the fissures. Brush across the crack to scrape paint off the brush and into the fissure. Make a stroke parallel to the crack in order to smooth the paint. Then tip off in the direction of the remainder of your paint job. Avoid the temptation to poke and gouge cracks and holes with the tip of your brush, as this will quickly wear out even the best brush.

Try to avoid a buildup of paint on your brush's ferrule by wire brushing, combing, or scraping with a putty knife to remove excess paint. Heavy paint buildup around the ferrule will increase the chance of dripping and may release lumps of dry paint into your work.

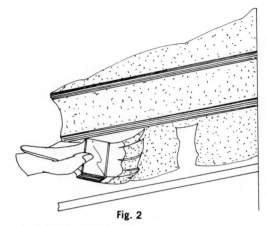

Fig. 2

Brushing Techniques. When using fast-drying paints on weatherboard, coat the bottom edge of one board. Daub on three or four spots of paint. Smooth with long strokes.

As with interior work, feather all edges. Try to stop work at natural dividers such as decorative molding or corners.

Special Techniques

When painting shingles, coat the bottom edge with paint. Work paint into cracks between shingles with strokes parallel to the crack. Finish up by smoothing paint on the shingle with a vertical stroke, from top to bottom of each shingle, or parallel with the grooves in horizontal shingles.

Masonry and whitewash brushes have thick, stiff bristles for working paint into the numerous small holes of cement surfaces. A circular motion works best with these brushes. Many whitewash brushes come with an extra long handle, so both hands can be used to guide the brush. Although lap marks seldom show with this circular application technique, straight finishing strokes will smooth out the coating.

Varnishes, lacquers, and enamels are an exception to the rule of working from a dry surface into a wet one. Load the brush and begin each new stroke at the end of the previous stroke. Work the material into the dry surface area. Because these finishes bubble with excessive brushing, they should be laid on with slow deliberate strokes. Check your work constantly, as these thin materials tend to run and dribble more than other paints.

See *Baseboards; Cracking; Cross-Brushing; Cutting-In; Doors; Enamel; Painting, Exterior; Painting, Interior; Trim;* and *Windows.*

BUBBLES

Form when the paint has been stirred excessively, usually with a stirring attachment for power drills, immediately before application. Varnish, shellac, and lacquer are subject to bubbling when overbrushed or overrolled during application. Let paint set 10 or 15 minutes after stirring and before use. Moving too fast with a roller is a common problem with all paints. Bubbles form. When the bubbles pop, they leave minute craters in the surface of the paint. To avoid bubbles, use slow, smooth brush and roller strokes.

BUTTED SIDE JOINTS

Commonly found in weatherboarding. If the joint has pulled apart, renail and caulk. Allow *caulking* to dry before priming. Top-coating a butted joint requires that paint be worked down into the crack. Make a brush stroke parallel to the fissure, then tip off the joint to the direction of the remainder of your paint job.

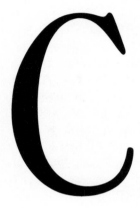

CABINETS AND DRAWERS

Instead of being finished with a natural finish or stain, cabinets and drawers should be coated with a glossy or semigloss trim enamel. This paint gives good wear because its tough durable finish allows frequent scrubbing to remove smudges and spills.

To paint cabinets, remove drawers and mask hardware with tape, or remove the hardware entirely. Sand shiny surfaces to provide *tooth* for the paint. Start on the bottom of the topmost shelf, working from the back to the front of the piece. Then paint backwalls, sidewalls, and the top of the shelves. Cover all the enclosed spaces, then paint the outside edges from top to bottom. Paint the doors, inside then outside, and leave open to dry. Paint only the front and front edges of drawers. Painting the entire sides of each drawer will destroy their smooth sliding action. Varnish, shellac, and lacquer are applied using the same procedures.

Allow cabinets and drawers to dry thoroughly, usually more than a day, before reassembling hardware or closing doors. If you fail to allow paint to dry thoroughly, it may stick around the edges of doors and drawers. The paint from one surface will pull off, leaving a groove, and build an unsightly paint ridge on the opposite surface.

CALCIMINE

A white or tinted wash consisting of glue, whiting or zinc white, and water and is used on plastered surfaces. In older houses, calcimine coatings may have been used on walls and ceilings. Unfortunately, *latex* and *oil-base paints* do not stick to this material. Calcimine must be removed during the preparation process. You can tell when you have calcimine on your wall by rubbing a finger across the wall. If your fingertip picks up a white powder, the wall should be washed before painting. Warm water, soap, and a stiff scrub brush will remove calcimine.

CASEIN

Many older homes may have walls coated with a casein paint. These paints were made from a protein found in milk and were used from the early 1930s through the late 1940s. Modern *latex* and *oil-base paints* will not adhere to this coating. They should be removed with warm water, detergent, and a stiff scrub brush before painting.

Casement Windows. The order of painting a casement window is (1) muntins, (2) horizontal and vertical edges of sash, and (3) facing around the opening.

CASEMENT WINDOWS

These windows swing in or out on hinges instead of sliding up and down like *double-hung* windows. Casement windows are usually made of *metals* such as aluminum or steel. They are more often used in brick or masonry homes than wooden ones.

Before painting casement windows, scrape them to remove all loose paint and *glazing.* If the metal is rusty, then wire brush it to remove the rust. Prime the metal with a metal primer prior to applying new glazing. When the glazing is dry, paint the window with a semigloss or glossy metal paint or oil-base trim enamel.

To paint casement windows, choose a sash tool and open the window as far as possible. Paint the muntins—the narrow strips of metal that hold the glass in place—first. See the illustration. Next coat the top and bottom edges of the sash, followed by the horizontal and vertical sections of the sash and finally the facing around the window. Because most casement windows are operated by a series of cranks, arms, and gears, be careful not to clog these mechanisms with paint.

CASINGS

Woodwork around windows and doors. They are usually painted with glossy or semigloss paint. When stained, casings are usually coated with a semigloss or glossy varnish.

See *Trim.*

CAULKING

A mastic substance used to seal cracks and small holes in a home's exterior surface. Caulking remains flexible enough to contract and expand with the wood or brick around it.

Many *moisture*-related paint failures can be prevented by caulking thoroughly. Although caulking may seem to be a tedious part of paint *preparation*, it will greatly increase a paint job's longevity when done properly. Caulking helps seal air and water leaks around windows and doors—saving dollars on your heating and cooling bills.

There are several types of caulking from which to choose. Ask your paint dealer to match a caulk to your particular job. The newer latex caulking materials last longer than the oil-base caulks because of their improved flexibility. Although latex caulks cost more, many people feel the easy water cleanup of this material is worth the added expense. The new silicone caulks are more of a rubber than a caulking compound. They seal cracks efficiently, but paint does not adhere to them easily. The very latest in caulk is the propellant-powered pressurized can caulking compounds. This caulking squirts from the can as a foam and settles into a concave-shaped bead as it dries. These materials are expensive and new; be wary of them.

Some manufacturers make a variety of colored caulks. Although these caulks may match your topcoat perfectly, they need to be painted over for maximum life.

Knife grade caulking comes in a can and is applied with a *putty knife* or spatula. Dig out the compound, work it deep into the crack, and then smooth with the working edge of your putty knife. The material should fill the crack so that it is flush with its surroundings.

Rope caulking comes in a coil and is pulled off in strands which are worked into cracks with the fingers. You may want to wear gloves while using this caulk.

Self-leveling caulking is useful on floors, decks, and porches. It is applied with a caulking gun and allowed to settle into the crack. Once it has cured, you can paint over it.

To prepare for caulking, remove all loose and deteriorating caulking from the crack (Fig. 1). A putty knife, scraper, knife or cold chisel, and mallet can be used to remove these materials. Dust the crack and prime with regular wood primer before applying new caulking. Do not apply caulking to bare wood. The wood will absorb the liquid in the caulk, rendering the material inflexible and unable to move with the crack.

Extremely small cracks should be widened with a putty knife or can opener to provide adequate footing for new caulk. Never apply to wet or oily surfaces. Do not try to apply the material when temperatures are below 45 degrees Fahrenheit. Adhesion will be affected by all three conditions.

Gun caulking is by far the most popular and efficient way to caulk your home. Several types of oil-base and latex caulks are available in easy-to-use 1-pound tubes. To load a caulking gun, turn the teeth on the plunger up, so

Fig. 1

Caulking. Clean all loose caulking from cracks prior to applying fresh caulking.

they disengage the catch of the trigger. Pull the plunger all the way back. Slip the cartridge, rear end first, into the cradle and then turn the rod so teeth engage the catch on the trigger. Cut the spout end of the tube at a 45-degree angle. This will leave an opening about ¼ inch in diameter. Poke a screwdriver or stiff wire through the hole to puncture the seal.

To apply caulking, turn the teeth of the plunger rod down so they engage the trigger. Squeeze the trigger gently until caulk begins to flow. Starting at the top or at one end of a crack move the spout along the joint. Feed a continuous bead of caulking into the crack. To stop the flow of caulk, turn the plunger rod so the teeth disengage. Pull the rod back, releasing pressure.

Caulking should be worked deep into cracks and have a slightly concave shape so water runs out. A convex shape will allow water to settle around the edges of the caulking. You may want to smooth the bead with

Fig. 2

Caulking. Smoothing caulking so that it is concave will keep water from collecting in the crack and causing deterioration.

your finger (Fig. 2). Allow caulking to dry thoroughly before painting.

See *Putty* and *Wood Fillers*.

CEILINGS

The paint job on a ceiling can make or break a room. No one notices ceilings with a good paint job, but everybody notices mistakes. Selecting the right paint and following the correct application techniques will make ceilings disappear.

Professional painters usually paint the ceiling of a room first. Drips and spatters can be corrected later. Because the ceiling is the largest expanse of unbroken area in a room, you should not start on a ceiling unless you have time to finish it without stopping. When these edges are painted over with new paint, *lap marks* will result. Fortunately, modern latex paints and improved tools have made lap marks the least of your problems.

Flat latex paints will cover most ceilings without lapping. When applying a semigloss enamel or flat oil-base paint, most lapping problems will be eliminated by working quickly and effectively. You may find, however, that with the latter paints two coats are necessary.

When shopping for a paint to put on your ceilings the salesman may suggest a paint labeled ceiling paint. The major difference between this paint and regular flat wall paint is the finish. Ceiling paints have a flatter finish than regular wall paints. They are also more delicate and harder to clean, so they should not be used on walls. Oil-base ceiling paints have the same characteristics except that they take longer to dry.

Latex no-drip paints are good for ceilings. Most have excellent one-coat coverage, and they are not as sloppy as thinner paints. No-drip paints are more expensive than regular paints and do not cover as much area.

Texture paint can be applied to ceilings just like regular paints. Usually a latex with sand or a compatible synthetic grit, texture paint creates a fine-grained, glare-free coating that works well on ceilings. When applying paint over a textured surface, count on using about 25 percent more paint than on a flat surface.

Acoustic tile should be painted with an *acoustic paint.* These paints do not bridge the holes in the tiles. Using a short nap when rolling will also prevent paint from clogging the holes.

The color or shade of a ceiling's paint can have quite an effect on your room's appearance. Ceilings darker than the walls will ap-

pear lower, while ceilings lighter than the walls will appear higher.

Before painting your ceiling, it must be properly prepared. Follow the same basic procedures as for interior walls. Priming is not usually necessary, although it is advisable when switching from one type of paint to another.

Although ceilings should be treated as if they are overhead walls, they frequently have a problem not commonly found on side-walls—water stains. These brown stains must be sealed with shellac or stain *sealer* (Fig. 1). When left untreated, water spots will burn through your paint job. If you happen to be using a latex paint, the stain may bleed through before the coating has a chance to dry. Ask your paint dealer for a suitable sealer.

Fig. 1

Ceilings. Water stains on ceilings should be coated with a sealer prior to painting.

To paint a ceiling, start by removing as much furniture as possible from the room. Push the remaining furniture to one end of the room and cover it and the floors with *drop cloths*. Remove all light fixtures and allow them to hang free. Patch all cracks and holes with *spackling compound*, sand rough areas, and seal stains. Cut in around the fixtures and edges of the ceiling with a 2 or 3-inch brush.

Begin painting in a corner of the room away from furniture and work across the narrowest expanse of ceiling toward the opposite wall. Paint in 3-foot-wide sections and feather the edges as best you can. When you reach the wall, work back in the opposite direction so that freshly painted areas blend together. By following this zigzagging routine, the lapping effect will be minimized. Try to paint facing a window or the dominant light in the room. The *angular sheen* of the light on fresh paint will make skips and other trouble areas show. You should correct them immediately instead of bringing your equipment back a second time.

Most people prefer to use a roller when painting ceilings. A 9-inch roller covers a lot of area quickly, and the paint-carrying capacity makes dipping less frequent. A 4- or 5-foot extension handle will allow you to reach the entire ceiling, even the area over protected furniture (Fig. 2). You may want to use a slightly longer nap on your roller when painting ceilings. The longer nap carries more paint and works around textured effects nicely.

Many people still like to brush their ceilings, although the work is often strenuous and messy. Use the largest brush that you can handle comfortably. Paint off a stepladder or scaffolding so that your head is 2 to 6 inches below the ceiling. Tip off paint in all directions to prevent unsightly patterns.

The crown molding running around the angle between the ceiling and wall can be painted several ways. When the walls are to be painted, the crown molding is usually painted the same color as the ceiling. For papered walls, you may want to match this molding to the remainder of the room's trim. Light molding makes ceilings appear higher and larger, while dark colors shrink and lower the appearance of the ceiling.

See *Cutting-In; Interior Paint; Painting, Interior; Preparation;* and *Sand Paint.*

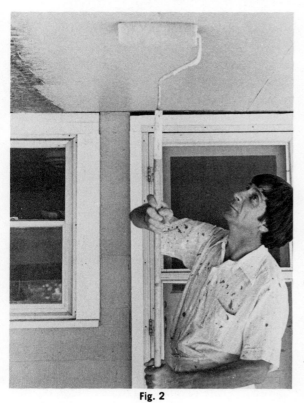

Fig. 2

Ceilings. A 4- or 5-foot extension handle for a roller will make painting a ceiling easy.

CEMENT PAINT

Inexpensive coating for *brick, masonry,* and stucco surfaces. More of a colored (usually white) layer of concrete than a paint, these coatings act as a *breather film*—allowing moisture within the wall to escape without causing blisters under the coating. This nonblistering characteristic makes cement paints especially useful on below-grade walls.

Most cement paints come in a powder which is mixed with water prior to application. These coatings are applied with a large stiff brush that is moved in a circular motion. The coating is worked deep into the porous surface of masonry walls. These coatings must be applied to damp walls, then cured by keeping them moist up to 72 hours after applications. Although made of cement, these paints are extremely fragile and make a poor base for other paints.

CHAIR RAILS

Wooden moldings around a room at the level of chair backs. When the area below the chair rail is finished with wood paneling or a similar material, the bottom section is called *wainscoting*. In most instances the chair rail is finished with the same material as the wainscoting. When the area below the wall gets painted the same as the area above the rail, the rail is painted a contrasting or matching *color*. Use a semigloss or glossy enamel so the molding will withstand the abuse it receives.

See *Trim*.

CHALKING

Some flat exterior alkyd paints exhibit chalking—a fine powder on the surface of a painted object. As these chalking paints oxidize, pigment particles form a powder on the paint's surface. Controlled chalking continues three or four years after application, and this gradual breakdown of the paint prevents an excessive buildup of old paint. Excessive paint buildup is one of the major causes of *alligatoring*.

Chalking. Chalking paints used on surfaces above masonry walls may cause the unsightly effects shown.

Chalking paint is not designed for use in all climates. In extremely wet climates, rain and snow will keep the house clean without the aid of chalking paints. In dry climates where there are no washing rains, chalking is also unnecessary.

The chemically induced chalking of paint has its advantages. It allows rain or a well-aimed hose to carry away dirt and debris, but a chalking paint should not be used above masonry or dark walls. See the illustration. The chalk will wash down to the lower wall and disfigure it. Chalk stains can be removed by scrubbing with a detergent and water solution.

Although paint manufacturers have perfected the rate of chalking in most high quality paints, excessive chalking can be caused by an inferior paint, improper application, excessive thinning, or a combination of all three mis-

Checking. Checking is a frequent problem on plywood and new siding.

takes. Chalking problems can be corrected by recoating the area with a nonchalking latex paint. Unfortunately, only latex primers and alkyd paint will stick to a chalking surface. Latex topcoatings do not adhere, because the powder prevents the paint from gaining a foothold in the substrate. In order to switch from a chalking to a nonchalking paint, both a primer and new topcoating must be applied.

Although primers and oil-base materials will stick to chalking surfaces, remember that dirt and chalk are present together. Dirt affects the adhesion of all types of paint, so scrub chalking areas with detergent and water before painting.

See *Preparation* and *Primer*.

CHECKING

A cracking of the paint parallel to the grain of the wood. See the illustration. This condition occurs frequently on plywood and new siding.

To correct checking, scrape away problem paint. Sand bare wood, prime, and apply topcoat. On new plywood a thorough sanding before the first coat of primer will help reduce checking. Checking forms many sharp splinters, so wear gloves and goggles when working with these surfaces.

CHEESIE

A term used to describe a paint film that is still soft. Slightly harder than *tacky*, but not totally cured, a film in this condition is subject to damage from very light pressure. Handle carefully when paint is in this stage.

CHINA WOOD OIL

This is another name for *tung oil*. This fast-drying oil is most often used in hard, clear, water-resistant finishes such as *spar varnish*.

CHIPS

Because of their tough shell-like nature, trim enamels tend to chip away with wear. Instead of the smooth degradation present with most paints, chip-prone enamels leave marks with sharp edges. These chipped areas must be sanded smooth, or the glossy finish of the next coat will highlight the imperfections.

See *Sanding*.

CLAPBOARD

Also known as weatherboard. It is a long thin board of increasing thickness from one edge to the other. It is nailed on homes in an overlapping fashion as an exterior siding. When painting clapboard, you will be confronted with a variety of situations. Generally, they involve working with new wood or previously painted wood that has gone bad.

New clapboard should be allowed to weather at least a month before priming. This

Clapboard. Rolling is a fast method of painting clapboard, but do not forget to cut in the edges of each board before rolling.

weathering period gives the wood a chance to bleed, dry out, and settle in before it is sealed with a paint film. Clapboard must be primed before applying a topcoat. Oil-base primers are usually recommended for the first coating of almost all clapboarding. This is not in deference to the wood as much as it is to the nails that rust in contact with most latex paints. Oil-base primers are especially suited for resinous wood, such as pine, and those woods noted for *bleeding* like cedar and redwood.

The topcoat can be either oil-base or latex, although many more homeowners are opting for the latex alkyd exterior finishes. You may want to consult your paint dealer to find out what climatic considerations can alter your choice of a paint.

Clapboard can be painted with a brush, roller, or spray gun. Brushing takes the most time, but this method produces the most thorough job if you are careful. Rolling cuts painting time in half, but it may not provide as thorough a job. See the illustration. The roller nap for rolling clapboarding should be at least ¾-inch long. Some professionals use 1¼-inch wool naps successfully. Spraying saves more time than rolling, although paint usually does not penetrate wood as well. Let your time schedule, available equipment, and personal preference be your guide.

New clapboard can be finished with a natural or penetrating stain. Penetrating oil-base semitransparent stains preserve the natural beauty of the wood. These stains are inexpensive, durable, and easy to maintain. Their water-repellent character combats mildew and moisture problems without *cracking, flaking,* or *peeling* like regular paint.

Some nonpenetrating finishes like varnish are not very durable. They may need to be replaced every year or two.

Previously painted clapboards go bad for many reasons including improper sawing at the sawmill, improper caulking, and inferior paint. In most cases clapboard can be scraped to bare wood, reprimed, and refinished without difficulty. Boards that are cracked, broken, rotten, or excessively grainy should be replaced.

To replace a clapboard, use a nail set to drive the nails all the way through the bottom edge of the board directly above the one you wish to remove. Pull out the unsuitable board. You may have to break the board into smaller pieces to facilitate removal, and you may need to dig parts of the board out from under the one above with a hammer and chisel. Prime both sides and ends of the replacement board. Allow them to dry. Priming all sides of the new board will extend the life of the replacement piece.

When the primer has dried, work the narrow edge of the new board under the bottom edge of the board still in place. Nail the bottom of the top board back in place, so nails pass through the replacement board. Countersink the nails and prime with an oil-base primer. When the primer dries, patch holes with appropriate *putty, spackling compound*, or *wood filler.* Do not forget to apply *caulking* to the butted side joints at the ends of the new boards. Apply topcoat when patching compounds are dry.

Paint can be removed from peeling and flaking clapboards by three different means: scraping, using chemical removers, and applying heat.

When scraping wood, be careful not to damage clapboard. Scrape with the minimum pressure necessary to remove damaged paint. When sanding, an orbital sander is the best bet. Belt and circular sanders damage wood by raising a tooth to which it is impossible to get paint to stick.

Heat is best applied with a heating iron designed specifically for the job. Paint is cooked off the board and then scraped away with a putty knife or scraper. Most rental stores carry suitable sanders and heat irons.

Chemical removers are brushed onto defective paint. They soften the paint for easy removal with a scraper or putty knife.

See *Brushing Techniques; Exterior Paint; Paint, Removing; Painting, Exterior;* and *Primers.*

CLEANING

In order for paint to look its best and last a long time, it must be applied to a properly prepared surface. The first step in almost any preparation routine is cleaning dirt, grease, and oil from the surface you intend to paint. A clean surface gives you a better chance of spotting problems and also prevents contamination of caulking, patching, and priming compounds.

Interior Cleaning

Walls, ceilings, and woodwork need a thorough scrubbing before painting. Pay particular attention to bathrooms and kitchens where grease and soap accumulate daily. Most surfaces can be cleaned with a detergent and hot water solution. Wax furniture polish should be removed with paint thinner or a suitable solvent. Although dirt and grease build up most in kitchen and bathrooms, check other walls. These substances must be removed, or new paint will not stick properly.

A large sponge and a detergent solution will remove most grease and dirt. Do not use a soap, as this material has a fatty base that adds to your problem. Rinse with clear water as you go.

Exterior Cleaning

Cleaning the exterior of your house is a big job. Use the best tools you can afford and avoid shortcuts. The cleaner your house is before you begin the actual paint job, the fewer problems you will encounter along the way.

If your house is small, you may need no more than a garden hose and an attachment which mixes detergent into the water stream. This should be enough to remove dirt on exposed areas. You will need to supplement the hose with a scrub brush under eaves facing a busy street.

For bigger houses, you may want to rent a high pressure sprayer. After renting a high power unit, read the operating instructions carefully. Many of the better units shoot out a narrow water jet at 600 pounds per square inch. Wear goggles and protective clothing. Strong detergents will cut through most dirt and grease.

Begin working on the house under eaves and cornices. Work downward toward the ground in 6 to 8-foot-wide swaths. Hold the nozzle about 8 inches from the wall and move the spray back and forth in smooth slow sweeps to wash off dirt. Flaking and peeling paint can be blasted off by holding the tip of the spray 6 inches from the wall and angling it at a 45-degree angle. Sweep each section in both directions to insure removal of all loose paint.

Patches of *mildew* can be removed by mixing bleach into the unit's detergent supply or by scrubbing affected areas with a solution of 1 cup bleach to 1 gallon of warm water. Never add bleach to an ammonia cleaner because a toxic gas will be created. When mildew disappears, flush the surface with clear water and allow to dry at least two days before painting.

Masonry

No paint will stick to masonry that is slick with oil or grease. Porches, patios, basements, and driveways must be washed of all animal, vegetable, and petroleum-base oils before painting. Detergents mixed with water and applied vigorously with a stiff brush will remove most animal and vegetable oils. Petroleum-base oils demand the use of a *degreaser*.

Degreasers are sold in powder, liquid, and aerosol form. Powders are the cheapest. Aerosols are the most expensive. Mix powders and liquids according to instructions and apply with a stiff brush. Aerosols are sprayed directly on the spot. After the degreaser has done its work, wash all residue down the drain with clear water. Masonry must be allowed to dry before painting. Surfaces affected by *alkali* and *efflorescence* must also be properly treated and washed before painting.

See *Fungi* and *Preparation*.

CLEANUP

Before you begin preparing a room for painting, move furniture out of the way. Cover all floors, furniture, and fixtures with *drop cloths* and newspaper. Keep a rag handy while painting. Use it to wipe up spills, splatters, and drips. Wet paint is much easier to remove from a surface than dry paint. Good preparation and clean working habits will reduce your cleanup chores to folding drop cloths, cleaning tools, rearranging furniture, and storing leftover material.

The first thing to do at the completion of a job is to pour extra paint back into cans. Put paint brushes, rollers, or spray machine parts into a suitable solvent. Do not wait for the paint to begin hardening before deciding to clean your tools.

One of the main reasons latex paints are gaining popularity is their easy cleanup. Simply run tools—brushes, paint pots, trays, and rollers—under running water. Keep brushes and rollers under until wash water runs almost clear (Fig. 1). Work paint out of the heels of brushes with fingers, fork, or brush comb. Do

Fig. 1

Cleanup. Roller naps clean up easily under running water when a latex paint is used.

the final wash in soapy water. Then rinse with clear water. Hang brushes up to drip dry or tap them on the toe of a shoe to knock out excess water.

There is also a spin drying apparatus on the market which makes drying brushes and rollers a quick and efficient process (Fig. 2). The tool clamps a brush or roller on one end, a handle is pumped up and down at the opposite end, and the brush or roller spins. The centrifugal force of this spinning forces water or thinner from the tool. To avoid spraying yourself, lower the brush or roller into a paper bag or trash can before spinning.

Oil-base paints, alkyds, and varnishes can be cleaned with *mineral spirits, thinner*, kerosene, or *turpentine*. Lacquers, catalytic epoxies, and enamels may need special solvents. Check the container's recommenda-

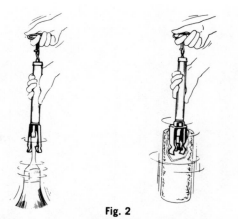

Fig. 2

Cleanup. Spin driers use centrifugal force to remove excess water or paint thinners from brushes and rollers (courtesy Shur-Line).

tions before painting with these materials to ensure that you have the proper solvent on hand.

Although oil-base paints are more difficult to clean than water-base materials, following the correct routine will simplify the process. Because paint thinners and solvents are expensive, you will want to get as many washes as possible from your fluid. To do this, pour a little thinner into your paint pot. Work on your cleanest equipment first. For example, clean your sash tool first, and then your 4-inch brush before washing the sides of your paint pot. This way you give all pieces of equipment a first wash with the same thinner. Pour this first wash thinner into a *gag bucket*.

Pour thinner for a second wash into a paint pot and rewash the brushes. Use your fingers to work the thinner well into the heel of the brush. Wash the paint off the sides of the paint pot. Three or four washes should remove all the pigment from your tools. For the final wash of nylon brushes, wipe out the paint pot with a clean rag and mix a solution of detergent and warm water. Do not over wash bristle brushes in water, as they will swell and lose their shape. Work detergent solution well into the bristles of the brush. Rinse in clear water and tap or spin out excess moisture.

Roller naps and frames can be cleaned in their tray. Like cleaning a brush in a paint pot, this washes two pieces of equipment with one batch of thinner. Follow the brush cleaning routine of repeated washings with fresh batches of thinner. Spin dry to fluff out the nap.

When the brushes are dry, store them for the next job. Run a comb through the brushes to align the bristles. Brushes should be returned to their original wrappers or secured in heavy brown paper. Cut a piece of paper bag twice as wide as the distance around the ferrule. Cut the paper twice the heel to the bristle tip length of your brush. Place the brush so that the handle extends beyond the edge of the paper, and the tips of the bristles reach the halfway point of the paper's length. Roll the brush up in the paper, then fold over and secure with rubber bands. Brushes should be hung up or laid on their sides for storage. Do not rest them on bristle tips, or the brushes will be deformed.

Fluff up the roller nap with your fingers to prevent matting during storage. Rollers should then be wrapped in brown paper. Cut the paper wide enough, so that the excess can be tucked into the ends of the roller (Fig. 3). Rollers can also be wrapped in plastic, but the plastic should be perforated to allow air circulation and prevent mildew. Stand them on end for storage, so a flat spot does not develop in the roller nap.

Pad applicators are cleaned with repeated washes in much the same way as rollers and brushes. If the pad is removable, take it off the handle before cleaning. Beware of cleaning foam rubber pads in thinner. The liquid may dissolve them. When wrapped in paper for storage, pads will last through many jobs.

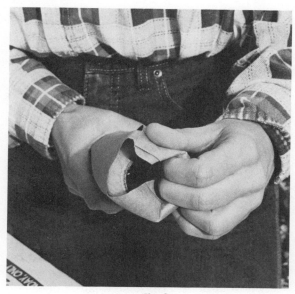

Fig. 3

Cleanup. Tuck the ends of a brown paper wrapper into a roller nap prior to storage.

Paint cans seal the best when their rims are free of dried paint. Clean rims thoroughly, then tap the lid in place with a hammer. Drape a rag over the can to prevent splatters. Do not throw any leftover paint away; you will need it for touching up later on.

Paint will keep the longest when enclosed in a container with little air. Small quantities of paint keep well when poured into small jars and sealed. Never store paint in plastic, unless it is the container the paint came in. Store all paint, thinner, and sharp tools away from children, pets, and open flames. Avoid direct sunlight and freezing temperatures.

By the time you finish cleaning your tools, recently painted walls should have dried enough for you to rearrange furniture, replace fixtures, and rehang drapes. Although painted walls may feel dry to the touch, the paint probably has not cured completely and will damage easily. Be careful when moving furniture.

There is no sense getting the brush you just cleaned dirty again for an error that could have been avoided. Most professionals recommend leaving furniture 6 inches away from walls for at least a week to prevent damage.

See *Applicators; Brushes; Rollers, Paint;* and *Thinners.*

CLOUDY

The term used to describe the opaque, milky-looking film which forms on varnish, lacquer, and enamel finishes when these coatings dry in a warm, humid environment. The best way to avoid clouding is to work with these coatings in fall, winter, or spring if your summers are hot and muggy. To correct clouding, sand the surface lightly and refinish in dry weather.

COAGULATION

A condition commonly found in old paints that have been exposed to extreme heat or cold. The defect resembles curdled milk and is caused by the *resin* particles sticking together. A paint in this condition is not worth saving. Throw it out.

See *Agglomeration* and *Curdling.*

COAL TAR SOLVENTS

These solvents are distilled from coal tar to make a crude petroleumlike product. Coal tar solvents can be used for cleaning oil-base paints from brushes. Wash brushes afterward with a higher grade *solvent* or *thinner* to prevent sticky residues from remaining in the brushes.

COATINGS

This is a modern term for any material that is spread over a *substrate* in order to protect it from weather and improve its appearance. Although this term is often meant to mean paint, it also includes varnish, shellac, lacquer, and other on-the-surface materials.

COATS, NUMBER OF

The number of coats of paint necessary for achieving the longest lasting and best looking job depends on several conditions: the condition of the substrate, color changes, application techniques, and what type of paint is being applied.

Interior walls that are in good shape (no *peeling* paint or extensive patching) may need no more than a single topcoat to regain a like-new appearance. Woodwork in such a room is likely to need only one coat of trim enamel.

In rooms with extensive patching, a substantial change in color, or a switch from one type of finish to another (from a flat wall paint to a semigloss enamel), a primer coat is necessary to build a solid base for the topcoating. In most cases the woodwork needs two coats of trim enamel. You might consider making the first coat a primer where the color change is substantial, or where trim requires much patching and sanding.

Outside, three coats of paint are recommended for a new wood surface. Generally, the three-coat system includes a primer and two finish coats. A variation is to use a primer over a *wood preservative*, then finish with a topcoating. Remember that a two-coat paint system lasts only half as long as a three-coat system.

On old outdoor paint surfaces that are in good condition (no extensive repairs, no flaking or peeling paint, and no bare wood), one topcoat may be sufficient. Do not expect one coat of paint exposed to weather or heavy use to last more than two or three years.

On bare wood consider spot priming the surface and applying a two-topcoat system over the entire surface. Spot priming saves paint, yet produces a measure of protection very close to a three-coat system.

In warm, dry weather, oil-base and alkyd paint should be allowed to dry a day or two before recoating. In cold, damp weather, oil-base paint may take up to a week to dry thoroughly. A time period in excess of two weeks should be avoided between primer and topcoat, because accumulating dirt and the effects of weathering reduce *adhesion*. Latex paint can be applied within a few hours of a previous coat of latex in hot, dry weather. Cool, damp weather may require a day or two between coats.

There may be spots on your house (under the eaves, for example) where you benefit by not painting as often as the remainder of the body of your house. Because weather does not attack these spots, they may need to be painted only every other time the rest of your house gets painted. You may consider giving it only one coat of paint, while the exposed portions of your house get two coats. Paint experts agree that overpainting can be just as damaging as underpainting. Excessive *chalking* or *alligatoring* are two indications of excess paint buildup.

See *Estimating Quantity of Paint, Finish Maintenance,* and *Paint, Choosing.*

COHESION

The ability of a coating to bind together to form a durable finish. Excessive thinning, cheap paints, applying a new coating over dirt and grime, or applying a paint over an *incompatible* substrate will cause cohesion problems. The first sign of a cohesion problem is usually *cracking. Flaking, peeling,* and *alligatoring* are advanced stages of the condition. To insure good cohesion, clean all surfaces thoroughly before painting. Buy a good quality paint. Follow the application and thinning instructions on the label carefully.

See *Adhesion* and *Intercoat Adhesion.*

COLOR RETENTION

The ability of a coating to preserve its original color. Sunlight, moisture, and age affect the color retention of different coatings. Count on some fading with the alkyd oil-base paints that advertise *chalking* as one of their traits. Because of this chalk-forming characteristic, these paints are sold in white or soft pastel tones. Latex paints hold color well without chalking. Latex paints are available in almost all the colors of the rainbow. Penetrating stains fade as they weather. The intensity of the pigments remaining in the fading surface can be used to judge when the siding needs recoating.

See *Colors* and *Yellowing*.

COLORS

Choosing the color for paint is often more difficult than choosing a type of paint. Although selecting a color from the virtually limitless array of possibilities may seem confusing, you can narrow your choices by following a few of the guidelines outlined in this section.

Color Basics

Colors are divided into two basic distinctions. One side is said to be cold and the other hot. The hot or advancing colors—yellow, red, and orange—seem to stimulate your eyes. The cold colors—blue, violet, and blue-green—are the soothing colors.

People who work with color have developed a color wheel. See the illustration. It is based on the colors produced when white light is refracted by a prism—the same effect as a rainbow. Sir Isaac Newton designed the first color wheel with seven colors; however, only six basic colors are used nowadays. The three primary colors—red, yellow, and blue—and

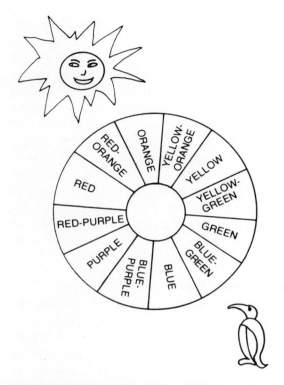

Colors. A color wheel helps make choosing contrasting and complementary colors easy.

the three secondary colors—orange, purple, and green (which are combinations of the primary colors)—are the basic colors of the modern color wheel. Indigo, Newton's seventh color, has been grouped with purple.

The colors falling between the secondary colors are known as tertiary colors—giving a total of 12 color groups from which to choose. The color wheel is best used to decide if two colors will go together. There are several methods of making this determination. One is matching colors on opposite sides of the wheel. Following this method, most shades of green will match well with most shades of red.

A variation of this method is picking colors that flank the color opposite another color on the wheel. Using this approach, shades of the red, purple, and blue-green group go good with yellow.

Another common method of determining matching colors is the triad approach. Colors that are one-third of the way (four spaces) around the wheel tend to match with each other. Yellow goes good with blue or red in the triad approach.

Experiment with the wheel, and you soon discover which method produces a combination most pleasing to your eye. You may find color combinations that violate these approaches and are still pleasing to your eye. Go ahead and use them. No two people have the same preference for color schemes.

Interior Paint Styling

Paint styling is a method of utlilizing the colors available to you in a way that benefits your house the most. Although there are no hard and fast rules in paint styling, using colors effectively will accent the good features of your house while camouflaging the unattractive aspects.

As a general rule, the ceilings are painted the lightest color, followed by the walls and woodwork. Trim (especially baseboards) is generally painted the darkest color in a room. It does not stop there. Light colors will make a small room seem larger and airier, while dark colors may make the same room seem small and cramped. Rooms that receive plenty of direct sunlight can be cooled with darker shades, while rooms that receive little direct light can be livened up with active, advancing colors.

By choosing the color schemes for interior rooms wisely, you can alter the appearance of your home. Light colors make walls look farther away and bigger than they actually are. Dark colors make the same walls look closer and smaller than they are. Yellow is a cheerful color, while red and orange are more active. Greens, blues, and purples are subdued colors. Gray is neutral.

Color selection can affect the apparent shape of a room, too. Subtle changes in the shade of a color will make a narrow room seem wider or deeper than it actually is. For example, you can bring the ends of a long narrow room in by painting the end walls a slightly darker shade than the sidewalls. It is usually best to bring only one wall in, preferably the one without windows or doors and the one you least often face.

Color is also useful for accenting the good features of a particular room or area. A breakfast alcove painted with warm colors appears bigger, brighter, and cheerier than it actually is. A living room painted in dark tones will give the room a subdued, stately look.

One of the most useful ways to use shade variations is raising or lowering the apparent height of your ceiling. Paints labeled ceiling white are extremely flat, reflecting very little light. The light they do reflect bounces back so blandly that your eyes do not even notice. You can lower the ceiling by painting it a shade slightly darker than the walls. A low ceiling can be raised by coating it with a bright white finish. The difference in shade does not have to be great to achieve the desired effect.

When planning the paint scheme for your house, it is not always advisable to consider the exterior and interior separately. By painting the eave on the north side of your house a light color, it will reflect more light into a room. If that room is painted with light, warm colors, a meager amount of light can be expanded into a surprising sum of illumination. Dark-colored eaves on the south side of your house will cut back on the amount of light reflected into a room. If that room is painted a cool color, the sun will be subdued.

Exterior Paint Styling

The colors you choose for the exterior of your house will be determined by its setting and the tone of the houses around yours. The exterior of your house has as many color tricks as the interior.

Light-colored houses appear bigger, while dark-colored houses appear smaller. Painting your house so that it is compatible with its surroundings—say trees or shrubs—will make it almost disappear. Remember that light colors reflect sunlight, thereby helping to keep your house cool, while dark colors absorb sunlight.

The color of your roof will determine, to some extent, what color the body of your house is. As a general rule, the body should be compatible with the roof. The trim should be compatible with the body to a greater extent than the roof.

By emphasizing horizontal instead of vertical lines with trim paint, you can make your house look shorter. Vertical lines such as corner pieces, painted a color lighter than the house's body, will add the appearance of extra height. Unattractive features like odd-shaped windows disappear when painted the same color as the body of your house. Porches and entranceways gain emphasis when painted in contrast to the body of your house. Outside, stairs appear wider when painted a light, bright color. If your house is chopped up—having many types of siding—you can disguise the fact by painting all parts of the body with the same paint.

It is easiest to maintain the existing color of your house, although moving to another color can be accomplished with the excellent *hiding power* of modern paints. Regardless of the quality of the paint, as it weathers the undercoating will show through. If the two colors are the same, you will hardly notice. Contrasting colors—especially a light over a dark—will produce a mottled appearance as the paint weathers. White and gray are the predominant colors used on exteriors, and moving away from them can be tricky. Move a shade or two at a time for the best results.

When choosing a color for the exterior of your house, carry the color sample to a window and check it in natural light. If the paint is to be used in a windowless room, check the color card under the same type of light found in that room. The source of artificial light will make a big difference in how a paint looks. Fluorescent lighting usually gives off a cool blue hue. Incandescent light casts a warm gold glow.

When the paint store must mix a color to match one already on your walls, take as big a piece of the old paint as you can. Make sure the salesman dries a sample of the mixed paint before comparing it to your chip. Paint tends to dry a slightly different color or shade from what you see in the can.

Mixing Your Own Colors

If you are dissatisfied with the choice of colors offered at the paint store, you can try your hand at mixing custom color paints. One of the first things you will discover is that matching two separate batches of paint is impossible. Either stick to smaller jobs or obtain a container large enough to hold all the paint you will need for a job. On a big job, like the exterior of your house, hand-coloring 10 to 15 gallons of paint is a long, tedious, and often frustrating job. It is best to leave the tinting to the paint salesman. He will provide a nearly perfect match between batches every time.

When tinting paint yourself, you will need a universal colorant. This pigment comes in many colors and works in most types of paint.

45

These pigments are color-saturated, and a small error can ruin a batch of paint. Mix the tint with a small amount of paint in a separate container before pouring into uncolored paint.

Begin by pouring an inch or two of paint into a clear plastic or glass container. Add tint according to the guidelines on the can's label. Stir until all tint mixes with the paint. When the paint in the cup is thoroughly mixed, pour it—a small amount at a time—into the uncolored paint. When you achieve the shade you desire, let the paint sit 30 minutes so the pigment will have a chance to blend with the paint.

There are many small tricks which will help you create a professional looking color scheme. In the final analysis it is your house, and you can paint it the way you like.

See *Pigments*.

COMPATIBILITY

The term used to describe the ability of one paint to mix with another. Most latex paints will mix with other water-base paints and with the alkyd and oil-base paints. When mixing paint produced by two different companies, you are asking for trouble. You are liable to end up with a paint that does not meet your expectations. Never mix interior and exterior paints. Each was formulated to withstand a different set of conditions, and you will end up with a paint which withstands neither. Leave the paint mixing to the manufacturers, and you will avoid any compatibility problems.

COPPER STAINS

Occasionally, copper gutters and downspouts will corrode in a way that stains the body of your house. The first step in curing this problem is coating the copper to prevent further oxidation. Clear coatings like varnish will preserve the natural look of the copper, but these materials must be reapplied every two or three years. Painting over copper is a shame, but primers designed for metal, top-coated with the new latex house paints, will effectively seal in the problem-causing metal.

Stains already on the house can be removed with a detergent and water solution and determined scrubbing. They can also be sealed in with shellac, *sealer*, or a primer. An oil-base primer works best, because the stain will bleed through latex paints in much the same way rusty nailheads penetrate water-base paints. A topcoat can be applied when sealer or primer is dry.

See *Metals* and *Staining Through*.

CORROSION

Corrosion in the form of oxidation and rust is constantly attacking the metal parts of your house. You will first notice corrosion when paint peels. Excessive corrosion will become painfully evident when rust streaks and stains begin to mar the finish of your otherwise sound paint job.

Because metals are corrosive in nature, you must keep a careful eye on the metal parts of your house. The problem should be corrected at the first sign of corrosion. It is much easier to refinish several quarter-size rust spots than it is a 3 by 4-foot section of metal. The secret to preventing corrosion is keeping the metal sealed against the intrusion of water and air with paint. To treat a corroded area, sand it, dust it clean, then coat it immediately with a metal primer. Semigloss and glossy paints are best for topcoats; they produce impervious finishes.

See *Metals* and *Rust Removal*.

COVERING POWER

The ability of a paint to coat a surface. The covering power of a coating is usually expressed in square feet of coverage per gallon of

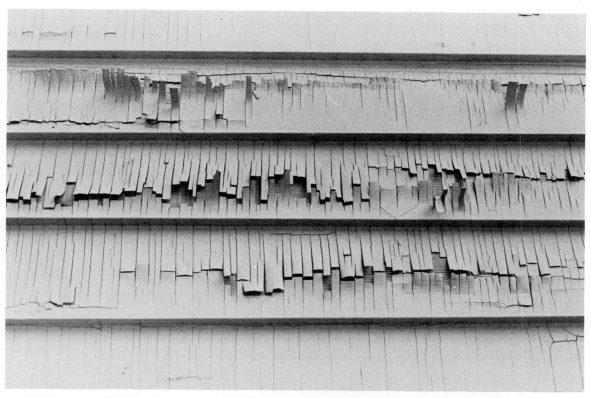

Cracking. Cross-grain cracking runs across the grain of wood siding. It is usually caused by a too thick buildup of paint.

paint. The type of coating, method of application, and the porosity of the surface have a great effect on the coating's covering power. Some latex paints may cover more than 400 square feet of smooth surface, while thin coatings like stain may cover only 200 square feet of absorbent weathered siding.

See *Estimating Quantity of Paint.*

CRACKING

One of the first hints of deterioration in a paint job. Unfortunately, cracks allow water to enter the paint job. This eventually leads to *flaking* and *peeling.*

The most common reason for cracking is improper application of paint. Applying a second coat of paint before the first coat is dry often leads to cracking. Using a topcoating over an undercoating or primer that is incompatible with the topcoating will also encourage cracking. Another common cause of cracking is moisture from rain or dew penetrating the pores in flat finish paints. The swelling and contracting of this moisture will eventually crack the paint film, exposing it to further deterioration.

To correct a cracking problem, scrape away all loose paint and sand the surface smooth. Coat with a wood primer, then apply a paint that has water-shedding characteristics. Gloss or semigloss finish paints shed water more readily than their flat finish counterparts.

Cross-grain cracking runs vertically from

the top to the bottom of clapboarding. See the illustration. These parallel cracks are caused by a too thick buildup of paint on the siding. This paint defect occurs most often on older houses that have been repeatedly painted with oil-base paint. Cross-grain cracking results from the thick paint coat not being able to expand and contract with the wood underneath.

Repairing cross-grain cracking is a difficult job. All the old paint must be removed through sanding, scraping, or heating until bare wood is exposed. Then the siding can be primed and given a topcoat without fear of a reoccurrence.

See *Alligatoring* and *Crazing.*

CRAWLING

A term painters use to describe a paint that will not stick or lay down on a surface. Crawling paint beads up into bubbles in much the same way that water beads on a waxed car. This frequently happens when trying to apply a latex paint to a surface with a glossy or semigloss finish or a surface contaminated with grease.

To prevent crawling, apply paint to surfaces that have been properly prepared and are free of grease and shine. If there is no way to avoid painting over a glossy surface, the *sheen* should be removed with a light sanding in order to provide *tooth* for the topcoat.

CRAZING

A term used to describe the formation of minute hairline cracks in a painted surface. Crazing cracks run in all directions and are a result of paint failing to expand and contract with the substrate. Application of a flexible latex paint over the problem area should cure this defect.

See *Cracking.*

CREOSOTE

An oily black penetrating wood preservative distilled from coal tar. Creosote is commonly used on wood exposed to a lot of moisture or positioned near or in contact with the ground.

The preservative can be brushed, rolled, or sprayed onto a surface, although overnight soaking is the best application method. Be careful when applying creosote because it kills vegetation.

If the wood is not to be painted, then a finish of creosote is the cheapest preservative to use. If you plan on painting over the treated wood, more expensive pentachlorophenol or copper naphthanate preservatives dissolved in light oils are easier to work with.

Creosote that has weathered more than a year may not bleed through paint. This preservative often inhibits adhesion up to eight years after application. To be on the safe side, all creosoted wood, no matter how old, should be coated with a *sealer* before applying a topcoat.

Small creosote stains can be killed with a sealer. Special stain sealers are available for larger creosoted areas, or you might try one or two coats of *aluminum paint* before applying a topcoat.

See *Wood Preservatives.*

CROCKING

A common condition in already dry latex paints when they are cleaned with a wet rag. The paint usually becomes lighter, so it no longer matches surrounding surfaces. Crocking is also possible in alkyd paints that have a built-in chalking characteristic.

Crocking is nearly impossible to avoid on flat finish wall paints; however, it seldom occures in semigloss or glossy trim paints. Use the latter paints when painting areas that you expect to wash frequently.

CROSS-BRUSHING

A technique used to work paint into cracks, especially at *butted side joints* in clapboard, when the crack is not large enough to caulk. Cross-brushing cracks involves passing the brush three times over the crack. The first brush stroke is made perpendicular to the crack in order to scrape paint into it. The second is made parallel to the crack to work the paint into it and smooth away excess paint. The final stroke is made to match the remainder of your job and is done with light, smooth pressure.

There is a high side to every butted joint. Try to make the final stroke from the high to the low side, so excess paint is not scraped off the brush into the crack. This extra paint will run and form a drip if not brushed out.

See *Brushing Techniques.*

CURDLING

A defect caused when the *resins* or *pigments* in a coating lump together. Old or cheap paints often exhibit curdling. If mixing does not eliminate the lumps, throw the paint away.

See *Agglomeration* and *Coagulation.*

CURTAINS

These wide expanses of sagging paint usually occur when oil-base or alkyd paints are applied too thickly. They are a common nuisance when painting metal with rust-inhibiting paints or when finishing large smooth doors with a glossy or semigloss trim enamel.

Curtains form during drying when the outside layer of the paint forms a skin. When the *vehicle* evaporates below this skin, the skin collapses without shrinking enough to smooth out the film. The paint droops in curtainlike wrinkles. *Sags* and *runs* are less severe forms of curtains. Correcting these defects is ac-

complished by sanding the surface smooth and applying a fresh coating at the proper thickness.

CUT BACK

The term is painter's slang for adding a *thinner* or *solvent* to make it less thick.

CUTTING-IN

The term used by painters to describe the process of painting around woodwork, corners, and fixtures on walls before they are rolled, sprayed, or brushed with a large wall brush. Inside you can use a 2 to 3-inch brush for working paint into all those places that are impossible to reach with a roller. Most of today's flat latex paints are nonlapping, which makes it easy to cut in around the entire surface of a wall before rolling.

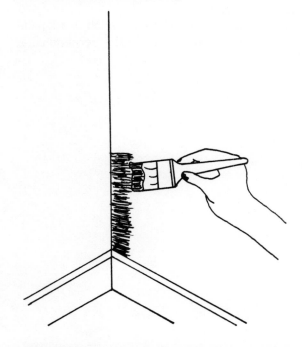

Cutting-In. To cut in, make several brush strokes perpendicular to the corner. Smooth out with a long parallel stroke.

Outside you will want to cut in around windows, corner boards, and trim with a 3 or 4-inch brush. Again, flat latex paints allow you to cut in a whole section before rolling or spraying.

Glossy enamels and alkyd paints may leave *lap marks* if you cut in too far ahead of roller work. With these paints, it is best to cut in several feet of edge and then catch up with your roller while the paint is still wet.

The general technique for cutting-in involves making brush strokes perpendicular to the edge of the corner or trim. Go back and smooth out the paint with strokes parallel with the edge. See the illustration. A 2 to 3-inch wide band is usually enough to allow access with a roller. For more precise work, say where two surfaces of a different color come together, you may want to try a technique known as beading.

Beading is a technique which floats paint into an edge without using the perpendicular strokes mentioned earlier. Use a trim brush with chiseled bristles, preferably one with a square cut tip. Dip the brush and grasp with your thumb on the opposite side of the handle from your fingers. Lay the flat of the brush on the wall ½ to ¾ inch away from the edge or corner. Make an arclike stroke, moving the brush up to the edge so that a bead of paint flows to within 1/16 to ⅛ inch of the edge. Steadily move the brush along the edge until the paint begins to thin to the point where it no longer comes out of the brush in a sufficient amount to coat the surface. Keeping the brush on the wall pull it away from the corner in a smooth arc. When the brush is safely away from the corner, remove it from the wall and redip in paint pot. The next stroke is begun in the wet paint of the previous stroke. By the time you reach the corner, the brush will continue the bead started on the preceding stroke.

See *Brushing Techniques; Painting, Exterior; Painting, Interior;* and *Trim.*

DECAY

Decay of the wooden parts of a house is due to prolonged exposure to extreme *moisture*. Punky, decaying wood will not hold paint effectively, leading to further decay.

When inspecting your house, look for decay behind shrubbery, in secluded corners where air circulation is slight, and anywhere you spot leaky guttering or downspouts. Wooden siding within 8 to 10 inches of the ground will often suffer decay problems. In all cases, the source of the moisture encouraging the decay must be stopped in order to prevent a reoccurrence of the problem.

The presence of *mildew* is often an indication of decaying wood. In advanced cases of decay, the deteriorating wood can be broken away from sound wood. The affected board should be replaced. Apply *wood preservatives* in areas of minor decay, then coat with a primer and topcoat.

See *Clapboard*.

DEGLOSSING

Paint should be applied to surfaces with tooth, or a slightly rough texture, in order to insure adequate *intercoat adhesion*. In most cases, washing a shiny surface with a detergent and water solution will dull it enough so that a topcoat can be applied. When a surface remains shiny after washing, the sheen can be cut with medium sandpaper or a commercial *deglosser*.

See *Preparation* and *Sanding*.

DEGREASERS

Chemical solvents designed to cut through and remove various types of grease. These materials are sold in powder, liquid, and aerosol form. Specific degreasers are designed to work with animal and vegetable grease or petroleum-base lubricants. Vegetable and animal fats accumulate in kitchens (spattered cooking oils) and bathrooms (soap films). Petroleum grease collects on driveways, carports, garages, and workshop floors.

Powdered degreasers are the least expensive, but they are also the hardest to use. The powder is spread over the stain, moistened, scrubbed with a stiff brush or broom, allowed to set, then rinsed away with clear water. Liquid degreasers are used in much the same way, but they are undiluted.

Aerosol degreasers are the easiest to use, but they are also the most expensive. Spray the degreaser on the stain, allow it to stand the recommended time, then wash residue away with clear water. Allow the surface to dry thoroughly before painting.

There are three precautions to follow when using degreasers. Most liquid and aerosol degreasers are flammable and toxic. They should be used in well-ventilated areas away from flame and heat. Degreasers will also kill grass and shrubbery, so do not wash these solvents onto the lawn. When removing grease spots from asphalt, make sure the degreaser is asphalt-safe.

DEPTH

A term used to describe the appearance that a coating is deeper than it is. Several coats of varnish or shellac will achieve a depth that is impossible with a single coat of these materials. Generally, glossy paints have more depth than flat wall paints. Lacquers have the most depth.

DISPERSION AGENT

This is a chemical added to paints to keep the pigments in suspension and prevent *curdling* or *agglomeration* prior to the paint drying.

DOORS

Doors get the most use, next to floors, of any part of a house. For this reason, they need to be coated with tough washable paints.

Glossy or semigloss trim enamels are the most widely used paints for doors. Stained doors need a coat of tough glossy or semigloss varnish to keep their finishes looking good. The same trim enamel that is used on the woodwork goes onto a door in most cases. You can use the same tools, too. If you plan to paint a door a different color than its jamb, paint the jamb when you paint the rest of the room's woodwork. Come back and finish the door after the jamb had dried.

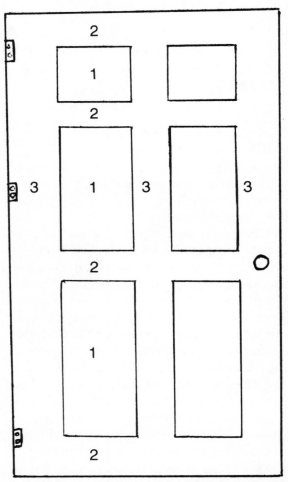

Doors. Follow this order when painting a door: panels, horizontal sections, and vertical stiles.

Paint jambs and stops from top to bottom. If the door opens toward you or into the room, paint only the face of the doorstop facing you. The top section of the stop, perpendicular to the door when closed, gets painted the color of the jamb's outside. If the doorstop is on your side of the door when closed, the top strip of the stop should be painted to match the inside jamb.

There are two ways to paint a door—while it is still hung or horizontal, after removing the hinge pins. You will save some time and get a smoother finish by taking down a flat door. Paneled or louvered doors are easier to paint when left hanging.

Paneled doors should be opened wide and secured with a doorstop to make working easier. Spread newspapers or drop cloths around and under the door. When painting a paneled door, follow the same pattern of movement that you would use on a window. Sand all imperfections, dust, then paint from the inside out, working from the top to the bottom of the door. See the illustration.

Paint the inside panels first, including the molding. Pull paint out of the crack where the molding meets the panel by working an unloaded brush into the crevice and pulling away from the molding to bring excess paint onto the panel. Check bottom corners of the molding often for runs and excessive paint buildup. Tip off panels in the direction of the longest dimension.

Paint the horizontal sections and feather the strokes well into the vertical stiles. Paint the stiles last. When the door is a different color on each side, paint the outside, or latch edge, the same color as the interior of the door when the door opens into the room. When the door opens to the outside, the latch edge should be painted the same color as the door's exterior surface. The inside, or hinge edge, should be painted the opposite color of the latch edge when the exterior and interior surfaces of the door differ in color.

It is best to leave hinges and latch hardware unpainted. Remove knobs and latch hardware if you can or mask with tape. If the hardware has been painted, paint according to latch edge/hinge edge instructions given earlier.

To remove a flat door from its hinges, pound a nail into the bottom of the hinge so that the nail drives the hinge pin out the top of the hinge. Replace the hinge pin in the section of hinge still on the jamb. Lay the door on sawhorses and paint with a trim brush. A short nap roller can be used on flat doors to speed up the job. Do not use a roller with varnish, as the roller tends to leave little bubbles in the finish.

This horizontal position will provide an extra measure of protection against *sags, drips,* and *runs.* Doors painted in this manner with a quick-drying latex paint can be turned over in an hour or two, although you will need to pad the sawhorses. It takes several days for paint to harden thoroughly.

Doors should be left open several days after painting to allow the paint to completely dry. If you do not open the doors, chances are the paint will stick along the stop and door edge. The first time you open the door, stuck paint will pull off and leave an ugly scar.

DOUBLE-HUNG WINDOWS

Windows that contain two *sashes* sliding up and down on runners along both sides of the opening. This type of window differs from a *casement window* where the sashes are hinged on one side, allowing them to swing in or out. The procedure for painting double-hung windows is basically the same on interior and exterior surfaces.

Choosing a paint for windows is a simple proposition: interior trim enamel on the inside, exterior trim enamel on the outside. Why? Windows receive more than their share of abuse. Doors and windows are the only moving parts on a house. Inside, a window's paint must be able to withstand condensation moisture and washing to remove smudges. Outside, a window is subjected to weathering without the flat, water-shedding characteristics of adjacent sidewalls. A window's paint must be impervious to water both inside and outside. Therefore, the use of a tough, durable coating of water-shedding glossy or semigloss enamel is essential. Settle for nothing else, and window deterioration problems will be kept to a minimum.

The first step in painting a window is removing its hardware; outside, this includes removing *screens and storm windows.* Scrape off all peeling or flaking paint and loose putty. Sand all rough areas. Outside edges and cracks in the trim around the window opening should be *caulked.* Nail holes should be patched with a *wood filler* or *spackling compound.*

Bare wood and places in the window sash where putty is missing should be primed. On problem windows, a coat of *wood preservative* prior to priming is a good idea. When primer is dry, windows can be *glazed.* The bottom puttied edge of exterior sashes and sills on the south and west sides of a house take the worst beating by the weather. These areas will need to be touched up more often than other parts of your house.

Painters have worked out a rather specific sequence for painting double-hung windows (Fig. 1). Inside, the inner sash should be raised and the outer sash lowered as far as possible. Outside, the procedure is reversed.

When sashes are in position, begin by painting the exposed muntins. These are the

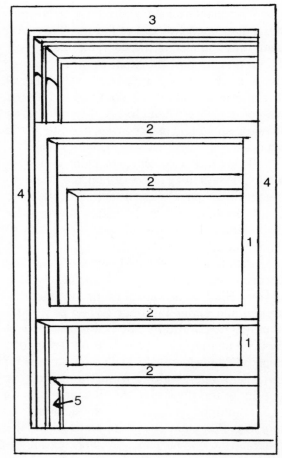

Fig. 1

Double-Hung Windows. The order for painting double-hung windows is: muntins /vertical pieces of sash (1), crosspieces of sash (2), top of frame (3), horizontal pieces of frame (4), and jamp (5).

strips of wood that hold the glass in on multiple pane windows. An inch-wide brush will work on the muntins. With a little practice, a 1½-inch beveled sash tool works just fine. Many of the new trim size *applicators* work well on windows. When painting over the muntin/ glass or putty/glass interface, run a bead of paint out about ⅛ inch onto the glass. This seals the crack against water and prevents early decay.

Some people mask off the glass with masking tape and then pull the tape from the glass when they are finished with the delicate work. Remove the tape before the paint dries, or you are liable to peel the paint off with the tape.

Other painters run a bead of paint out to about ¼ inch onto the glass, when the paint has dried, they use a utility knife and straightedge to score a line through the excess paint. They scrape away excess paint with a window scraper. Move the scraper blade in toward the muntin with the blade parallel to the score line. Peel off a small section of paint at a time.

If you are really steady with a brush, you can float a bead of paint out onto the glass the desired ⅛ to 1/16-inch overlap. Regardless of which method you choose, painting windows is a painstaking and slow business. Take your time and do them right the first time, so you will not have to touch-up a second time.

When muntins have been painted, coat the crossbar at the bottom of the outside sash. Move both sashes back to within an inch of their closed position. Paint the muntins and crosspieces on the outside sash. Repeat the order for the inside sash, but do not move up or down (Fig. 2).

When painting the casing around the window opening, begin with the top horizontal. Then work down the sides. Next paint the inside jamb, unless it is aluminum, in which case it does not need painting. Many people prefer not to paint the insides of the jamb. Correctly, they believe that over the years multiple layers of paint will make the window extremely difficult to move up and down. If your windows feel tight, you may want to fol-

Fig. 2
Double-Hung Windows. Raise the inside sash of double-hung windows so that you can paint the top horizontal piece.

Downspouts and Gutters. Peeling and flaking steel gutters must be wire brushed and sanded smooth before painting.

low this advice. If your windows feel loose and rattle in high winds, painting the inside of the jamb will snug up the window and help block air leaks.

When paint is dry to the touch, replace hardware. Move sashes up and down to make sure the paint does not stick them shut. Leave the windows open at least ½ inch for several days to prevent binding of the new paint.

DOWNSPOUTS AND GUTTERS

A system of troughs and pipes designed to carry water off a house's roof and away from the building. Many paint problems such as rust stains and excess moisture can be cured by properly installed and maintained guttering and downspouts. There are aluminum, copper, plastic, steel, and wood gutters and down-

spouts. Each has its own method of painting and maintenance.

Aluminum

Aluminum guttering and downspouts come with one of two finishes: baked on enamel or unfinished. Although aluminum does not usually corrode except near the ocean, many homeowners prefer to paint the gutters to match their homes. Unfinished guttering should be allowed to weather a year. Wipe it with a special metal conditioner or mineral spirits to remove factory grease and powder. Follow with a metal primer or *aluminum paint* before applying a topcoat.

Factory-finished enamel guttering and downspouts are not usually painted over. Although they may look a little out of place unpainted, they will be an eyesore in a short time if you try to paint over the slick enamel. Paint tends to peel and flake off the slick enamel almost as fast as you put it on. If you want to paint downspouts and gutters with this finish, the entire surface area must be prepared by sanding or applying a deglosser before painting in order to provide *tooth* for the paint.

Copper

Copper gutters are best left unpainted. Copper weathers naturally into a distinctive bluish-green patina. If, however, the gutters are leaking onto other parts of your house and disfiguring it, you can remove all the corrosion with a sander and seal with an exterior varnish. This finish, however, requires almost yearly recoating and may not be worth the trouble.

Plastic

Plastic guttering is finding its way into the market at an increasing rate. It comes in a variety of colors, never fades, flakes, or peels. Getting paint to stick on plastic is difficult. So plastic is not usually painted.

Steel

Like aluminum, steel guttering comes in a baked on enamel finish or galvanized. Galvanized gutters should weather for at least a year before they are painted. This allows most of the oil and dust to wash off. Even with this precaution, paint will flake and peel off gutters and downspouts if they are not primed with a metal primer. Before painting galvanized guttering, wipe the surface with a solvent-soaked rag or one of the solvents intended specifically for galvanized metals. Coat immediately with a good oil-base or alkyd metal primer. Apply a topcoat when the primer is dry. Glossy or semigloss latex or oil-base alkyd metal paints

are the best topcoats, but trim enamel will often do the trick.

All loose paint must be removed on old rusting and peeling gutters before painting. See the illustration. Sand rough and rusty spots to bare metal and prime with a zinc-base primer. Apply regular primer over this and then a topcoat.

Enameled steel guttering should be left unpainted, as all types of paint have difficulty sticking to the slick finish. The guttering can be painted after deglossing.

Wood

Wooden gutters are rare. They require a fresh coat of paint every two or three years. Periodic touch-up whenever deterioration begins to show is essential, because collected water will quickly rot the wood.

Before painting, clean out debris and allow several days for drying. Scrape off loose paint and sand rough spots. The inside of the guttering should be painted with a coating of thinned asphalt roof paint. A second coating can be applied two days after the first coat.

On the exterior, bare wood should be sanded and primed with an appropriate primer. When the primer dries, apply house paint. Two coats of trim enamel usually work well.

See *Metals*.

DRIER

A term used to describe a material added to a coating to make it dry more quickly. In epoxy paints a drier is added in order to make the material react and harden into a useful coating. A drier increases the rate of *evaporation* in conventional coatings.

DROP CLOTHS

Protective sheets used to cover floors and furniture when painting. They will save you much cleanup time if used properly. Although just about any nonporous material—from old sheets to newspapers—can be used as a drop cloth, some materials work better in different situations than others.

Paint stores sell drop cloths made of canvas or cotton fabric backed with a rubberized finish. Although these cloths are the best for stopping splatters and spills from reaching your rug, driveway, or furniture, they are expensive. These cloths last a lifetime with proper care.

Plastic sheeting up to 4 mils thick works well as a drop cloth. The plastic sheeting is not absorbent, though, and paint will remain wet on it for a long time. Plastic should not be used to cover floors. If plastic is used, you will soon be walking in wet paint. When you step off the drop cloth, the paint on the bottoms of your shoes will mar rugs and floors. If you must use a plastic drop cloth on the floor, place a newspaper or rag at the doorway so you can wipe your feet before leaving the room. Plastic works well on furniture.

The relatively small size of newspapers makes them handy for covering light fixtures or slipping under doors. They also make a good pad on which to rest your paint pot or roller tray. Newspapers soak up drips and spills before damage can be done.

DRY

The term used when a paint has set up enough, so it can be handled or painted over without fear of wrinkling. The drying time for latex paints is usually a few hours. Oil-base paints usually dry overnight. Follow the recommendations on the can to be safe.

DRY FILM THICKNESS

A term used to describe the buildup of a coat-

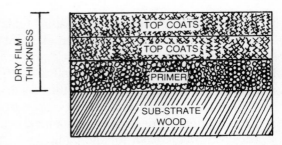

Dry Film Thickness. On new wood it takes at least three coats of paint to build adequate dry film thickness.

ing after it has dried. The thickness of a coating is important for two reasons. A paint film that is too thin will weather away quickly. The paint will lose its ability to protect the surface, and you will end up repainting more often than necessary. Also, a paint applied too thickly will not be able to bend and flex with the *substrate*. This condition may result in *alligatoring, cross-grain checking*, and other *peeling* and *flaking* problems.

As a general rule, the paint on your house should be about 4.5 to 5 mils thick for an oil-base system and 3 to 4 mils thick for a latex system. See the illustration. A mil is one-thousandth of an inch (.001). As the paint on your house weathers, it naturally gets thinner. Repainting builds the dry film to its proper level. On relatively sound paint, this may mean no more than one coat of paint. On new wood, three coats will be required to build a sufficient *film thickness*.

See *Finish Maintenance*.

DRYING OILS

The *vehicle* in oil-base paints. These vegetable or petroleum-based oils carry the paint *pigments* and particles onto a surface and then evaporate, leaving behind a dry paint film.

DRYING TIME

The estimated time it will take for a paint to thoroughly dry, or dry to the point where another coat of paint can be applied. The can label will give an estimation of drying time, although the actual drying time will vary according to weather conditions. Cool, humid weather requires a considerably longer drying time than hot, dry conditions.

DRYWALL

One of the most common interior wall materials in use. These drywall or Sheetrock gypsum wallboards are nailed to the wall studs to form smooth ceilings and walls. Although the preparation methods for both new and old surfaces are similar, each has its own set of problems.

New Drywall

New drywall must be allowed to breath and dry thoroughly before it is sealed behind a layer of paint. New drywall will cure in about two weeks in all but the most humid conditions. If you cannot wait this long, apply one coat of latex primer. Wait at least one month before applying a finish coat.

Before painting a drywall surface which has aged sufficiently, dust thoroughly and apply a latex primer. Do not use an oil-base primer, as it tends to raise a nap on the paper surface of the drywall. Most new drywall requires a primer coat and two topcoats to look its best.

Old Drywall

On old drywall, tack and nail holes should be spackled, allowed to dry, and then sanded smooth (Fig. 1). Holes up to about an inch in diameter should be stuffed with paper or joint tape. The stuffing should be recessed below flush to form a footing for the first layer of patching plaster. Smooth on a layer of patching plaster with a taping knife, feather the edges,

Fig. 1
Drywall. Nail holes and other small holes should be filled with spackling prior to painting.

and allow to dry. Because the patching plaster will probably shrink during drying and leave a depression in the hole, apply a second coat of spackle or joint cement to bring the repair flush with the wall surface. When this second coat of patching material has dried, sand smooth with fine grit sandpaper.

Large holes up to 8 inches in diameter should be repaired with plaster and hardware cloth. Holes larger than 8 inches in diameter will require replacing the damaged section of wall with a new piece of drywall.

To repair with plaster and hardware cloth, first remove all lose and crumbling pieces around the edges of the hole. Cut a piece of the wire screen, so it is an inch or two larger than the hole. Thread a piece of string through the center of the screen. Hang the screen inside the hole, keeping it in place with the string (Fig. 2).

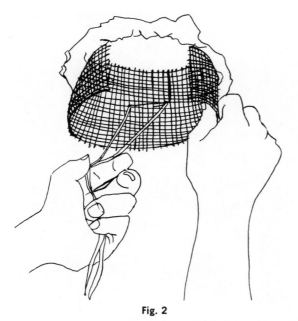

Fig. 2

Drywall. For large holes in drywall, cut a piece of screen several inches larger than the hole and insert into the hole. Hold in place with a string.

Wet the edges of the hole and work patching plaster to the inside edges of the hole. Pull the screen into position behind the hole, so that the edges of the screen settle into patching plaster. You can work the screen into place by pulling on the string.

Place a dowel over the exterior of the hole. Tie a string around it, so that the screen is held snugly in place. Work the plaster into the screen until it pushes through the screen. Fill the hole with plaster until almost level (Fig. 3). Let stand until plaster has set. Cut the string with scissors and remove the dowel (Fig. 4). Work the plaster into the hole, covering the string and filling the hole till flush with the surrounding wall. Feather edges of the plaster and allow for drying. When the plaster has dried, smooth on a finish coat with a taping knife, feathering edges beyond the edge of the previous coat (Fig. 5). When dry, sand smooth.

Allow a week or more of drying time before applying primer.

When replacing a damaged section of drywall, remove all loose and crumbling material around the edges of the hole. Cut a piece of drywall board as close as possible to the size and shape of the hole. Fit the patch into place and secure with drywall nails (Fig. 6).

On the last stroke of your hammer for each nail, dimple the wallboard by driving the nailhead just below flush. This creates a small depression around the nail. Do not break the paper. Spread joint cement over the dimple with a taping knife and feather edges beyond the dimple. Allow for drying and reapply more cement, feathering edges beyond the first application. Allow for drying then sand smooth with a fine grit sandpaper. Use circular motions and try not to raise a nap on paper of the nearby drywall.

The joints between two pieces of drywall are handled in a different manner than dimpled nails. Spread a 1/16 to ⅛-inch layer of joint cement over the joint with a 6-inch taping knife

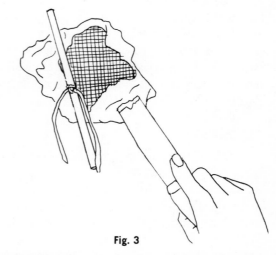

Fig. 3

Drywall. Fill the hole with patching plaster. Make sure the plaster keys behind the screen.

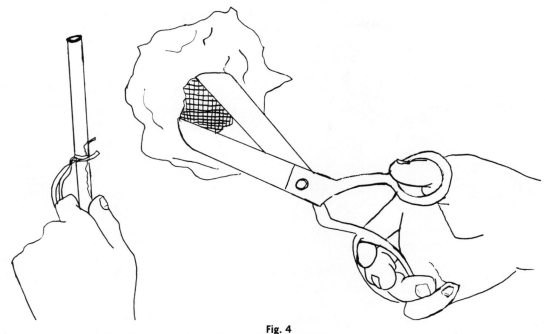

Fig. 4

Drywall. Cut the string with scissors when the plaster has dried.

(Fig. 7). Feather the edges and use long, smooth strokes. While the first application of cement is still wet, lay the end of a roll of joint tape at the highest point of the seam. Unroll the tape along the seam, so it is centered over the joint. Smooth the tape into place by mash-

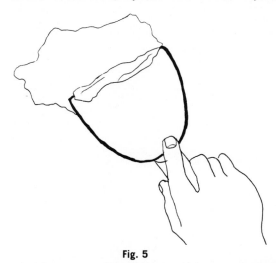

Fig. 5

Drywall. Smooth the final layer of plaster over the hole and allow for drying.

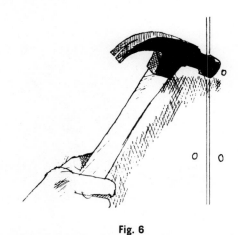

Fig. 6

Drywall. Secure drywall with drywall nails. The last stroke of the hammer should push the nail just below flush (courtesy Hyde Tools).

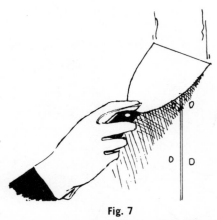

Fig. 7

Drywall. Spread a thin layer of joint compound over the crack where the two pieces of drywall meet (courtesy Hyde Tools).

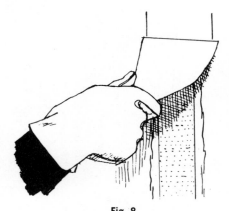

Fig. 8

Drywall. Spread a thin layer of joint compound over the tape with a taping knife (courtesy Hyde Tools).

ing it with long smooth strokes of the taping knife (Fig. 8). The tape should settle into the first application of cement. Work in 2 to 3-foot sections until you reach the end of the joint. Tear off the tape and smooth the end onto the wall. Next, smooth a thin layer of joint cement over the tape, feathering it out an inch beyond the first application (Fig. 9). Make sure the tape is completely covered and that the cement is as smooth as possible. Allow to dry thoroughly.

When the second application has dried, apply a finish coat of cement (Fig. 10). This layer should be very thin, feathered out 5 to 6 inches beyond the center of the seam. A finishing knife is best for this job; however, on small jobs the taping knife can be used. Allow the finish coat to dry and then sand smooth with a fine grit paper (Fig. 11). Be careful not to rough up the paper on adjacent drywall.

After repairs have been made, but before painting, wash walls with a detergent and

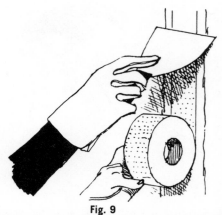

Fig. 9

Drywall. Smooth joint tape into place with a taping knife (courtesy Hyde Tools).

Fig. 10

Drywall. Use a finishing blade to smooth on a final coat of joint compound (courtesy Hyde Tools).

Fig. 11

Drywall. When the final layer of joint compound has dried, sand with fine grit sandpaper (courtesy Hyde Tools).

water solution. Unseen grease and dirt accumulate on the walls and hinder the ability of new paint to adhere to them. While washing walls, inspect for stains, *bleeding*, and other indications of water seepage. Try to determine the source of the moisture and correct it. Seal stains with shellac or an oil-base sealer such as Loc Tite.

On old walls with few repairs, the new one-coat latex paints may let you get away with a single coat of paint. Highly patched walls and substantial changes in color or shade will require at least two coats of finish paint. A primer first coat is not a bad idea if the wall is in really

bad shape. Follow the primer with a suitable topcoat.

See *Paint, Choosing; Painting, Interior; Plaster; Preparation;* and *Sanding.*

DURABILITY

The ability of a paint to resist wear and tear. Various types of paint are made with different chemical compositions, so they will have maximum durability for their intended use. The *resin* content of a paint is the major determinant of durability. The more resin a paint contains, the tougher it will be. Glossy paints contain the most resin while flat wall paints have the least. This is the reason semigloss and glossy enamels are used on woodwork and trim instead of flat wall paints. Flat paint is durable enough for covering walls with a low sheen surface, but it is unsuitable for the repeated use and washings to which woodwork is subjected.

Improper application techniques, inadequate surface preparation, and overthinning will contribute to a reduced durability. For maximum durability, choose the right paint for the job and apply it correctly.

See *Abrasion Resistance; Paint, Choosing;* and *Toughness.*

EAVES

The extension of the roof beyond the wall of a house. Eaves present some interesting problems when painting time comes. The major problem associated with eaves is that they are either too wet or too dry for paint to adhere properly.

Water leaking through the eaves of a house will not attract much attention until *blistering* and *peeling* paint or *mildew* and *decaying* wood make the problem obvious. Water running around flashings on the roof and leaky *downspouts and guttering* are two common causes of excess water under the eaves. Vents installed in the bottom of *soffits* will reduce *moisture* problems by aiding air circulation.

Scrape loose paint, sand rough spots, and prime bare wood before coating the eaves with house paint. The best paint to use on eaves with a moisture problem is a *breather film* latex house paint. If you are painting over wood which has been attacked by rot, apply a coating of *wood preservative* before priming to stop the problem.

Sound eaves are seldom affected by water. The problems of *chalking* and *alligatoring* result from a lack of water. Many oil-base paints are designed to chalk and then have the chalk and accumulate dirt washed away by rain. Because rain seldom reaches the eaves of a house, excess chalking problems are a concern with oil-base paints.

A simple way to reduce the amount of chalking under eaves is to hose them down once or twice a year to remove dirt and chalk buildup. Another way to reduce chalking is to paint the eaves only when they need it—say, once every other time you paint the body of the house. The only way to completely eliminate the problem is by using a nonchalking paint. Flat exterior latex paints are noted for their nonchalking characteristics. Latex paints will not stick to chalking surfaces, so a good non-chalking oil-base or alkyd primer must be applied to chalking areas before painting with water-base paints.

If your house has open-ended rafters, you may want to spray them with paint. The maze of angles in an open-rafter eave cannot be easily reached with a brush. A good airless spray is appropriate. Spray paint eaves before painting the walls of the house. This allows you to lean against the wall without getting paint on your hands and clothing. Open eaves are the most difficult part of a house to prepare and paint.

See *Painting, Exterior.*

EFFLORESCENCE

A white crust of salt deposited on masonry surfaces from which water evaporates. Although efflorescence is most common in below-grade walls, the problem will often occur on above-ground cinder block walls into which water is leaking. Efflorescence also tends to form on freshly plastered walls, but it can be brushed off once the plaster wall has cured.

Water-induced efflorescence problems require a little effort to correct. The only way to eliminate these problems is by finding the *moisture* source. When leaks have been patched, remove the deposits. Even the best paints will not adhere to this powder.

To remove efflorescence, mix 1 part *muriatic acid* in 5 parts water. When mixing acid and water, always pour acid into water. When handling acid, wear rubber gloves, long sleeves, and goggles. Brush this solution onto the wall and rinse with clear water when the efflorescence has dissolved. Because the rinse water may draw more salts to the surface, paint the wall as soon as it is dry to the touch. A good concrete primer, top-coated with a

nonbreathing latex paint, should cure the problem.

See *Alkali and Masonry.*

EGGSHELL

A paint finish with a *sheen* falling between flat and semigloss. Shinier than flat paints, but less washable than a semigloss, eggshell finish enamels are used most often on woodwork receiving little wear and tear.

ELASTICITY

The ability of a paint to stretch and contract with the surface beneath it without *cracking.* Most latex paints have a higher elasticity than their oil-base counterparts.

See *Flexibility.*

ENAMEL

Although enamel is called a paint by most people, it is really a pigmented clear finish more akin to varnish than true paints. Enamels come in three basic finishes—flat, semigloss, or glossy—and in three materials—latex, alkyd, or oil-base. You may have trouble finding the color you want in a high gloss latex, but your paint dealer should have a glossy alkyd enamel which fits your needs.

Types

Latex enamels are replacing oil-base enamels as the coatings most often used for trim work and on kitchen and bathroom walls. Latex enamels dry to a hard washable surface in a few hours and do not leave behind the odor associated with their oil-base counterparts. Latex is easier to use, because it can be cleaned up with soap and water. Latex enamels are more weather-resistant than alkyd or oil-base materials, and these water-base enamels are also more *alkali*-resistant. Glossy latex enamels are not as shiny as the oil-base or alkyd glossy enamels.

Alkyd enamels are a little tougher and more reliable than latex enamels in heavy wear areas such as doors and baseboards and in situations where water contacts the paint— say, on windows that sweat during the winter. Outside, oil-base enamels are the least weather-resistant, but they work well over properly primed *metals*.

Finishes

Of the three common finishes offered in enamel paints, glossy is the most durable, because it contains more resin than semigloss or flat finish enamels. Glossy enamel is the only really waterproof enamel, and it is also the most resistant to repeated washing with water and detergent.

Semigloss finish enamels stand out less than glossy finish enamels, because they have less *sheen*. Although semigloss enamels keep trim work inconspicuous, they also wash well due to their resin content. Many concrete and wooden porch floors are painted with semigloss porch and deck enamel.

Flat enamels are useful in rooms where you want flat finish walls with a nonporous surface. An example is in a laundry room where *moisture* is seeping through a wall, causing the paint on an exterior wall to peel. A coating of flat enamel will provide a vapor barrier that stops the moisture migration while presenting the low sheen characteristic of flat wall paint.

Application

Applying an enamel paint can be a tricky proposition, because different brands of latex, alkyd, or oil-base enamels behave inconsistently. Latex enamels tend to be slippery. They may be applied in a coating that is too thin. Although latex enamels do not *sag* and *run* as often as alkyd or oil-base enamels, be sure to check your work for thin spots.

Oil-base enamels are sticky and subject to overapplication, which results in running and sagging. Avoid the temptation to lay these paints on too thick. Two normal to slightly thin coats produce a more durable finish than one thick coat.

Use slow brush strokes when applying enamels in order to prevent *crawling*. Unlike most paints, enamel should be laid on beginning in the already wet paint, then brushed out and tipped off into the dry areas. By *feathering* the final strokes of each brush load of paint onto the dry surface, *lap marks* can be eliminated.

See *Brushing Techniques* and *Trim*.

EPOXY PAINTS

These paints contain special resins that make them some of the most *durable, abrasion-resistant* and chemically-resistant coatings available. Instead of drying through the evaporation of *solvent* or *thinner*, these materials harden chemically. They are also more expensive than standard paints.

Epoxy coatings are available in premixed form and in two-component mixes. Although premixed epoxies are easy to clean up and can be used directly from the can, they do not wear as well as two-component epoxies. When two-component epoxies are used, a catalyst or hardener is mixed into the pigmented material just before application. Two-component paints harden quickly and often require special thinners (listed on the label) for cleanup. These coatings have a limited pot life and must be used within eight hours after mixing.

Epoxy and *urethane paints* produce a slick impervious coating over nonporous surfaces such as ceramic tile, fiberglass, bar tops, swimming pools, and metal surfaces. These coatings will not adhere to oil-base, alkyd, or latex paints. Preparation must include stripping away all old paint—even the sound stuff. Oil-base and alkyd paints can be used over an epoxy paint, although deglossing of the epoxy coated surface is necessary to insure adequate *adhesion*.

Epoxies give off toxic fumes during their drying period, so they should be used only in well-ventilated areas. These materials are also tricky to apply, and the label should be followed exactly to prevent mishaps. Unlike latex or oil-base paints, mistakes with epoxies are not easily corrected.

Clear epoxies and urethanes can be used to lock copper, brass, and bronze hardware in a tarnishproof shell. Remove the hardware, clean it with fine steel wool or metal polish, then dip into clear epoxy. Allow the hardware to dry before handling.

EQUIPMENT

The proper selection and use of painting tools, whether working inside or out, are essential for a good paint job. In addition to items like hammers, screwdrivers, wiping rags, rubber gloves, and goggles, you will need specialized tools to do the best job possible.

Interior Tools

For patching plaster or drywall, you need a 1½-inch-wide *putty knife*, a 6-inch taping blade, fine sandpaper, and a sanding block (Fig. 1). A finishing knife is useful on large drywall finishing jobs. Get a sponge and bucket for detergent and water washing solutions. These solutions can remove all old dirt and grease from surfaces prior to painting. A *tack cloth* comes in handy for picking up dust. *Drop cloths* keep dripped paint off your furniture and carpets. A trim guard makes working around

Fig. 1

Equipment. The basic tools necessary for painting inside the house.

woodwork and trim easier. *Masking tape* or a window scraper makes cleaning glass easier. A brush comb keeps your brushes' bristles straight. Thinners are necessary for cleaning brushes used to apply paints other than latex. Most interior jobs can be accomplished with a 2-inch trim brush and a 4-inch wall brush. Painting will be easier if you also have an angular sash tool. A 3-inch wall brush may also speed the process of *cutting in* before rolling. For rolling a 9-inch spring tension roller frame with a cover or nap, an extension handle, tray, and grating are necessary. It is easier to paint out of a pail than a gallon bucket. A *pail* with a bail works best.

Special painting jobs like refinishing wooden floors may require heavy-duty power tools. Power sanders and high power vacuums

Fig. 2

Equipment. These tools will help you do a professional job when painting outside.

can be rented at local stores. When painting cinder block walls in the basement, you may want to use one of the stiff bristle masonry or whitewashing brushes to save wear and tear on your regular brushes.

Exterior Tools

Outside you need to substitute a hooked paint scraper, wire brush, electric paint remover, and power sander for the plaster and drywall tools you used inside (Fig. 2). When working with masonry, you may also need a cold chisel, mallet, trowel, and jointer. A caulking gun and putty knife are used during preparation. For applying paint, you need a 4-inch wall brush and a sash tool for the trim. Special *applicators* speed painting on shakes and shingles. An *airless sprayer* saves much time on extra large jobs. You need extension and stepladders to reach the high areas of your house. *Drop cloths* keep paint off your lawn, bushes, and driveway. A tool called an S-hook holds your paint pail as you paint while on an extension ladder. Thinners are necessary for paints other than latex.

See *Brushes; Ladders; Rollers, Paint;* and *Spraying Paint.*

ESTIMATING QUANTITY OF PAINT

You do not have to be a mathematician to estimate the amount of paint you need for a paint job. Yet many people fail to measure the area they wish to cover. When they get to the paint store, they make a guess at how much paint they need. Buying too little paint requires an extra trip to the paint store. Buying too much paint wastes money. Get the area of those interior rooms or exterior walls measured before you go to the paint store to buy paint.

Interior

Measuring the area you plan to paint inside is quite simple. Measure the distance

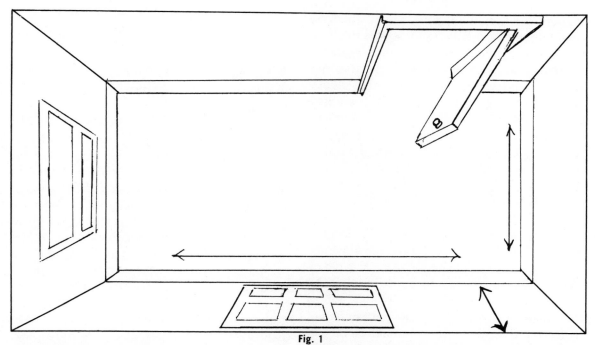

Fig. 1

Estimating Quantity. To estimate the area of an interior room, measure around the baseboard and multiply by the height of the room.

around the diameter of the room. Multiply that number by the ceiling height, and you have the total area of the walls in square feet (Fig. 1). Subtract the area of windows and doors in the room to get the area of the walls. Windows usually account for 15 square feet each, and doors cover an area of about 21 square feet.

Because most ceilings are flat and unobstructed, determining their area is even easier than finding the area of walls. The area of the ceiling is simply the width times room length.

Here is how to figure the area for a room 20 feet long and 10 feet wide with an 8-foot ceiling. The distance around the walls of the room is 60 feet. Multiply that by 8 feet, and the total area of the walls is 480 square feet. The area of the ceiling is 200 square feet (10 by 20). Divide these numbers by 400 square feet of coverage (the average area of coverage for 1

gallon of interior paint), and you will have the paint requirement.

The wall area, 480 square feet, divided by 400 square feet of coverage per gallon, equals 1 gallon and 1 quart of paint. Do not worry about the space taken up by window and door openings, unless these openings are especially large or numerous. You can use leftover paint for touching up later. If you decide to subtract the area of the windows and doors from the wall area, add the areas given earlier for windows and doors and subtract this total from the wall area of the room. If the 10 by 20-foot room has one door and two windows, this adds up to 51 square feet. Subtract 51 square feet from 480 square feet to get 429 square feet. You still need a little more than 1 gallon of paint for complete coverage. Buy a little extra to be safe.

The 200-square-foot ceiling of this room

69

requires ½ gallon of paint. Two hundred square feet divided by 400 square feet of coverage per gallon equals ½ gallon of paint.

To figure the amount of trim paint you need for windows and doors, use this guide. Windows average 15 square feet each and doors 21 square feet apiece. If the room has two windows and one door, that is 51 square feet total. (Two times 15 for the windows plus 21 for the door equals 51 square feet.) Divide 51 square feet by 400 square feet of coverage per gallon, and you need 1 quart of paint for the trim, excluding baseboard. Figure the baseboard at 1 square foot of coverage for every 2 linear feet. The 60 feet of baseboard in this room require enough paint for 30 square feet of coverage. Buy at least a pint for the baseboard.

For special cases like stairwells, finding the area to be covered is a little more difficult. Measure the length of the wall and its tallest height (usually at the head of the stairwell). Multiply these figures and divide by two. The figure you have is the area for one sidewall of the stairwell. In most cases a stairwell has two sidewalls, so you do not need to divide by two. The measurement for one sidewall, undivided, equals the area of both walls. Do not forget to figure the area of the headwall (height times width). Add this to the area for the sidewalls, and you know rather precisely how much area the stairwell contains.

It is also helpful to remember that new drywall and plaster soak up paint more rapidly than previously painted walls. You need to figure a little extra paint for the first coating of these walls. Remember, too, that cinder block walls soak up paint and have a reduced rate of coverage. Coverage is figured the same way for these absorbent walls, except that the coverage per square foot per gallon will be less, probably 250 to 300 square feet per gallon.

Exterior

The method for estimating the amount of paint you need to do the job is almost the same as for interior work. Measure the distance around your house and the height to the eaves (Fig. 2). Multiply these two numbers, and you get the total area of the body of your house below the eaves. Gables are equal to one-half their width times height.

Assume your house is 25 feet wide and 45 feet long, with eaves 11 feet above the ground. The area around your house is 1,540 square feet (140 feet multiplied by 11). Next add in the area of the gables, say 8 feet by 25 feet, or 200 square feet. Two hundred square feet divided by two equals 100 square feet for each gable. Because most houses have two gables, multiply by two to get 200 square feet of gable area. Add this to the total area of the below eave body—200 plus 1,540 equals 1,740 square feet of body. Divide this area figure by 400 square feet of coverage per gallon of paint to get the amount of paint needed to cover the body of the house (1,740 divided by 400 equals a figure of 4 gallons and 1 quart of paint.) Do not subtract the area of windows and doors from this final area.

To figure the area for trim paint, remember that windows and doors equal about 15 and 21 square feet, respectively, Let's say your house has eight windows and three doors.

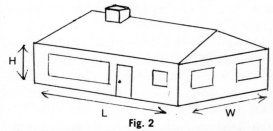

Estimating Quantity. The length around a house multiplied by its height produces an estimate of the area of the house's body.

You need enough paint to cover 183 square feet. Fifteen square feet per window times eight windows equals 120 square feet, plus three times 21 square feet per door equals 63 square feet. Adding these two numbers together totals 183 square feet of trim. Divide this area by 400 square feet of coverage per gallon of paint, and you need 2 quarts of trim paint.

Guttering is usually figured at 1 square foot for each linear foot. Assuming the house in the illustration has guttering along its length on both sides, you need enough paint to cover 90 square feet. (Forty-five feet times two sides equals 90 feet.)

Weathered siding and cinder block absorb more paint than previously painted surfaces. You will probably get less than 400 square feet of coverage per gallon. Applying a penetrating stain to weathered siding usually gets less than 400 square feet of coverage per gallon, too. You may not need a whole gallon to cover 400 square feet on sound wood. For more specific details about how a certain type of paint covers different sidings in your area, consult your paint salesman.

See *Colors, Covering Power,* and *Paint, Choosing.*

EVAPORATION

A process whereby a liquid becomes a gas. Evaporation is the process that most coatings use to dry. In water-base paints, the water evaporates into the air, leaving behind a residue of paint pigments, solidifiers, and binders that form the paint film. In oil-base paints the *volatile* oils evaporate, leaving behind the protective coating. The higher the temperature and the lower the *relative humidity*, the quicker evaporation will take place.

A few coatings like the two-component *epoxy paints* do not dry in the normal sense of the word. Instead of containing a vehicle that evaporates, a catalyst causes the material to harden into a tough protective film.

See *Dry.*

EXTENDERS

Low cost *pigments* added to a paint in order to increase its *hiding power* or its coverage without adding substantially to the paint's cost. Many manufacturers add extenders during the manufacturing process. You should not attempt to extend paint in this way, as the alteration can cause the paint to perform at less than optimum levels.

EXTERIOR PAINT

House paint is the commercial term for coatings designed for use on the exterior of a house. As a rule, house paint refers to the paint used on siding and other wall material. Trim paints come in exterior blends, as do special coatings for *metals, masonry*, and *natural finishes*.

House paints are made in both latex and oil-base materials. The vehicle of most *oil-base paint* is usually an alkyd resin with *turpentine* or *mineral spirits* also used as a *vehicle. Latex paint* vehicles consist of fine particles of a resin emulsified in water. Most homeowners choose latex house paints almost exclusively for their painting needs. Latex is easy to clean up, quick to dry, and easy to handle. There are certain situations where an oil-base paint is required. The most notable are *chalking* or rusting surfaces.

Exterior paints are designed to build a tough flexible film in order to stand up to a variety of weather conditions, pollutants, and physical abuses. Through the years a pattern has developed which matches certain paint characteristics—*sheen*, for example—to various areas of the house. Because a glossy finish is easier to clean and resists scuffing more than flat paints, the shiny paints have been adopted for use on trim and other high traffic areas.

All manufacturers do not build the same characteristics into their paints, and not all areas of the country have the same climate. Your paint salesman is an invaluable help when deciding which house paint performs the best.

Wooden siding or *clapboard* can be finished in one of two ways. You can apply a material that penetrates the wood or a coating that builds a barrier on the wall's surface.

The barrier-forming house paints come in latex, oil-base, and alkyd materials. The finishes of these paints range from glossy to flat. Flat paints make walls seem less noticeable, because they diffuse light. Flat paints also tend to hide flaws in siding. Latex flat house paint has the ability to breathe, allowing *moisture* to pass from the wall into the air without *blistering* or *peeling* the paint. Some flat alkyd paints produce a chalk compound that allows dirt and debris to be washed away by rain. Glossy or semiglossy house paints prevent dirt buildup, but they are subject to blistering and peeling if the wall has a moisture problem. Most house paints work well on wood, *masonry*, and *shingles*, although there are a few combinations of old and new paint that do not work. Latex paints, for example, do not adhere to chalking alkyd paints. An oil-base primer that is compatible with the latex topcoating is required.

Exterior primers penetrate the substrate while building a flexible film onto which topcoating is applied. Although most topcoatings can be used on most types of primer, it is best to follow the *specifications* on the topcoating's can.

Penetrating stains are commonly used as a preservative and beautifier for shakes, shingles, and other rough-cut sidings made from cedar, fir, and redwood. These are resinous woods that have a habit of *bleeding* through surface coatings. Most penetrating stains are oil-base materials, although some new latex stains are beginning to appear on the market. Stains range from almost clear to nearly opaque, and in damp conditions they breathe, preventing blisters from forming under the topcoating. The natural look can also be achieved by coating siding with one of the commercially available *wood preservatives* or *water repellents*.

Although the trim on a house can be finished with flat house paint, generally trim is set off from the body of the house with a glossy or semigloss finish paint. Available in both latex and alkyd materials, these paints have good color and gloss retention, excellent durability, and have relatively easy workability. Regular house paint may not retain its gloss, as long as a trim paint and chalking paints may discolor adjacent surfaces when used on trim.

Trim such as doors, windows, and shutters are usually painted with a glossy or semigloss enamel paint. These paints are available in both latex and alkyd. They build a waterproof film through which water cannot penetrate to the wood. This reduces swelling, which would make windows and doors stick, while providing an *abrasion resistant* surface.

Most exterior masonry, when painted, is coated with a latex or *rubber-base paint*. The alkali in cement products attacks most oil-base paints. The same is not true of latex paints. The latex paints also have the ability to breathe, reducing blistering and peeling problems. Concrete porches and steps, or wood porches and steps, are usually coated with a *porch and floor paint*.

Exterior metals usually take a house paint if they are not in bad shape. Excessive rusting, peeling, and *flaking* may require priming with a zinc-base primer prior to topcoating. Enamel trim paints and oil-base house paints help to prevent rust. Latex paints may encourage the problem.

See *Colors, Estimating Quantity of Paint, Finish Maintenance*, and *Painting, Exterior*.

FADING

The loss of color, or depth of color, on darker paints. This fading is due to heat, weathering, and other conditions, including improper application or excessive thinning of the paint prior to application. As dark paint weathers, the thickness of the paint film thins until it reaches a point where a lightening of its color is noticeable. This deterioration is one of the first signs that the paint film is becoming too thin to stand up to the weather. Although not a major problem, fading can be reduced by using light-colored paints or by painting over an old paint with a color that closely matches the color of the older paint.

See *Color Retention; Paint, Choosing;* and *Yellowing*.

FALSE BODY

A term used to describe paints that have been made artificially thick by the manufacturer. One-coat, dripless paints are good examples of false-bodied paints. In order to achieve the desired film thickness, these paints have been treated so they are thicker than standard paints.

FASTNESS

The ability of a paint to withstand exposure to heat, rain, and dirt without *fading*. Latex paints are the fastest paints for exterior use, because they are formulated not to chalk. Many oil-base alkyd paints are designed to chalk. This *chalking* creates a white powder on the surface that tends to lighten it. Most penetrating stains are very fast and fade only as the pigment is lifted from the wood by weathering.

See also: *Color Retention* and *Paint, Choosing*.

FEATHERING

A method of stroking with a brush or roller that produces a paint edge which fades to nothing.

It is useful when applying all paints, especially glossy oil-base paints, to large flat surfaces.

To feather paint, the last stroke of your brush should end up in an unpainted area. As you move into the dry area, slowly lift the brush off the surface so there is less pressure on the brush tips until the brush has finally lifted free of the surface. The result is a ragged featherlike edge. This edge is less prone to leave *lap marks* when covered by the next brush or roller load of paint.

The feathering technique should also be used when working plaster, patching compound, or *spackling* into a hole or crack. As you move away from the hole, bear down harder on the blade until no more material is sticking to the wall. Lift the blade. You should have a barely discernible transition between the patching material and the wall surface. An edge like this will not show up when painted.

See *Brushing Techniques* and *Walls, Patching*.

FIBERGLASS

Glass in fibrous form is not normally painted; however, it does grow dingy with age and weathering. If you decide to paint fiberglass, it is accomplished using the same basic procedures as other painting jobs: *preparation*, priming, and applying a topcoat.

To prepare fiberglass for painting, wash the surface with a detergent to remove dirt, grease, and *mildew*. Sand thoroughly to raise a *tooth*. Wipe with a *tack cloth* or solvent-soaked rag to remove dust. Apply a primer. An epoxy paint works best on fiberglass in most cases. Allow the primer to dry thoroughly before applying a topcoat.

See *Swimming Pools*.

FILM THICKNESS

The depth at which you apply a paint. Most paints grow thinner as they dry; therefore the film thickness of a wet paint is more than the dry thickness.

Primer coats on wood should measure 1.5 to 2 mils (thousandths of an inch) in thickness. This is just enough to cover the grain of the wood. Most weekend painters tend to spread primer paints too thin. When the paints dry, they fail to build a sufficient *substrate* for the topcoats.

Topcoats should be applied so they are approximately 1.5 or 2-mils thick when dry. To achieve the desired 4.5 to 5-mil thickness for oil-base paints and the 3 to 4-mil thickness for latex paints, you need two topcoats on new wood. Old paint in good condition usually requires no more than a single coat of paint to bring it back to optimum film thickness.

You should notice when rolling on paint that the longer the roller nap, the thicker the paint film. Roll out paint sufficiently so that it does not *run* or *sag*. Spraying generally puts on a thinner paint film, but several passes will build a sufficient film thickness. Remember that several thin films of paint are better than one that is extra-thick.

See *Finish Maintenance* and *Coats, Number of*.

FINISH MAINTENANCE

The best way of deciding when to paint your house is to let the paint tell you that it is time for recoating. This way you can keep an optimum amount of paint on your walls, and it will do the best job of preserving and protecting your house. A good way to accomplish this is by setting aside time each year to inspect your house.

Exterior

When is the proper time to repaint? For all practical purposes, the best time to tackle the whole job is when touching up takes about half as long as applying an entire coat. Because you have been touching up periodically, most of the old paint should be in good enough shape to require only a single coat of paint. With the new latex house paints, five years is a pretty good estimate for the time period between complete recoatings.

Many people delay the huge task of painting the entire exterior of their house, until the paint begins *flaking* and *peeling* from the walls. Patches of bare wood are showing by this time. The paint job is magnified by the extra preparation required.

Some homeowners paint their entire house at the first sign of peeling or flaking paint. They may be hampering the effectiveness of the paint by applying a new coat when the house really does not need it. They end up with an excessively thick paint film that does not bend, expand, or contract with the substrate. The result is *alligatoring*, which necessitates the removal of all the paint before recoating.

An old paint job that has been allowed to weather to the point where much bare wood remains after scraping and sanding may need two coats of paint: a primer followed by a topcoating. The primer is applied over all surfaces, whether bare wood or sound paint. This provides a uniform surface for the topcoating.

There are a couple of paint system choices on new wood. The first is a two-coat system. In this method a primer is applied over the bare wood and then coated with a topcoating. Depending on the weather conditions, you can expect signs of aging in two to three years with this system. The three-coat system is better. A primer coat is followed by two topcoatings. This system can be expected to last up to five years before weathering begins to show.

During your yearly house inspection, you may find that certain sides of your house, usually the south and west, deteriorate more rapidly than the others. You may be able to put off a paint job for the entire house by painting these problem walls with a coat of paint. By the time it weathers a second time, the other walls should be ready for a new paint job.

Interior

Accumulating grease and dirt tip you off that walls and woodwork need to be painted. Before you dive headlong into the project, try washing the grime with a detergent and water solution. Modern paints are designed to be washed, and you may discover that a thorough washing delays the need to paint for a year or two.

Excessive paint buildup is not usually a problem inside the house. Interior paints are generally thinner than exterior paints. A thorough washing each year wears away a thin layer of paint, simulating the weathering that takes place outside your house. Certain walls and pieces of woodwork, notably doors, get excessive wear. By patching them up from time to time, you can keep them at the same level of wear as the remainder of interior surfaces.

See *Coats, Number of; Painting, Exterior;* and *Painting, Interior.*

FIRE-RETARDANT PAINTS

These paints, also known as intumescent coatings, slow the spread of fire by foaming when exposed to high temperatures. See the illustration. Available in flat latex, these paints do not burn. They are most often used in garages, workshops, and basements near furnaces.

Fire-retardant paints should be applied exactly as the can directs for maximum effectiveness. A coating that is too thick will run off

Fire-Retardant Paints. Fire-retardant paints foam to slow the spread of fire (courtesy Fuller-O'-Brien Paints).

the wall in the event of a fire. A coating that is too thin may not be thick enough to slow the spread of fire.

Most fire-retardant paints are adversely affected by water. They should not be washed.

FIXTURES, ELECTRICAL

Electrical fixtures such as lights, switches, and outlets should have their cover plates removed before painting, even if the plates get painted the same color as the wall. There are two good reasons for this precaution. The first is as a preventive measure against electrical shock while painting the covers. If the plate is painted in place, wet paint may conduct enough electricity to produce a nasty shock. The second is that when covers are painted over while in place, paint seeps behind the plate and dries. When you remove the plate, the dry paint will pull away part of the finish on your wall.

When painting the cover plates for wall switches and outlets, lay them face up on a piece of newspaper. Paint with a brush. Do not forget to paint the screws.

Ceiling lamps can be unscrewed from the ceiling and left to hang while *cutting in* around

them. Cover the fixtures with plastic or newspaper to protect them from drips and splatters. Replace when the paint is dry.

FLAKING

A paint failure caused by water entering cracks in the paint. Water makes the surface beneath the paint expand and contract. The paint falls off in flakelike patches. Flaking is commonly an advanced form of *alligatoring*. It can be controlled by eliminating the source of *moisture*, removing defective paint, properly preparing the surface, and then repainting with a primer and topcoat.

See *Blistering* and *Peeling Paint*.

FLASHING

A paint problem identified by an unevenness of *sheen* across a newly painted surface. It can be caused by improper preparation of the surface, poor application techniques, and exposure of wet paint to dew or mist while drying.

See *Blushing*.

FLASH POINT

A term used to describe the temperature at which the volatile solvents used in some coatings ignite in the presence of sparks or an open flame. Common coatings with low flash points are oil-base paints; clear finishes such as shellac, varnish, and lacquer; epoxy paints; and thinners and solvents. The flash points of these materials are lowered when they are applied with a spray gun, so be extra careful when applying volatile coatings. Most latex coatings are not flammable.

FLAT FINISH PAINTS

Paints that produce a surface without *sheen* or *gloss* when dry. Flat finishes are used most often on walls and ceilings. They soften the light and hide imperfections in the wall's surface. Unfortunately, flat finish paint is not as tough as semigloss or glossy finish paints. It weathers a little faster than these shinier paints, has less *abrasion resistance*, and will not withstand repeated washing.

FLATTENING AGENT

Chemical added to clear varnishes and lacquers to produce a dull *sheen*. The effect is of a hand-rubbed look straight from the can. This material is added at the factory and comes in cans labeled as flat or hand-rubbed finishes.

FLEXIBILITY

The ability of a paint film to bend, stretch, and contract with the surface beneath it without *cracking*. Most latex paints have greater flexibility than alkyd or oil-base paints.

See *Durability* and *Toughness*.

FLOATING

The tendency of *pigments* to separate from the *vehicle* during drying. The result is a mottled surface of dubious quality. Floating is a common problem in old or cheap paints.

FLOORS, WOOD

Many people shy away from refinishing floors because the job seems so difficult. You need not be afraid to tackle a floor refinishing project. The floor is the same size as the ceiling. Modern tools and products have made floor refinishing relatively easy.

Preparing the Floor

The first step in reworking a floor is removing the furniture and then scrubbing with a solution of detergent and hot water. Mop the floor in sections, much the way you paint a ceiling, and wipe dry immediately to prevent swelling the wood and raising a grain. Rinse

the floor with clear water and allow it to dry thoroughly.

While the floor is drying, make an inspection to decide which method of renovation your floor needs. Hopefully you will find that the washing removed all the dirt and accumulated wax and that the present topcoat is sound. Simply apply another topcoat to make your floor look like new.

You may discover that your floor is beginning to show signs of wear. Dullness in high traffic areas is a good clue. A fresh topcoat will bring your floor up to par with a minimum of work.

You may find that spots in front of doors or a favorite chair have worn through, although the remainder of your floor appears intact. These worn areas can be patched up before applying a topcoat to the entire floor.

Spots worn to bare wood may not match the remainder of your floor without a little work with stains and finishes. Sand the bare wood to remove raised grain and then wipe with a *turpentine*-soaked rag. If the bare spot matches the surrounding finish, you can go ahead and revarnish without the spot showing. If the spot and finished floor show different tones, you may have to stain the spot before revarnishing.

If there are many worn spots on your floor, you may decide it is easier to sand the entire floor with a drum sander before refinishing. Before you rent the necessary equipment, consider using a renovator on your floor.

Floor renovators are penetrating finishes modified in a way that allows them to clean the floor while reconditioning the previous finish. Renovators work best on floors finished with a penetrating type finish or varnish. They do not work on shellacked surfaces.

To use the renovator, the floor must be washed, scrubbed, and dried. Sand any bare spots before applying a renovator. Apply material in small patches, so you can reach the entire area of each section. Try to make the edges of each section coincide with the cracks between boards. This reduces the chance of *lap marks*. Spread the renovator with a brush and let it stand 10 to 15 minutes so the material soaks in. Scrub with steel wool. Wrap the steel wool around a two by four or a brick to make

the work go quicker. Wipe the area with clean burlap rags and then move on to the next section.

With a little planning, you can be applying and removing the renovator in alternating sections instead of waiting for one section to dry before wiping. To alternate tasks, coat a section adjacent to the first section you coated while the renovator is setting up. Come back

Fig. 1

Floors, Wood. A drum sander cuts old finish from a wood floor quickly with a minimum of effort.

and wipe the first section, apply renovator to a third section, then come back and wipe the second section. Alternating the application and removal sets up a rhythm that wastes very little time and reduces monotony, because you are switching from one job to another every 5 to 10 minutes.

Allow the renovator to dry overnight. The floor will have a dull sheen the next morning. A high gloss finish can be produced by waxing or by coating with a varnish.

The finish on your floor may not be doing its job simply because it is overage. Like all other coatings, floor finishes break down over a period of time, so they need to be removed and replaced periodically. The time period may stretch from 10 to 15 years between complete stripping and refinishing, but eventually it must be done. A floor finish that chips or flakes away when scraped with a coin or putty knife is overage. It will not take a new topcoating. The old finish needs to be removed before refinishing.

Before stripping a floor, remove the shoe or toeplate from the baseboard. Use a pry bar, but be careful not to damage the molding. Save the trim so that it can be replaced when the floor is finished. Check for loose boards and nails that project above the surface of the floor. Renail loose boards and countersink nails that project above the surface of the floor.

The next step is *sanding*. Renting a drum sander and disk sander will make the job easier (Fig. 1). Drum sanders plug into wall outlets. An electric motor drives a sandpaper-covered drum that cuts about 1/16 inch off your floor. The drum pulls the unit along and can be controlled by tilting the sander up or down to achieve the desired cutting speed and depth. Tilt the sander back so that its drum is off the floor, turn it on, and lower gently until it begins to bite the floor. You have to pull back a little

on the handle to prevent the sander from taking off, but with a little practice you can remove just the amount of finish needed. Always lift the sanding drum at the beginning and completion of each pass in order to prevent gouges in your floor.

Sand with the grain, usually along the length of the boards. Overlap 3 to 4 inches on each pass. When you have finished sanding the floor for the first time, switch to a medium paper. Make as many sandings as necessary to expose the bare wood. Some areas require a little more work than others. Change to a fine grade sandpaper for the final pass.

The drum sander will not reach right up to the baseboard, so you have to sand around the edge of the floor with a disk or vibrating sander. Again, work with the grain and try not to gouge the floor with the edges of the sander. Vacuum the entire floor, and you are ready to apply a finish system.

Stains

If you want to stain your floor, this step follows sanding and vacuuming. Penetrating wiping stain, colored penetrating sealers, non-grain raising stains, and colored varnish can all be used to color the wood. With the varnish, you will not be able to top-coat with shellac. These two materials are not *compatible*. If you thin the varnish stain, it produces a suitable surface for finish varnish. Allow stains to dry overnight before coating.

Choosing a Finish

Wiping stains and non-grain raising stains need to be sealed before top-coating. Most of the colored penetrating sealers and colored varnishes will act as primers and accept a topcoat.

On floors, just as on other painted surfaces, two average thickness coats of a material will outlast one heavy coat. As a general rule, you need to apply two to three coats of material in order to build a topcoat system. You have a choice between varnish, penetrating sealer, shellac, or lacquer as a topcoating system.

The penetrating sealers are the easiest to use. Simply brush them on and wipe them off after they have been absorbed by the wood. Shellac is also an easy finish to use. The penetrating sealer or shellac finishes are also easy to patch up, because they seldom show lap marks. On the surface, finishes like varnish and lacquer are more difficult to touch up.

Glossy floor finishes show dirt and scratches the most. Semigloss surfaces do not show dirt and scratches as readily, but they do not clean as easily as their shinier counterparts.

If you want to finish the job by waxing, make sure not to use a water-base wax. Select either a paste or liquid floor wax. Wax can be useful for covering up scratch marks as the floor ages. It can also prevent premature aging by lubricating the surface.

Finish Systems

Penetrating wood finishes embed themselves in the wood. They do not sit on the surface as most other finishes do. These finishes are the easiest to patch, longest wearing, and require the least maintenance. Penetrating wood finishes are about the easiest to apply. Pour the finish over a strip of floor about as wide as you can reach. Spread the material with a brush or rag and let it soak in for half an hour (Fig. 2). Wipe dry and move on to the next area. Repeat this application/removal process until the floor has been treated. Allow to dry overnight. Repeat the application and wiping process the next day, then allow to dry overnight before use.

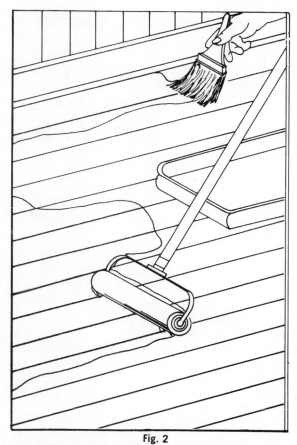

Fig. 2
Floors, Wood. A special applicator makes applying a floor finish easy.

Shellac is a topcoat that is easy to use and patch. It is susceptible to water damage and must be kept waxed for maximum wear. Shellac should be applied in three or four coats using a 3-pound cut. Thin the first coat to allow penetration into the wood. Use straight shellac for subsequent coats in order to build a finish on the wood's surface. Allow each coat to dry at least three hours before sanding and recoating. The final coat should dry at least 24 hours before waxing.

There are many varnishes that can be used to build a floor finishing system. *Acrylic varnish, phenolic varnish, polyurethane var-*

nish, *urethane varnish,* and *vinyl varnish* are discussed in this book. Varnish systems also need a coat of wax for maximum longevity. Although varnish has good *abrasion resistance,* scratches through to the wood show up readily. Varnishes are also more difficult to patch.

These materials should be brushed or rolled on to build a three to four-coat finish. The first coat of varnish should be cut with 1 part *thinner* for every 8 to 10 parts varnish. This encourages the first coat to penetrate the wood. Subsequent coatings are applied at full strength. Each coat should be sanded before applying the next. Several days after the last topcoat has been applied, the floors should be waxed to prevent dulling of the surface.

Lacquer dries faster than varnish, but it produces the same built-up finish. You should not apply lacquer over fillers or stains other than wiping and non-grain raising varieties. Lacquer attacks the other types of finish and severely limits the life of your finish.

A lacquer primer is usually applied first. Work quickly as lacquer dries in an hour or less. The material is toxic, so the work area should have plenty of ventilation. Lacquers are flammable. All pilot lights and other spark-producing appliances should be unplugged or turned off.

Sand lightly between the primer and the first coat of lacquer. Apply a second coat of lacquer and allow to dry overnight. The final coat of lacquer should be thinned 1 part thinner to 5 parts lacquer before application. Allow to dry overnight. Wax before the furniture is moved to preserve the glossy sheen.

See *Porch and Floor Paints.*

FLOW

A painter's term used to describe the leveling of a paint. The more flow a paint has, the fewer brush marks remain in the dried surface.

Some shellacs, lacquers, and varnishes have a lot of flow. Apply them sparingly to prevent *runs* and *sags. Texture paints* have very little flow, allowing them to produce the desired effect.

FROSTING

An opaque or milky appearance in a drying clear finish such as lacquer. This defect is common in lacquers applied in hot, humid conditions. The lacquer is designed to dry quickly, but the humidity prevents this and frosting occurs. Use lacquers only on days with a low *relative humidity* and moderate temperatures. Spring and fall are usually ideal.

See *Blushing* and *Cloudy.*

FUNGI

A large group of molds, *mildews,* smuts, and rusts that feed on organic materials, including your house and some house paints. They appear as splotchy brown, black, or gray discoloration.

See *Fungicides.*

FUNGICIDES

Chemicals that prohibit the growth of fungi. These materials are added to paints that will exist in moisture and temperature conditions conducive to fungi growth. Some types of fungi actually feed on various paint ingredients.

In addition to adding a fungicide, fungi growth can be curtailed by using a *glossy finish* paint. Shiny surfaces prevent moisture from entering a paint film, reducing the ability of fungi to grow.

See *Mildew* and *Mildewcide.*

GABLE

The triangular section of wall at the ends of a house under the inverted "V" of the roof line. Gables are usually painted to match the body of your house.

See *Estimating Quantity of Paint* and *Painting, Exterior*.

GAG BUCKET

Slang for the bucket in which professional painters keep used *thinner*. Pour all used thinner in a 5-gallon bucket and let it stand a few days. The paint *solids* will settle out. The clear thinner can then be poured off and reused. Use this thinner to clean brushes and rollers. Do not use it to thin paint.

GLAZING

A puttylike substance used to seal panes of glass into a window sash. Glazing compounds are designed so they do not thoroughly harden for several years. This delayed drying allows easy removal if glazing becomes defective or glass needs to be replaced.

If your house has glazed windows, then removing and patching old glazing will be a part of your exterior *preparation* scheme. The sun beats down the hardest on the south and west sides of a house, so you will probably find the most cracked and loose glazing on these sides. Defective glazing allows moisture into the window frame and sash, leading to peeling and flaking of paint and glazing. Prolonged exposure to moisture causes rotting of wood or rusting of metal sashes and frames.

Loose glazing can be worked free with a hooked scraper or *putty knife*. Be careful not to break glass. Brush all dirt out of the area to be glazed. Prime with a good primer that is compatible with the finish paint you plan to use. Allow the primer to dry overnight, then apply glazing.

To apply glazing, dig a ball out of the can and roll between your palms to warm it up.

Fig. 1

Glazing. Roll glazing into a rope before applying to a sash.

Fig. 2

Glazing. Overfill "V" formed by glass and sash with glazing.

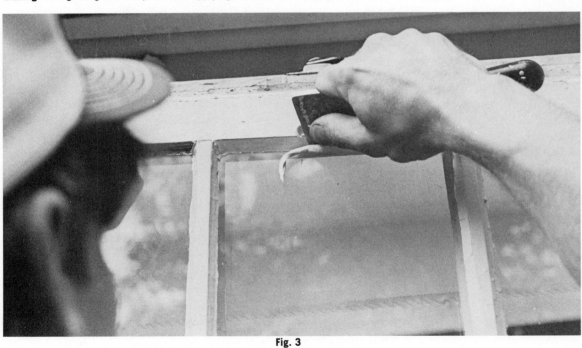

Fig. 3

Glazing. Press down hard with a putty knife when removing excess glazing from a window sash.

When it is pliable, work into the joint between the frame and pane of glass with your fingers. Some professional painters roll the glazing into a rope before working it into the sash (Fig. 1). This produces a more uniform application of the glazing. Try to overfill the joint and work the putty deep into the "V" formed by the glass and sash (Fig. 2). Lay your putty knife in one corner of the window, so the edge of the knife rests on the glass and the angle is about 45 degrees. This produces a beveled bead of glazing that is more suited for allowing water to run off. Draw the knife to the other corner of the window pane (Fig. 3). Bear down hard on the knife, so it cuts off the excess glazing while forcing the remaining compound firmly into the joint. You may want to go back over the putty with a finger, running it along the glazing opposite the direction you moved the knife, to smooth the putty. Glazing compound should dry about a week before top-coating.

See *Casement Windows* and *Double-Hung Windows*.

GLOSS RETENTION

The ability of a *glossy* or *semigloss finish* to hold its *sheen*. The harder the coating is when it dries, the longer it will hold its original gloss. Trim *enamel, varnish, lacquer,* and epoxy finishes contain enough *resins* to offer good gloss retention.

As a rule, latex enamels have less gloss retention than oil-base and alkyd enamels. Epoxy has the best gloss retention of all the coatings.

See *Durability* and *Hardness*.

GLOSSY FINISHES

These finishes have smooth, shiny *sheens*. Glossy paints contain more *resin* than their flatter counterparts, which makes them more wear-resistant. Glossy finishes do not have the minute pits that give *flat finishes* their textured appearance. Dirt and water find little to stick to, and they tend to wash off easily. Paints with a glossy finish are especially suited for use on doors, windows, and trim—both inside and outside your house.

See *Paint, Choosing*.

GOUGES

Relatively small cavities that most frequently occur in woodwork and trim. If gouges are too deep to sand out, they should be filled with a *wood filler* or a *spackling compound*. When the filler has dried, sand smooth and spot prime, if wood is to be painted. If the damaged piece is stained, stain the patch to match surrounding areas. Apply a finish coating.

GRAIN CHECKING

This paint problem first appears as little cracks running parallel to the grain in a wood surface. See the illustration. Left uncorrected, grain checking eventually leads to *flaking* and *peeling* of paint. This problem most often occurs on wood that has not been sanded smooth prior to painting. Plywood often shows signs of grain checking.

To solve a grain checking problem, scrape loose paint from the surface. Sand smooth. Prime with an oil-base primer. Applying a latex primer may cause the wood to swell and lead to *grain raising* problems, which will eventually produce grain checking. Allow the primer to dry; then top-coat.

GRAIN RAISING

When raw wood is exposed to water, the fibers in the wood absorb the moisture and swell. When the wood dries, little ridges remain in the surface. This roughness prevents paint

Grain Checking. Grain checking eventually leads to more severe paint deterioration.

from sticking. Raised grain should be sanded smooth before priming. Some latex primers cause the grain to raise again, so it is best to treat bare wood with an oil-base or alkyd primer.

GUMS

Thick resins from various plant and fossil sources. Gums are occasionally used in natural finishes, but they are being replaced by petroleum-based materials.

H

HAIRLINE CRACKS

Fine fissures that appear in paint or plaster due to an uneven expansion and contraction of the surface. Hardly noticeable by themselves, hairline cracks allow water to enter the paint film. This moisture leads to more severe problems such as *peeling* and *flaking* paint. Hairline cracks can usually be corrected by painting with a paint, such as latex, that has a good *bridging* characteristic.

HARDNESS

The measure of the ability of a paint film to withstand physical abuses such as scratching and abrasion. Paints with more resins—the *glossy finishes*—dry harder than flat wall paints. Two-component epoxies and urethanes are the hardest paints.

HIDING POWER

The ability of a paint to cover and color the surface to which it is applied. Clear shellacs and varnishes have very little hiding power and are not meant to hide the subsurface, but to accent it. *One-coat paint* is made with an extra measure of *pigment* so that it has as much hiding power as possible. As a general rule, dark paints have more hiding power than light ones.

HOLDOUT

A painter's term used to describe the ability of a *primer* to cover and seal a surface. A primer with good holdout produces a substrate with a uniform surface, so that subsequent topcoats have an even gloss and color.

HOLIDAY

Painter's slang for a missed or skipped place on a painted surface.

HOT SPOTS

A disintegration of paint caused by *alkali* in the wall. This defect is most common on *masonry* materials outside the house and on fresh plaster walls inside. Allow outside masonry walls to weather at least six weeks before painting. Allow fresh plaster inside to cure thoroughly before painting. Latex paints are less susceptible to hot spots than oil-base paints.

See *Efflorescence* and *Muriatic Acid*.

I

INCOMPATIBLE

A term used by painters to describe types of paint that cannot be mixed with one another, or paints that cannot be applied over a different type of paint. Oil-base and latex paints cannot be mixed. Latex paints will not stick to *chalking* oil-base paint. In both cases the combination is incompatible.

See *Paint, Choosing*.

INERT

A term used to describe chemicals with active properties. Many of the *pigments* added to paint are inert. They do not dry as the vehicle does, and they do not make paint stick together as *binders* do. They are added for color or to make the paint less costly.

INHIBITORS

Chemicals that retard rust and corrosion. They are added to many metal paints.

INTERCOAT ADHESION

The ability of one coat of paint to stick to another. Primers coated with the appropriate topcoating have excellent intercoat adhesion. Some topcoatings also stick to old paint, provided the two are *compatible*. Few paints stick to glossy enamels, unless the enamel's *sheen* is cut by *sanding* or application of a commercial *deglosser*. Few paints stick to surfaces that are dirty or greasy. Maximizing intercoat adhesion requires thorough *preparation* and the application of the proper coating for the surface.

See *Intercoat Peeling* and *Paint, Choosing*.

INTERCOAT PEELING

Caused by a lack of *adhesion* between a topcoat and the surface beneath it. See the illustration. The tip-off for intercoat peeling is a situation in which the topcoat peels; yet the paint beneath it remains sound. This paint failure can occur on the interior or exterior of a house.

Intercoat Peeling. When a topcoat is incompatible with a substrate, intercoat peeling results.

The reasons for intercoat peeling are many and varied: waiting too long a time between priming and top-coating; leaving the underlying surface too smooth, hard, or glossy for the topcoat to stick to; using a cheap paint on a difficult surface; or by painting over dirt and moisture, which prevents penetration of the topcoat.

To produce the best *adhesion*, a topcoat should be applied within two weeks of the primer coat. Gloss can be removed from a surface with steel wool, fine sandpaper, a strong detergent, or one of the commercially available *deglossers*. Grease and oil can be removed with *mineral spirits, thinner*, or *degreaser*. *Chalking* and dirt can be removed by thoroughly washing the surface with a deter-

gent/water solution. An extra precaution against intercoat peeling on chalking surfaces is painting over the affected area with a primer before applying a topcoat.

See *Peeling Paint*.

INTERIOR PAINT
Specially formulated for use inside your home. Because interior paints are not as tough and weather-resistant as their exterior counterparts, they should not be used outside. Seventy-five to 80 percent of the painting you do inside involves ceilings and walls, so interior paints include the *flat, glossy*, or *semigloss finishes* available in *latex, oil-base* or *alkyd paints* designed for these surfaces. Interior primers, trim paints, clear coatings, and spe-

cial finishes are also available for inside work.

Primers

There are two basic types of interior primers: latex and alkyd. These paints dry to a flat finish and provide a good bridge between the substrate and topcoating. Latex primers work well on plaster, drywall, concrete, cinder block, or over old flat paints. They should not be used on raw wood, as they raise a grain that must be sanded smooth. They do not stick to glossy surfaces. Alkyd primers do not raise grain on bare wood, but they do raise a nap on drywall's paper coating. Although alkyd primers are less popular than latex primers because they must dry overnight before applying a topcoat, they provide a *compatible* undercoating for most topcoatings. Alkyd primers should not be used on masonry surfaces prone to alkali.

Wall Paints

Wall and ceiling paints are available in three materials: latex, alkyd, and oil-base. Most homeowners prefer the convenience and quick-drying time of latex paints to alkyds. Latex paints are also porous, allowing the wall to breathe, while alkyd paints present a nonporous surface.

Although interior walls are usually painted with a flat latex paint, special situations may arise where a semigloss or glossy finish is desirable. Such an instance may be in the kitchen or bathroom where an easy-to-clean, moistureproof finish is a must.

Most interior walls are usually painted with a flat finish paint. Flat finishes reduce glare and help hide imperfections in the wall. Latex adheres to most clean surfaces painted with flat oil-base or latex paints. Latex paints may not stick to alkyd paints or high gloss enamels. Latex paints may also cause the ink in certain wallcoverings to bleed. The water in latex paint can cause wood fibers to swell, producing a rough surface, so they should not be applied to unprimed wood. Latex paints work well on masonry walls and often prevent the occurrence of *alkali* damage.

Alkyd wall paints are not as popular as latex paints, because they require a *thinner* for cleanup. Although alkyd paints produce a tough nonporous surface that is more durable than that of latex paints, they do not adhere to bare masonry or plaster. The paints may raise a nap on drywall's paper coating. Drywall should be primed with a latex primer before top-coating with an alkyd paint. Alkyd paints may take up to a full day to dry, effectively preventing the application of a two-coat job in a single day.

Oil-base interior paints are made by very few manufacturers nowadays, and with good reason. Oil-base paint emits a strong odor, is extremely slow to dry, and is difficult to handle. Oil-base paints have been almost entirely replaced by latex and alkyd paints, and they are not really worth your trouble.

Ceiling Paints

Ceilings are usually painted with a flat latex or alkyd paint. Special paints labeled ceiling paint dry to a finish that is flatter than flat wall paints. Alkyd ceiling paints contain an extra measure of *pigment* to increase their *hiding power*. Ceiling paints also tend to have more *body*, so they do not drip and splatter as much as conventional wall paints. In most cases one coat is sufficient. Do not use a ceiling paint on walls, or you end up with a flat finish that is unattractive.

Trim Paints

Most interior trim is finished by painting or staining. Because these parts of your house receive heavy wear and tear, they need a tough, washable coating with good *abrasion resistance*. Latex, alkyd, and oil-base trim enamels are available for painted woodwork. Doors, windows, molding, and baseboards require a semigloss or glossy paint to stand up to the constant wear they receive. Although alkyd trim enamels produce a slightly tougher finish than latex enamels, latex enamels are gaining popularity because of their easy cleanup.

On woodwork where you want the natural grain of the wood to show through, it is necessary to apply a clear finish like varnish, shellac, or wood sealer over stained wood. Varnish is by far the toughest finish, although it is more expensive than shellac or sealer. Varnish is best used on floors, stairs, and other high-use surfaces.

Shellac is fast drying and inexpensive, but it cannot be used over other coatings because the vehicle in it dissolves other coatings. Shellac also may be stained by water, so it cannot be used on woodwork that needs frequent washing.

Most interior stains are oil-base wiping stains. They are applied to raw wood, so the pigments soak into the wood. Stain should be finished with a sealer or varnish to protect the wood. Do not use latex stains on woodwork, because they raise a grain that makes the surface unpleasingly rough.

See *Painting, Interior*.

J

JALOUSIES

Windows with movable, horizontal glass slats. The slats are angled to admit ventilation and keep out the rain. The term is often used to describe the movable *louvers* in exterior and interior shutters.

When painting the movable louvers on shutters, only a very thin coat of paint should be applied to the area where the louvers fit into the vertical rails. Just as soon as the paint is dry enough to touch, move the louvers so that possible paint seals will be broken.

Use a glossy or semigloss trim enamel for jalousies. Use a glossy or semigloss trim paint for outside work. The same paint used on woodwork and trim is fine for inside work.

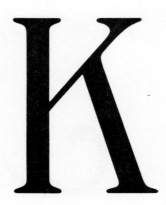

KNOTS IN WOOD

Lumps or knots can be aggravating problems in new wood both inside and outside your house. In most cases the knot leaks resins that attack the paint coating and quickly stain through it. The knot must be sealed before refinishing, or the problem reoccurs.

To seal a knot, scrape all excess resin off the area and sand. Paint with a straight *shellac* if the new topcoat is to be clear, or an opaque *sealer* if you plan to top-coat with a colored paint. Lightly sand the knot when the first sealer coat is dry. Apply a second coat to complete the seal. When the second coat of shellac or sealer dries, apply a topcoat.

Knots with missing holes need to be filled with a *wood filler*. Sand the repair smooth and then seal with shellac or sealer as outlined earlier.

See *Bleeding*.

LACQUER

Commonly used in the home to coat floors, metal, furniture, and bar tops. Clear lacquer allows the natural look of wood to show through while protecting it against alcohol and other staining liquids.

Most lacquers are made to be sprayed or brushed onto a surface. Colored lacquers, made primarily for metal, are best applied with a spray gun to prevent *lap marks* and to obtain the smoothest surface possible. Sanding between coats is necessary. The last coat should be thinned with lacquer thinner before application.

Lacquer is difficult to handle. Application is tricky, so many homeowners are afraid to use it. The material dries quickly, which produces *lap marks*. The coating often attacks finishes over which it is applied.

Cleaning up lacquer scares many people. Regular paint *thinner* does not cut lacquer.

Instead, special and expensive solvents must be used. Lacquers are also one of the most toxic and flammable coating materials around.

LADDER JACKS

Brackets that attach to the rungs or rails of an extension ladder in a way which forms a base to support planks or a walk board. See the illustration. This combination of ladders, ladder jacks, and boards produces a raised platform from which you can work on the high areas of a house. Many rental stores stock ladder jacks. If your house has much work more than 10 feet high, you may want to rent a pair. The time you save not having to move your ladder every 10 minutes is worth the price.

Ladder jacks should be secured to the ladder at the height desired. The support arms should be adjusted until the crosspieces on which the planks or walk board rests are level. The jacks should be 2 or 3 feet from the wall. A

Ladder Jacks. Ladder jacks will transform a pair of extension ladders into a second story work platform.

plank or walk board is rested on the arms to form a platform from which to work. Be cautious, though, as this setup provides few handholds should you lose your balance.

See *Ladders*.

LADDERS

Stepladders are of a fixed height, hinged at the top, and self-supporting. Extension ladders can be made longer or shorter to reach different heights. Extension ladders need a solid surface against which to lean.

Stepladders and extension ladders come in wood, aluminum, or fiberglass. They are generally typed according to their strength. One system of ladder typing suggests that Type I ladders hold up to 250 pounds and are considered suitable for industrial use. Type II ladders are rated up to 225 pounds and are considered adequate for commercial, light mechanical, or handyman work. Type III ladders are classed as household ladders, and

they have a duty rating of 200 pounds. Type III ladders are the lightest and easiest to handle. They should fulfill most home fix-up needs.

Next to the spray outfit, ladders are the most expensive equipment you need for painting your house. Fortunately, a homeowner usually needs only two ladders for painting. Inside you need a stepladder tall enough so that you can reach the highest point inside your house from the third highest step. Outside you need an extension ladder 3 feet taller than the highest painted point on your house. This can be a substantial distance, because a two-story house with a gabled roof may reach 25 feet above the ground.

The choice of material for your ladder depends on your preference. Wooden ladders are sturdy and useful around electrical lines. Aluminum ladders are lighter in weight and last longer than wooden ladders, however; they are flimsier. Ladders with fiberglass runners and metal rungs are electricproof and heavy. These ladders are also the most expensive. At any rate, the ladder you choose should carry a UL (Underwriters' Laboratories) seal.

Stepladders

Stepladders are self-supporting ladders that can be used where all four feet rest firmly on the ground when the ladder is fully open. A spreader holds the two side rails in position while in use. The size of a stepladder is measured along the front edge of the front rail. There should be no more than 12 inches between steps. Each step should be flat on top with a brace underneath. Every stepladder should come with a paint shelf. This shelf should close within the supporting rails when not in use. For maximum safety, a stepladder should come equipped with rubber nonskid shoes.

The stepladder should be fully open and

the spreader bars locked in place before climbing. Make sure all four feet rest securely on the ground when climbing. Always climb or stand in the center of the steps. Never climb the back of a stepladder. Only one person should be on a stepladder at a time. Do not climb higher than the second step from the top, or the ladder may become top-heavy and topple from under your feet (Fig. 1). Never set up a stepladder directly before an unlocked, closed door. Either lock the door or open it so that someone coming through the door does not knock the ladder from under your feet.

Extension Ladders

Extension ladders are a necessity for most outside painting. These ladders are designed so that one set of rails and rungs travels

Fig. 1
Ladders. Never climb higher than the second step from the top when working from a stepladder (courtesy Bestt Rollr, Inc.).

in a set of guides on the other section. This allows the ladder to be adjusted to various working heights. Although extension ladders are measured by the length of an individual section, 12 feet for example, their total working height is less than the sum of the lengths of the two sections. Thus, a 16-foot extension ladder does not permit you to reach a 32-foot height because of the necessary overlapping of the two sections (usually 3 feet or more). A ladder of two 16-foot sections allows you easy access to 25 feet.

Before climbing on an extension ladder, it should be thoroughly checked. All rungs should be tight in their side rails. Rung locks should open and close easily. Side rail guides should be secure and in such a position that they prevent the top section from tipping out of the bottom section.

To stand an extension ladder up outside the house, place the foot of the ladder against the house's foundation. The two sections should be fully collapsed to reduce the chances of the foot of the ladder from kicking away from the wall. Starting at the top end away from the wall, walk the ladder hand-over-hand up to the wall. This process should be fairly quick, so the momentum of the ladder helps with the lifting.

When the ladder is against the wall, move the bottom out a foot or two, so the ladder leans against the house on its own. Raise the top section to the desired working height. It is much easier to raise the top section while the ladder is nearly straight up and down than if it is leaning against the house at a working angle. When the ladder is extended and rungs are locked into position, move the base of the ladder out from the house one-quarter of the working height (Fig. 2). If you are working at 16 feet, the ladder's base should be 4 feet from the house. Less than 4 feet results in a ladder

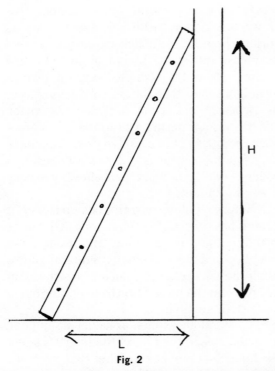

Fig. 2

Ladders. An extension ladder's base should be away from a wall the distance equal to one-quarter of the ladder's working height.

wooden ladders with a clear wood *preservative, shellac,* or *varnish*.

Safety

Ladders are the most dangerous equipment you use while painting. When climbing on a ladder, always grip the side rails or rungs with two hands. Always face the ladder while climbing. When working, try to keep one hand on the ladder at all times. If you need both hands free, lock yourself in positon by inserting a leg through two rungs and catching your toe on a side rail or rung. Do not reach too far to a ladder's side. Keeping your belt buckle within the side rails generally prevents overreaching (Fig. 3). Never climb with wet shoes. Hard-soled shoes with heels are the best.

position so steep that it is capable of falling away from the house. More than 5 feet results in a ladder that bounces excessively as you climb it.

To take the ladder down, move the base in to the house's foundation and lower the top section. Again, walk the ladder down, moving rung by rung away from the house. Go slow here, or momentum will work against you. The ladder will feel heavier than it actually is.

When not in use, an extension ladder should be hung horizontally in a dry storage area with a fairly constant temperature. The hardware on wooden, aluminum, and fiberglass ladders needs to be lubricated occasionally. Never paint a ladder. The paint will cover up cracks and other signs of weakness. Coat

Fig. 3

Ladders. When working off a ladder, keep your belt buckle within the side rails and hang on with at least one hand at all times (courtesy R.D. Werner Co., Inc.).

Never climb higher than where the top rung is parallel with your belt.

Do not hold a paint container with your hand while working off an extension ladder. Invest in a pot hook or make one by bending a coat hanger into an S-shape. Do not climb with tools in your hands. Raise and lower them with a rope.

Extension ladders should have rubber nonskid pads on their feet, so they do not slip on concrete or asphalt. When positioning a ladder on these surfaces, tie a rope around the bottom rung and secure it to the building, so the ladder cannot slip out from under you. If you are forced to use a ladder on an uneven surface, use a brick or flat board to build up the low side. Dig a shallow hole in the high side, so the side rail on this side is even with the lower side.

When moving an extension ladder around outside, be wary of electrical wires. Metal ladders should not be used near electrical wires, as they conduct electricity. Be careful with wooden and fiberglass ladders, too. If they are wet, the moisture carries an electrical charge.

Never set up a ladder in front of a closed, unlocked door. Someone is liable to come through the door and knock you off the ladder.

Finally, to prevent marring a freshly painted surface with the top of your ladder, wrap rags, socks, or gloves over the ends. Fresh paint needs several weeks to harden thoroughly.

See *Ladder Jacks*.

LAP MARKS

Caused when the meeting edges of two sections of fresh paint are not *feathered* sufficiently. See the illustration. This leaves a distinct border of paint two coats thick, resulting in a

Lap Marks. Lap marks are a result of insufficient feathering.

change of color or tone that does not match the remainder of the paint coating.

Luckily, flat finish latex paints do not show lap marks readily. Many of the oil-base, enamel, and glossy trim paints produce lap marks if not handled carefully. To prevent lap marks, feather all edges of wet paint before moving on to a new section. Apply paint from wet to dry areas of the surface.

See *Brushing Techniques*.

LATEX PAINT

A water emulsion of a synthetic rubber or plastic obtained by polymerization and used as a paint coating. These water-base paints have virtually replaced oil-base paints for most home fix-up needs. The major attraction of latex paints is that water and soap are the only things needed for cleaning equipment. Drips and splatters can be wiped up easily with a damp rag. Another advantage of latex paint is its quick-drying time. Most latex paints dry sufficiently for recoating in less than two hours, while oil-base paints normally require a full day of drying time before recoating.

Although latex means rubber, latex paints contain no rubber. Instead, they are made from *synthetic resins*, usually acrylic or vinyl, that have many rubber-like qualities. For this reason, latex paints are more *flexible*, have less *fading*, and are easier to use than most oil-base paints. Flat latex paints also breathe by allowing moisture to pass from the wall to the outside, eliminating many of the *blistering* and *peeling* problems associated with oil-base paints. The following four types of latex paint will cover virtually all the surfaces inside or outside a house.

Enamel

Latex enamel paints work well on doors, windows, floors, and walls when you need a long lasting, durable, and easy-to-clean surface. Latex enamels have better *hiding power* and superior *color retention* when compared to most oil-base enamels.

Latex enamels come in *glossy* or *semigloss finishes*. Semigloss finishes work well on trim and the walls of kitchens and bathrooms where a tough, water-resistant finish is needed. Unfortunately, latex glossy paints are not as shiny as their oil-base counterparts. Latex glossy paints are not as washable as oil-base paints, and they are not available in as many colors. Still, many painters find that the benefits of these paints outweigh the disadvantages.

Primer

Latex primers are gaining acceptance because of their easy cleanup, quick-drying time, and because almost any paint can be applied over these primers.

Outside, latex primers seal cedar, redwood, and fir, which are notorious bleeders. Some manufacturers recommend two coats of primer over these woods. Latex primers offer excellent *adhesion* for topcoatings. They are *mildew* resistant and can be applied to slightly damp surfaces. This last feature allows you to begin painting earlier in the morning, later in the evening, or a couple hours after a light rain without fear of the paint *peeling* or *blistering*. Primers, like other latex paints, dry in an hour or so.

There are a few drawbacks to using latex primers. The most important one is that the water in these paints raises a grain on bare wood. This *grain raising* may lead to accelerated deterioration of the paint film. Latex primers should not be used on rust-prone metals such as the nailheads in *clapboard* siding.

Inside, latex primers are good on plaster, wood ,drywall, and masonry surfaces. Latex primers have good resistance to *alkali*, dry quickly, and cleanup easily with water. Water-base primers also make an excellent bridge between two types of paint—say, an oil-base paint already on a surface and a new latex topcoating. Be careful when painting over wallpaper, as the moisture in these paints may cause the paper to peel.

Topcoating

Latex topcoatings are the most popular finish paints. Outside the house, latex topcoatings have many advantages over oil-base paints. They can cover a wide range of surfaces—from metal and masonry to wood and asbestos shingles. Latex topcoatings dry fast. They can be applied to damp surfaces, and their breathability reduces blistering and peeling. Flat latex finishes are made so that they do not chalk. This adds *color retention* and an overall cleaner appearance to their list of pluses.

One disadvantage of exterior latex paints is that they are slippier than oil-base paints; therefore, they may be applied too thin for maximum coverage. Latex paints cannot be applied over *chalking* surfaces without first priming the surfaces with an oil-base paint.

Inside, latex topcoatings adhere to almost all surfaces, except some alkyd paints or surfaces with a glossy finish. Once dry, latex topcoatings tend to have a little less *abrasion resistance* than oil-base or alkyd paints.

The best masonry paints are vinyl latex topcoatings. The topcoating should be applied over a *block filler* or latex primer. Some latex concrete paints are available in a limited number of colors. Before using latex on masonry, make sure that masonry is listed on the label as a suitable substrate for the paint.

Many latex paints cover properly primed metal and do just as good a job as their oil-base counterparts. The metal must be completely sealed in a nonrusting primer. Some latex paints stick to galvanized metal and aluminum, but it is usually best to prime these surfaces first.

Trim

Most latex trim paints are enamels. They slide on easily and stick to most nonglossy surfaces. Although these paints dry quickly, they are not as durable as the oil-base trim paints. Like other latex paints, the main advantage in using a latex trim paint is that it is easy to clean up.

See *Paint, Choosing; Paint, Exterior;* and *Paint, Interior.*

LEAD

Until recently, lead was added to paint to en-hance its *hiding power*. No coatings sold for home use today contain more than the legal minimum amount of lead. Lead is a highly toxic substance that has been replaced in paint by *synthetic resins* and *pigments*.

LETDOWN

Painter's slang for adding a paint of lighter color to a darker paint in order to lighten the dark paint's color.

LEVELING

Smoothing out of a paint as it dries. A coating with good leveling qualities dries without brush or roller marks. This characteristic is important for glossy, semigloss, and clear finishes.

To insure correct leveling, paints should be applied to properly prepared surfaces with the right type of brush, roller, applicator pad, or spray. Painting in direct sunlight or on hot surfaces often causes paint to dry without leveling.

See *Brushing Techniques.*

LIFTING

A paint problem that occurs when a topcoating penetrates the substrate, especially old paint, and causes it to wrinkle, peel, or form *bubbles*. Epoxy paint is a material notorious for lifting previous surfaces. Lacquers, too, have a tendency to lift other paints. To prevent lifting, use topcoatings *compatible* with their undercoatings, or remove all old paint before applying a primer compatible with the topcoating.

LINSEED OIL

A *drying oil* pressed from flax seeds. It is one of the oldest and most common *vehicles* for oil-base paints and varnishes.

Linseed oils are available in two forms: boiled and raw. Raw linseed oil penetrates wood more quickly than boiled oil. Boiled linseed oil that has been heated and treated chemically yields a richer finish than raw linseed oil.

See *Drying Oils, Safflower Oil, Soybean Oil, Tung Oil,* and *Vegetable Oils.*

LOUVERS

Painting louvers can be a tricky problem. Louvers are used in many places on the ex-

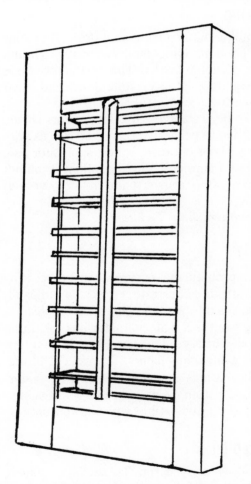

Louvers. The order for painting movable louvers is: back of slats, front of slats, frame, and adjusting bar.

terior and interior of a house. Outside, they serve as covers for the vents on gabled ends of a house. They are also used for shutters and fancy doors. Inside, they are often used for doors for cabinets, closets, and cupboards.

Exterior

Louvers in the gabled ends of your house should be painted to blend in with the remainder of the wall. Most louvers are either metal or wood and can be painted with the same paint used on the siding.

Louvered window shutters, whether functional or merely decorative, should be removed as part of the preparation. They do not really need painting. You often find louvers with *peeling* or *flaking* paint. Scrape old paint away, fill cracks with *spackling,* sand smooth, and then dust thoroughly before painting.

Spray painting is the easiest and quickest way to paint louvers. You will not ruin a good brush trying to poke and gouge paint into the myriad angles in louvers, and overspray is easier to control when working on these small objects. You can paint louvers in a garage or workshop when it is impossible to work on other parts of your house.

If you do not have a spray gun use these brushing techniques on louvers. A ½-inch brush usually works best on the slats, while a 2-inch sash tool makes painting the frame easy. Choose a slow-drying oil-base trim paint for louvers. You do not want the paint drying and lapping before you have finished a particular side.

Paint the backside of the slats first. Any paint that drips through to the front can be corrected when you paint that side. When you paint the front side, any paint that drips through to the back is usually out of view. To avoid paint buildup in the corners, begin painting at one end of each slat. Smooth on the paint toward the center of each piece. Begin again at the opposite end of the slat and smooth on the paint until the slat is covered. Paint the frame with a larger brush, then turn the louver over and check for drips on the front side. Brush these out and set the louver aside to dry. When the paint on the backside has dried, paint the front in the same manner.

Interior

There are two types of louvers inside— those with stationary slats and those with movable slats. Both types should be removed, if possible, and spray painted. Stationary slat louvers are painted following the same procedure mentioned earlier.

Movable slat louvers make the job more tedious. Open the slats so they are horizontal. See the illustration. Working from the side opposite the adjusting bar, paint as much of the slats as possible. Turn the louver over and paint the inside edge of the adjusting rod. Close the louver's slats, but wedge a stick into one of the staples so that the slats do not close

completely (a ¼ to ½-inch space is usually sufficient). Finish the front sides of the slats, then switch to a larger brush and paint the frame. Paint the front of the adjusting rod last and then set aside to dry.

LUSTER

A term used to describe the appearance of *depth* in a finish. Luster is usually most pronounced in floors and woodwork where multiple layers of varnish, shellac, or lacquer have been applied.

LYE

A powerful alkaline substance, usually sodium or potassium hydroxide, used to make soaps. This substance is occasionally added to solutions used to wash down the exterior walls of houses prior to painting. Unfortunately, lye tends to leave a soap film that if not totally washed from the surface, will reduce the paint's *adhesion*. Lye as a cleaning detergent has largely been replaced by cleaners containing trisodium phosphate.

M

MARINE PAINT

Designed to protect boats against the corrosive effects of weather and water. These paints contain more *resin* or epoxy than the standard house paints in order to increase their wearing qualities. Unfortunately, marine paints are considerably more expensive than house paints. The type of marine paint applied to different sections of a boat depends heavily on the material comprising that structure.

More than on your house, the surfaces of a boat must be thoroughly prepared before applying any marine paint. This preparation includes removing all loose or flaking paint, then sanding the surface smooth. Never use steel wool, because the minute particles left on the surface speed up rusting problems. When the surface has been physically prepared, wipe with a thinner-soaked rag or *tack cloth* right before painting. Marine paint should be applied to perfectly dry surfaces in all cases. A drying time of several weeks is necessary for wood—several days for metal and fiberglass. Apply marine paints when the atmosphere is dry and the temperature is between 50 and 85 degrees Fahrenheit.

Aluminum

Below the waterline, fouling aluminum bottoms can be painted with a nongalvanic tin antifouling paint. Where fouling is not a problem, apply etching primers to new, bare metal, or a zinc-chromate primer to weathered bare metal, after washing with a phosphoric acid wash. Topcoatings *compatible* with these primers should be used.

Above the waterline, aluminum should be washed with phosphoric detergent, primed with an etching primer, then top-coated with a sturdy marine enamel. Epoxy and silicone enamels produce the longest lasting protection. For a clear finish, remove all corrosion with a deoxidizer and top-coat with a *nonyellowing* varnish.

Corrosive Metals

Below the waterline, remove all corrosion and loose paint, prime with a suitable metal primer (usually zinc base), then top-coat with marine paint. Use a glossy epoxy where fouling is not a problem and a noncorrosive (tin) antifouling paint where it is.

Above the waterline, corrosive metals should be scraped, wire brushed, or sandblasted to remove all old paint and corrosion. Wipe with a benzene or *mineral spirits* solution. Prime with two coats of red lead primer and follow with two or three coats of a marine enamel paint. Silicones and epoxies are the best bets.

Fiberglass

Below the waterline, most fiberglass boats seldom need painting; however, fouling may force you to apply an antifouling paint. Choose a vinyl bottom paint containing tin or copper antifouling additives. Hulls without a fouling problem can be primed and top-coated with an epoxy primer followed with an epoxy enamel or alkyd marine enamel.

Above the waterline, choose from several types of paint. Epoxies or silicones are recommended. Silicones hold their looks better than epoxies, although epoxies stick well and have excellent *abrasion resistance*.

Wood

Below the waterline, caulk all defects with a compound compatible with the finish you plan to use. Prime all bare spots and then apply two coats of a marine paint specified for wooden hulls. Epoxies and alkyd marine enamels work best.

Above the waterline, wood can be painted or sealed in a clear surface coating of varnish. When painting with an epoxy enamel, choose an epoxy primer. When using alkyd or silicone enamels, choose a primer compatible with these finish paints. Two medium coats of finish paint, with light sanding between coats, last much longer than one heavy coat. Varnish can be applied over previous varnish finishes, provided the surface is sound and the *sheen* has been cut with sandpaper or *deglosser*. On raw wood, seal with varnish cut with thinner before top-coating. Epoxy and alkyd spar varnishes work best on wood.

MASKING TAPE

A tape, with an adhesive on one side, that is used to cover a surface not to be painted. The

Fig. 1

Masking Tape. Masking tape will help make straight lines when cutting in windows.

Fig. 2

Masking Tape. Masking tape takes the drudgery out of painting windows.

tape can be used to mask the line between floor and baseboard. The glass in window sashes can be protected by masking tape in order to prevent getting an excess amount of paint on the glass (Figs. 1 and 2). When you pull the tape off the glass, a straight line of paint remains on the glass (Fig. 3). Tape is also useful on odd-shaped windows such as those with curved sashes. Masking tape comes in handy for securing newspaper and drop cloths around fixtures in order to protect them against paint drips and splatters.

When applying tape, pull short segments (6 to 8 inches at a time) off the spool and lay these along the line to be masked. When one section is firmly in place, pull off another measure of tape and lay it onto the surface. You end up with a continuous piece of tape on the surface without the trouble of wrestling with long pieces of the tape. If the tape strays from the line, pull it up and reapply. To keep paint from seeping under the tape, rub it down tight with

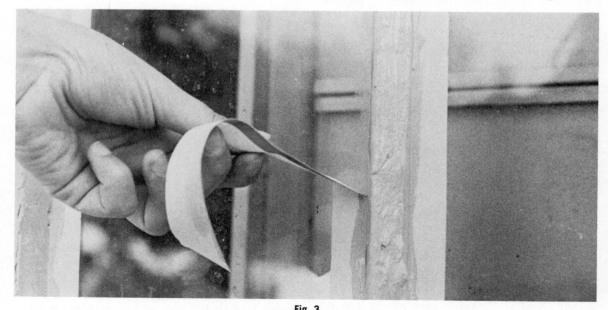

Fig. 3

Masking Tape. Pull tape from the sash while paint is still wet. A professionally straight line will remain.

the handle of your putty knife or thumb. The tape should be removed when paint is dry to the touch. Pulling it off while the paint is still wet may smear the paint. Allowing the paint to dry thoroughly before removing the tape may cause the paint to be pulled off in a way that leaves a ragged edge.

Masking tape was originally developed for use when spray painting. It is generally used to seal the edge of newspaper or plastic along a line where the sprayed paint is to stop, or to hold drop cloths in place to prevent *over-spray* from reaching surfaces not intended to be painted.

MASONRY

Keeping a nice finish on masonry surfaces used to be a time-consuming and repetitive chore. *Whitewash* and *calcimine* were the common masonry finishes, and each required annual or semiannual recoating. Nowadays homeowners have a variety of long lasting, low maintenance coatings for masonry surfaces including *latex* wall paints, *cement paint, rubber-base paints*, and special alkyds.

Unlike other surfaces, masonry walls and floors must be allowed to weather before they hold paint. This requirement is necessitated by the alkaline nature of cement products. Water pulls a substance known as *alkali* to the surface where it attacks the bonding agents in paint, especially oil-base ones, and causes them to flake and peel off the wall or floor. New concrete should weather at least six months to a year before it is painted. You can be relatively certain that most alkali and *efflorescence* formation has stopped when these white powders no longer form on the surface. Do not let the wall age too long, or the mortar joints may begin deteriorating to the point where they require extensive patching and filling before painting.

To patch cracks and deteriorating joints in masonry, follow these easy steps. Chip or dig away all loose material from cracks and joints. Stir together sand, cement, and water to form a patching mortar thin enough to trowel, but not so thin that it sags. Dampen the crack with water—an old paintbrush is useful for this job—then trowel mortar into the hole. Use the edge and point of the trowel to make sure no pockets of air remain in the patch. Smooth the patch and keep it damp for 48 hours, so the concrete cures properly. To match the texture of cinder block, poke the patch gently with a handful of broomstraws an hour or so after application. Like any new concrete, patches should be allowed to age before painting.

Some manufacturers now make latex concrete patching compounds. These materials are ready for painting as soon as they are thoroughly dry. Many masonry *caulking* compounds are also available for patching smaller cracks and holes.

Like most other surfaces, the prepainting preparation of masonry depends on the condition of the surface. In most cases the surface you want to paint is in one of three conditions: new, bare and thoroughly aged, or already painted with another coating.

Aged Bare Walls

When a masonry wall is bare and aged to the point where alkali no longer forms, you have the easiest type of masonry surface to paint. Wire brush the wall to remove dirt and grit, then hose down with clear water. Remove grease or oil spots with a strong detergent or *degreaser* and allow for drying. Recheck for efflorescence or alkali. If present, treat the wall with *muriatic acid*, rinse, and allow it to dry. Coat with a primer, *sealer*, or *block filler* before applying a topcoat.

Like wood or metal surfaces, most masonry requires a good primer coat before top-coating. The choice of a primer depends largely on the specific characteristics of the wall. Porous masonry surfaces can be smoothed and sealed with block fillers. These coatings generally come in a powder. When mixed with water and then brushed onto walls, they supply a good base for latex, cement paint, rubber-base coatings, or special alkyds. A primer coat of masonry conditioner is good insurance when working on a wall that is chalky or dusty. This material seals and hardens marginal surfaces. Almost any paint can be used over this preparation.

Your wall may be in really good shape, and you can bypass the primer coat and apply a topcoat. Rubber-base paints are recommended, because they prevent the infiltration of moisture. They can be applied directly to bare masonry and cinder block; however, brick must be sealed before application of this material. Remember that latex paints are more alkali-resistant than oil-base or alkyd paints.

Cement paint can also be applied to bare masonry. Cement paint actually produces a new surface on brick, stucco, and concrete by adding a thin layer of colored cement. Unfortunately, this material forms a poor base for other finishes, and it is not as sturdy as the name implies.

New Masonry

New masonry is not as easy to prepare for painting as weathered masonry. Although it is best to allow masonry to age six months to a year before painting, a paint job can be applied in as little as two months by following this method of preparation. Before concrete or cinder blocks are painted for the first time, they should be etched with muriatic acid. This neutralizes the alkali inherent in cement mate-

rials. A solution of 1 part muriatic acid to 4 parts water applied with a stiff brush over the entire wall neutralizes most alkali. Rinse with clear water and allow to dry thoroughly before continuing preparations. Wear gloves, goggles, and long sleeves when working with muriatic acid. Confine this acid wash to the surface you are working on, because it bleaches or stains adjacent surfaces.

When the wall has dried, check for alkali and efflorescence. If these problem materials do not reappear, the wall can be painted with a variety of coatings based on the same methods for coating bare weathered walls.

Previously Painted Walls

Old paint that is peeling or chalking excessively should be removed from masonry walls before painting. Coatings such as whitewash and calcimine should always be removed even if the surface looks sound, because the chemical composition of these materials prevents other paints from sticking.

Old paint can be removed from masonry surfaces mechanically and chemically. Mechanical methods include scraping, wire brushing, and sandblasting. Wire brushing and scraping are time-consuming jobs, and sandblasting is beyond the capabilities of most home handymen. If you do not feel like contracting a sandblasting job, chemical removal may be for you.

Mix 1 pound of lye in 3 quarts of water and brush this solution on the wall with a stiff brush. When paint has softened, wash it off with a hose. Etch the newly exposed surface with muriatic acid and allow it to dry. At this point you can treat the wall as if it is a weathered bare masonry surface.

If the old paint is sound, wash with a detergent and water solution. Allow for drying and apply an appropriate topcoat.

Application Techniques

Spraying is the fastest method for applying a paint to a masonry wall. Spraying paint may not get the coating down into the porous surface of the masonry. Rolling is the next fastest way of applying paint to masonry walls. Use a ¾-inch or longer nap and roll slowly, so the paint has a chance to sink into the wall's pores. Cement paints should not be rolled on; instead, they should be brushed.

If you plan to use a brush for applying paint to a masonry surface, select a stiff bristled one. Do not use your favorite 4-inch nylon wall brush, because the masonry wall wears the brush considerably during the job. A stiff whitewash brush with an extra long handle is the best choice, because it works the paint into the masonry's pores with a minimum of effort, and they do not wear quickly. When applying paint to a masonry surface, use circular motions to work the coating into the wall. Brush out with lighter finishing strokes.

When applying latex paint to masonry surfaces, moisten the surfaces with a fine mist of water. This prevents the surface from sucking the moisture out of the paint and causing it to dry too quickly. The moisture also reduces the amount of paint you use. A masonry conditioner or block filler reduces the absorption rate of porous walls.

When painting horizontal surfaces such as porch, garage, or basement floors, you can pour out the paint and then spread it with a roller. Rubber-base paints work well on floors, because they are not slippery and have good *abrasion resistance*. Two coats of average thickness are superior in wear to one thick coat.

On below-grade (underground) walls apply a paint that breathes or allows moisture to pass through the paint. Cement paints and latex paints work best.

See *Brick*.

METALS

The easiest and cheapest way to keep moisture, oxygen, and dirt—the three main causes of deterioration in metals—away from these materials is to seal them in a paint coating.

Paint adheres to metal best when the surface is shiny and bare with all traces of corrosion removed. You can usually get a satisfactory bond on previously painted metal surfaces by wire brushing all loose paint and rust from the surface before priming (Fig. 1). As with all primers, quality counts in the coating's ability to prevent oxygen and water from reaching the metal and causing rust. Two coats of primer are generally better than one, and they should be top-coated as soon after drying as possible.

Fig. 1
Metals. A wire brush will clean up most metal good enough for painting.

Fig. 2

Metals. A trim brush is a good way of coating decorative metals around the house.

Primers work on metals in two ways. Most metal primers contain chemicals that counteract the acid necessary for rust and corrosion formation. Primers also form a waterproof film on the metal and produce a bridge between the metal and topcoat.

Most manufacturers say that their ordinary house paint can be used on guttering, downspouts, screens, grills, *louvers*, railings, and other metal parts of a house. Additionally, some companies make self-priming topcoatings. Although these coatings are slightly more expensive than regular house paints, their ease of application and enhanced durability make them a worthwhile choice. Most of these metal paints can be applied directly to properly prepared metal. They dry to a hard glossy or semigloss finish, and two coats are

better than one (Fig. 2). The gloss on the initial coat should be cut with sandpaper or a *deglosser* for best *adhesion*. Metal paints are thinned with mineral solvents and some, like *aluminum paint* (powdered aluminum suspended in an oil or alkyd resin), provide a shiny metallic finish that is very durable. Different metals in varying conditions of deterioration require specific methods of preparation, priming, and top-coating.

Aluminum

Aluminum does not rust, but pits and a white powder forms on its surface as it weathers. The powder can be wire brushed or washed off with a detergent and water or a commercial product before painting. Latex paints stick well to aluminum, but some manufacturers recommend a zinc oil-base or alkyd primer prior to top-coating.

Many *downspouts and gutters* are made of aluminum; most have a baked-on enamel finish. These gutters do not need to be painted. If you decide to paint over the slick factory finish, rough it up with sandpaper or a deglosser to provide *tooth* for the next coat of paint. Alkyd and latex trim enamels generally stick best to this surface.

Copper, Brass, and Bronze

Copper, brass and bronze are usually not painted outside; instead, they are allowed to weather. This produces a bluish-green patina that many people find attractive. Unfortunately, copper gutters may stain other surfaces if the corrosion that forms on them is allowed to continue. If you want to remove this corrosion to prevent staining adjacent surfaces, use a fine steel wool or one of the commercial copper cleaners. When the metal is clean, paint with a clear acrylic varnish to retain the natural copper color. If you plan to paint the copper with an opaque paint, use a fast-drying latex primer prior to topcoating.

Copper, brass, and bronze hardware is not normally painted inside; instead, it is lacquered at the factory. If this finish wears away, remove remaining lacquer with lacquer thinner. Polish the meal and refinish by dipping pieces in *polyurethane varnish* or a clear epoxy coating. To paint these metals, remove old finish, prime with an alkyd primer, and topcoat with a compatible paint. Enamels generally work best.

Galvanized Iron and Steel

Many items around the house are made of galvanized iron or steel. These include mailboxes, downspouts, gutters, roof flashing, louvers, and garbage cans. New galvanized iron or steel usually contains an oil that is applied at the factory. This oil prevents paint from sticking to the metal's surface. The oil wears off naturally after a few months exposure to the weather. If you want to paint sooner, the oil can be removed by wiping the surface with a thinner-soaked rag. Most manufacturers recommend a zinc chloride or zinc dust primer under a compatible topcoating for galvanized metals. Two coats of topcoating are better than one.

Rusting galvanized iron or steel should be treated as if it was untreated steel. Remove all rust with a wire brush or sandpaper before coating with one or two coats of a rust-inhibiting oil-base or alkyd primer. When the primer has dried, apply two or more coats of topcoating to finish the job.

Steel and Iron

Steel and iron are tricky materials to keep painted. These materials must be scraped, sanded, or wire brushed to remove rust before priming. Apply a rust-inhibiting alkyd or oil-base primer containing zinc or red lead. Some special latex metal primers work on steel and iron. Top-coat with a compatible latex, oil-base, or red lead paint. Although red lead paint does not produce as nice a finish as other top-coatings, it does offer good protection against rusting.

See *Rust Removal and Wrought Iron*.

MILDEW

A fungus that causes discoloration of paint in areas of high humidity and low air circulation. See the illustration. Mildew is common on exterior walls behind bushes or around windows and doors that sweat during the winter. Most mildew is black, but it can also be red, green, or brown.

Distinguishing mildew from discoloration due to dirt is a relatively easy proposition, because household bleach easily kills this fun-

Mildew. Mildew must be removed from walls prior to painting, or it will reoccur.

gus. Dab a little bleach on what you suspect is mildew. If it is mildew, the discoloration fades and disappears in a few minutes. If nothing happens, the discoloration is probably due to dirt rather than mildew.

Some paints are more vulnerable to mildew than others. Paints that contain zinc pigments are less susceptible to mildew than those that use a titanium pigment. Soft (flat finish) paints are more likely to be affected by mildew than hard (glossy finish) paints. Oil-base paints using *linseed oil* as a *vehicle* are also susceptible. Mildew feeds on the oil in most oil-base paints. Porous latex paints applied over linseed primers are extremely vulnerable to attack by mildew. Acrylic latex paints afford the most mildew protection.

Before attempting to remove mildew, scrape all loose paint from the area. This procedure may reveal hidden patches of mildew. To kill mildew, scrub the affected area with a stiff brush using a solution of 1 quart bleach and 1 cup detergent mixed into a gallon of water. When clean, rinse thoroughly with clear water. Wear rubber gloves and goggles during this procedure, and try not to splash the cleaning solution.

As soon as the area is dry, treat with a *wood preservative* or *mildewcide*. Then apply an alkyd primer containing zinc oxide. Top-coat with an acrylic latex paint, preferably one containing a mildewcide, and the problem should not reoccur.

You may be able to paint over a slight case of mildew with a paint containing a mildewcide. It is usually better to wash with a bleach, detergent, and water solution before doing any refinishing.

Mildew on shake or shingle siding should be washed with a bleach and water solution, allowed to dry, and then coated with one of the penetrating wood preservatives. Apply a stain

over the preservative if desired, but remember that oil is a source of food for mildew.

MILDEWCIDE

A paint additive that reduces the ability of mildew-causing fungus to attack a paint. Many primers normally contain a form of mildewcide, because they are made with zinc or zinc oxide. Mildewcide additives are designed to be mixed into a topcoating prior to application.

See *Fungicides*.

MINERAL SPIRITS

Petroleum-base *thinners* made to match the drying capacity of more expensive *turpentine*. Odorless and clear, mineral spirits are more expensive than paint thinner, so they should be reserved only for thinning oil-base paints that specify them as a thinner. Use a cheaper thinner for cleanup chores.

MITTEN APPLICATOR

It simplifies the painting of pipes, metal furniture, *wrought iron*, and places inaccessible to brush or roller. Most mitten applicators are covered on both sides with lamb's wool, so they can be used on either hand. A plastic liner keeps the paint from soaking through to your hand.

Dip the palm of the mitten into a tray of paint, then spread the paint on the surface. These mittens can be cleaned and reused just like any brush or roller.

MOISTURE

Most of the damage to the paint on your house is a result of one form of moisture or another. Water, ice, and vapor all conspire to *blister, peel,* stain, and flake the paint on both the interior and exterior of a house.

The two most common classifications of moisture problems are internal and external.

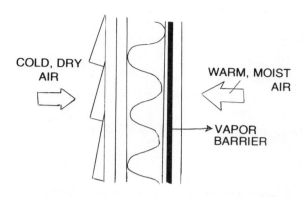

Moisture. A vapor barrier will prevent moisture from penetrating walls and peeling paint on the exterior walls of a house.

Internal moisture problems are a result of moisture vapor inside a wall trying to escape through the paint layer on the wall. The tremendous pressure of the vapor causes the paint to blister, then flake and peel off the wall. External sources of water include cracks and crevices in a paint film and the substrate, as well as large leaks resulting from inefficient *downspouts and gutters* or leaking roofs.

Exterior moisture is probably the most common kind of water problem you encounter while repainting a house. The first step in correcting a moisture problem is determining the source of the unwanted water.

When water gets inside walls through a leaky roof, the trouble spot must be found and corrected. If the gutters overflow during heavy rains or drip on painted surfaces long after a rain has passed, you may need to install additional downspouts or rehang the gutters so they have more fall.

Keep an eye on trees and shrubbery close to the house. Leaves and branches that rub on a painted surface hold moisture and cause peeling and flaking problems.

You have a potential exterior moisture problem where two pieces of wood or other material meet. Wood and other materials such as metal or masonry expand and contract at different rates when exposed to temperature and moisture changes. Consequently, cracks in the paint develop along these joints. Water is allowed to enter. Water increases the rate of expansion and contraction of wood, causing paint to peel and flake. The only way to keep cracks from allowing moisture to enter a surface is by making the joint waterproof.

The old peeling paint should be scraped away, and the bare wood is then sanded smooth. Paint the defect with a *wood preservative*. When the preservative has dried, apply a coat of primer, allow this primer to dry, then caulk with a good water-resistant caulking compound. When caulking has dried, top-coat with two coats of house paint.

Some porous, flat finish alkyd, oil-base, and latex paint systems hold water on their surface for extended periods. This allows water an opportunity to penetrate into the paint and wood. If the bond between paint and wood is weak, the paint peels. Choosing a nonporous paint reduces this problem.

Water repellents can be used to reduce the water penetration of wood siding. These preservatives are sold by lumber dealers and some paint stores. They contain *fungicides, resins,* and waxes that cause water to run off instead of penetrating into wood siding. They are especially useful on cedar or redwood siding where moisture may cause bleeding and discoloration of painted surfaces.

On masonry walls, excessive moisture can cause *efflorescence* that leads to blistering and peeling of the paint. As with wood walls, the source of the moisture must be eliminated to keep the problem from reoccurring. Many paint manufacturers make a waterproof sealer paint for concrete. These work best on preventing exterior moisture problems; however, they may peel when used over interior mois-

113

ture problems. Porous latex paints are generally best for coating masonry surfaces susceptible to interior moisture problems.

Interior moisture vapors are perhaps one of the most difficult problems to identify and correct. The water vapors released through bathing, washing clothes, and by humidifiers may be working their way from the inside of your house through the walls toward eventual evaporation into the outside air. Interior moisture is probably the culprit when paint problems are localized to the wall area outside bathrooms, laundry rooms, kitchens, or other high moisture areas in a house. To correct this problem, you need to stop the moisture from reaching the outside wall.

Several measures can be taken to help keep moisture out of walls. One of the most effective is to put a vapor barrier under the plaster, drywall, or paneling of inside walls. See the illustration. Asphalt-coated paper, aluminum foil, and plastic film are good vapor barriers. Renovation of insulation in your house should always include replacing the vapor barriers.

Additionally, vapor barriers can be made by applying semigloss or glossy enamel finish paint to inside walls. Glossy enamels are the most waterproof paints around, and they can be used effectively in bathrooms, kitchens, or laundries as vapor barriers. An exterior blistering problem can often be eliminated by preventing moisture from entering interior walls. As an added bonus, these finishes stand up to repeated washings.

Moisture can also be reduced by venting moisture out of a room before it has a chance to penetrate the walls. Another tack is the ventilation of wall space. Most hardware stores sell small metal vents that are pushed into the appropriate size holes drilled in problem walls. These vents are positioned so that they are sheltered from rain by the eaves. The vents allow moisture vapor to escape. Avoid clogging the vents with paint when refinishing exterior walls.

MULLIONS

The slender framing that separates the panes of glass in a window. Mullions are usually made of the same material as the frame. They should be painted with the same paint as the window frame.

See *Casement Windows* and *Double-Hung Windows*.

MURIATIC ACID

A commonly used commercial term for hydrochloric acid. Muriatic acid can be used to etch smooth concrete surfaces so that they hold paint better, or to counteract the *efflorescence* and *alkali* present on cement products.

An etching solution can be made by mixing 1 part muriatic acid with 5 parts water. Pour the acid into the water; never pour water into an acid. Work the solution into the concrete with a stiff brush while wearing gloves, goggles, and protective clothing. When the solution stops bubbling, rinse with clear water. This solution should not be used where it can rinse or splatter onto shrubbery or lawns, as it kills the plants. When the concrete is dry, it can be finished using standard *masonry* painting procedures. One gallon of dilute muriatic acid solution should cover 100 square feet, depending on the surface's porosity and absorption rate.

See *Brick*.

NAILS

These fasteners are encountered in three situations during home painting chores: in *drywalls, trim,* and outside where they hold exterior walls in place. As a rule, you never notice nails until they go bad by popping loose or rusting.

To prevent rust, use stainless steel or aluminum nails. You may also have to cover nails used to repair drywall. Raised nails should be driven ⅛ inch below the surface of the drywall, so a dimple is formed. Do not break the paper. Apply a thin, evenly spread layer of joint compound over the dimple with a taping knife. When this cement is dry, add a second larger layer. Be sure to *feather* the edges carefully. Complete the repair job by sanding the patch smooth. Be careful not to rough up the paper on adjacent drywall. Prime patch with a latex wall primer before top-coating.

Nails in woodwork occasionally pop loose. They should be countersunk with a nail set and a new nail driven in nearby. These nail holes should be filled with a vinyl *spackling compound* or plastic *wood filler.* Sand the dried patches with fine sandpaper and seal with primer before top-coating.

Outside, rusting nails can mar the beauty of an otherwise sound paint job. See the illustration. Use sandpaper or steel wool to remove rust stains. Clean the nailhead until only shiny metal remains. Countersink the nail ⅛ inch and paint with an oil-base or alkyd waterproof primer. When the primer has dried, fill the hole with spackling or *putty* and allow to dry. Sand patch smooth and top-coat with appropriate finish paint.

Rust stains on *shingles* or *shakes* cannot be removed by sanding. Instead restain the shingles or shakes with a dark opaque stain to hide the defect.

See *Rust Removal* and *Staining Through*.

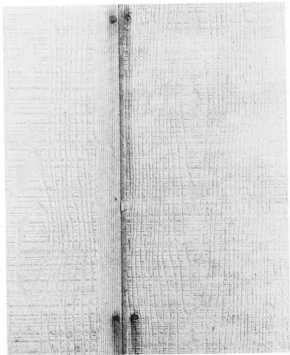

Nails. Use nonrusting nails to prevent rusting nails from marring exterior siding.

NATURAL FINISHES

Many homeowners want the natural beauty of the wood inside and outside their house to show through. There are many natural finishes for wood. Natural finishes generally work in one of two ways: by forming a film on the surface of the wood or by penetrating the wood.

The film-forming coverings are useful inside where weathering is at a minimum. No really good film type clear wood finishes have been developed for exterior use. They begin to discolor, *crack,* and *peel* within a year in most cases. Because of this, penetrating finishes are the most popular for exterior natural finishes.

Penetrating finishes are recommended for natural looking outside finishes, because they do not leave a coating on the surface that

may *blister, flake*, or crack. They are also easy to recoat, because they seldom need scraping or sanding as surface paints do.

Penetrating finishes usually spread at a rate of 400 to 500 square feet per gallon on planed and smooth wood. They can be applied with a brush, roller, or spray gun, although brushing insures deepest penetration and hence the most durable protection. Rough-cut and weathered surfaces may achieve a *spreading rate* of only 200 to 250 square feet per gallon.

Apply only one coating of a natural finish to a new wood. After a year of weathering, additional applications can be made. This wait allows wood to become more uniformly absorptive, so the finish looks its best. A double coating of penetrating finish lasts up to 10 years.

Virtually all penetrating finishes are oil-base, although a few companies have introduced latex natural finishes lately. Most use *linseed* or similar *vegetable oil* as a *vehicle*. These materials afford good water repellency and *mildew* prevention. All penetrating finishes can be coated with colored stains later if you decide to alter the color of your siding.

Inside, natural wood trim or paneling should be sealed to preserve its natural look. One coat of *shellac* is usually sufficient to achieve this goal. When shellac dries, the surface should be sanded lightly with fine grit sandpaper and wiped clean. Linseed oil can be applied to give your trim a natural hand-buffed look, or you can finish with a clear *varnish* that allows dirt, fingerprints, and smudges to be wiped off. Varnish also protects the wood against nicks, scratches, and gouges.

See *Stains* and *Wood Preservatives*.

NONTOXIC

Very few of the materials used in painting

should be considered nontoxic or nonpoisonous. Although some water-base materials claim to be nontoxic, they can have harmful effects when ingested. Treat any ingestion of a paint product according to the recommendations on the material's label.

See *Safety*.

NONVOLATILE

These materials do not evaporate. Most *binders, pigments,* and *extenders* fall into this category.

See *Evaporation*.

OIL-BASE PAINT

The paint uses an oil—usually a *vegetable oil*—as a *vehicle* for spreading the *pigments* and solids onto a surface. These paints are thinned with *turpentine* or *mineral spirits* type *thinner*.

Some solvent-thinned paints, like catalyzed *epoxy paints, polyester,* and *urethanes,* are not considered oil-base paints. *Enamels* made from *varnish* or resin bases are included in the oil-base group.

Although latex paints are gaining popularity, oil-base paints are durable, resist staining, and give good one-coat coverage. Oil-base paints also resist *moisture* and can be used on some dampness-related problem areas. Oil-base paint must be applied to absolutely dry surfaces. An oil-base paint applied to fresh plaster, for example, wrinkles and *peels* because of its moisture-holding capabilities.

Oil-base paints come in three basic finishes: glossy, semigloss, and flat. Gloss and semigloss finishes work best for trim. Use flat finishes for sidewalls and ceilings. There are also special oil-base paints for *masonry* and *metal*.

Alkyd

Alkyd oil-base paints are made from a reaction of alcohol and acids that produce a resin. The resin is then mixed with a vegetable oil (that usually acts as the paint vehicle).

Alkyd paints have excellent *covering power* and dry to a hard, tough, nonporous surface. They are washable and resist wear better than water-base paints.

Enamels

Enamels are clean finishes carrying some sort of pigment. They are free flowing and dry to a hard shell-like finish.

Oil-base enamels tend to be stickier than water-base enamels. This characteristic often leads to overapplication, which results in *sags*. While working with oil-base enamels, constant rechecking of your work for drips and runs is a must. Runs can be worked out by a few light strokes with an unloaded brush.

Glossy enamels are the best waterproof paints for use on trim and high moisture areas. Although most enamels are available in either oil-base or latex, many professionals prefer to use only oil-base enamels. They believe that the oil-base paints produce better serviceability and a nicer look when properly applied.

Because porch floors get heavy wear and are exposed to all forms of weathering, they demand a glossy oil-base enamel for lasting protection. *Porch and floor paints* come in a variety of colors and can be rolled or brushed on.

Primers

Oil-base primers are designed to penetrate the wood surface while leaving a layer on top for the second coat, or topcoating, to stick to. Most oil-base primers are noted for their penetrating characteristics. The wood-preserving qualities found in oil-base primers are often missing in latex primers. In addition to providing a surface for topcoatings, oil-base primers also resist *bleeding, rust,* and moisture problems.

Oil-base primers must be applied to absolutely dry surfaces, and they take a long time to dry. Three days is not an uncommon drying time, making these paints unsuitable for one-weekend jobs.

Rustproofing

Oil-base paints do a good job of locking out moisture on rust-prone metals. Oil-base primers cure rusting nailheads in clapboard if the nails are wire brushed to bare metal before painting.

Downspouts, gutters, and wrought iron benefit when coated with a good oil-base paint. On problem areas, coat the metal with a zinc-base metal primer before top-coating with an oil-base paint.

Topcoatings

Oil-base flat paints can be used on all surfaces where a latex finish coat can be applied. Because they are less convenient than water-base paints, oil-base topcoatings are losing popularity.

Alkyd oil-base flat paints adhere and cover most surfaces well, except for unprimed masonry or metal. On damp surfaces, oil-base topcoatings may peel and blister more easily than latex, because they do not breathe like their water-thinned counterparts. Alkyd paints adhere to chalking surfaces better than water-thinned paints.

Trim

Oil-base glossy or semigloss trim paints contain more resin than flat paints and are excellent for exterior and interior trim work These paints, usually enamels, provide good wearing qualities and self-wash by allowing rain to carry off accumulated dirt. Shiny trim surfaces also tend to add an extra dimension to the house by highlighting flat finished walls.

See *Paint, Choosing; Painting, Exterior;* and *Painting, Interior.*

ONE-COAT PAINT

Many manufacturers advertise paints guaranteed to cover existing surfaces in good condition with one coat of paint. No paint takes the place of a primer and topcoat combination over bare wood. One-coat paints work well if you paint your house every four or five years, before the old paint has a chance to get out of hand.

One-coat paints come in both latex and oil-base. These paints take advantage of extra *pigments* and a richer *vehicle* than regular paints in an attempt to provide more *covering power, adhesion,* and *durability* than their two-coat counterparts. Special drying agents keep the extra thick film of paint necessary for one-coat coverage from wrinkling.

OPAQUE

A term used to describe a coating that is not transparent. House paints that totally hide the *substrate* are opaque. Stains that allow the grain of a wood to show through are less opaque than paints. Clear finishes like shellac or varnish are transparent.

See *Depth* and *Hiding Power*.

ORANGE PEEL

An orange peel defect is due to faulty application techniques for certain finishes. Many quick-drying finishes such as shellac and varnish have these fine wrinkles if they are rolled or sprayed onto a surface. This effect can be good or bad, depending on whether the paint is supposed to have such a finish or not.

An orange peel or wrinkle effect is a common finish on many types of metal furniture. These paints come in aerosol cans and wrinkle as they dry to produce the desired dull texture effect.

OVERSPRAY

The term for paint that leaves a spray gun nozzle and does not land on the surface being painted. Paint drifts a long way in a breeze if you are not careful. The best way to reduce overspray is to paint on a calm day and not to thin the paint too much.

Overspray can be kept off trim or glass by covering the surface you do not want painted with newspaper, plastic, or *drop cloths* held in place with *masking tape*. Make sure the edges of these coverings are sealed tight, because overspray has an amazing ability to penetrate the smallest holes.

See *Airless Sprayers* and *Spraying Paint*.

OXIDATION

The combining of a metal with oxygen to form rust or corrosion. This deterioration occurs on almost all *metals*. Paint does not adhere to oxidating surfaces.

The best way to prevent oxidation is to seal a material prone to oxidation behind a coating that prevents the intrusion of water and air. Do not use a paint with breathability; instead, choose a gloss or semigloss alkyd paint, or a paint designed for use on metals.

See *Rust Removal*.

P

PAILS

Paint stores carry a variety of paint pots ranging in size from 1- or 2-quart capacity all the way up to 2 gallons. Paint pails are made of different materials. The expensive pots are metal and the cheap ones are waxed cardboard or paper, while moderately priced plastic pails fall in between. The distinguishing feature of paint pots is their shape. Unlike paint cans, pails have lips that curve outward instead of inward. This prevents many of the knuckle scraping and paint smearing episodes encountered when painting out of a gallon paint can. Paint pots also have bails or wire handles that allow the pail to be carried around.

Professional painters have found painting out of paint pots so efficient that seldom, if ever, do they paint out of the can in which the paint came. The shape of the pails allows the paintbrush to be slapped on the side of the container to remove excess paint, instead of the slower method of scraping paint off the brush on the paint can's rim. The pail also doubles as a sink in which to clean tools when the job is done.

Pouring paint out of a paint can, or painting from a can, leaves a residue of paint in the can's rim. To keep this buildup from interfering with your job, and to make closing the can easier when the job is completed, punch holes in the bottom of the rim with a nail and hammer. See the illustration. Paint drains back into the can instead of clogging up the groove. When you close the can, an airtight seal is obtained. Punch holes only in gallon or larger cans because smaller cans may buckle, thereby preventing effective closure.

Another trick for making your pail more efficient is to drill a couple of holes on one side of the pail just below the rim. Thread a stiff wire through the holes. The wire creates a resting place for your brush when not in use.

121

Pails. Use a nail to punch a hole in the bottom of a paint can lip. This way paint will drain back into the can instead of drying in the rim.

When too much paint gets into the heel of the brush, you can remove it by scraping the brush on this wire. The paint runs back inside the pail instead of dripping down the outside of the pail where it is wasted.

PAINT, CHOOSING

Paint choice is simplified if you remember that a paint is designed to produce a film that sticks to a surface in order to beautify and protect it from weathering, dirt, and cleaning chemicals. To perform effectively, the paint must remain flexible enough to expand and contract with the surface below it. There are paints for every surface around your house. Unfortunately, there is no single paint that can be used in every situation. Different paints are manufac-

tured to meet the needs of varying surface materials.

Most paints consist of two parts: a solid (pigment) and a liquid (*vehicle*). Pigments can be opaque or transparent. The vehicle can be either a latex or an oil-base liquid. Oil-base paint generally contains a *vegetable oil* (usually *linseed*) or a modified alkyd resin, a *solvent* such as *mineral spirits* or *turpentine*, and a small amount of drier in the vehicle. The vehicle for *latex paint* is usually an acrylic or vinyl resin suspended in water. The performance characteristics of various paints depend on the type of pigment used, the ratio of pigment to vehicle, and the specific properties of the vehicle.

By being familiar with the condition and material making up the surface you wish to paint, selecting a paint is much easier. Ask your paint salesman for advice. He knows the type of paint that stands up best under the conditions you mention. He also knows the climatic patterns associated with the area in which you live.

Although the latex/oil-base distinction is the most obvious difference among paints, other characteristics such as interior/exterior and *glossy, semigloss*, or *flat finishes* are also relatively easy to identify. The ability of various paints to work on specific surfaces is often more difficult to pin down. The table gives you a pretty good idea of what paints are suited to various surfaces. It is not comprehensive, though, and you should ask a paint salesman for advice before deciding which type of paint to buy.

See *Alkyd Paints, Colors, Estimating Quantity of Paint, Exterior Paint,* and *Interior Paint.*

PAINT, REMOVING

Most homeowners find they are applying paint

Table. Paint, Choosing. Paint Choices for Various Surfaces.

Surface	Alkali resistant enamel	Alkyd ext. masonry paint	Alkyd flat enamel	Alkyd floor enamel	Alkyd glossy enamel	Alkyd semigloss enamel	Aluminum paint	Cement-base paint	Epoxy enamel (opaque)	Epoxy finish (clear)	Ext. house paint (oil)	Ext. house paint (latex)	Lacquer	Latex ext. masonry paint	Latex int. flat wall paint	Latex floor enamel	Latex glossy enamel	Latex semigloss enamel	Metal primer	Pigmented wiping stain	Porch and deck enamel	Portland cement paint	Portland cement metal paint	Primer (latex)	Primer (oil)	Shellac	Spar Varnish	Transparent sealer	Trim paint	Urethane enamel (opaque)	Urethane finish (clear)	Varnish	Water repellent preservative	Wood stain (penetrating)
Wood																																		
Flooring, int.				x					x	x			x			x					x									x	x	x		x
Frame windows			x		x	x					x	x					x	x						x	x				x			x		
Natural siding																											x	x				x	x	x
Porch and floor																						x		x	x				x					x
Shingle roof																																		x
Shutters and trim					x	x											x	x						x	x				x					x
Siding					x	x					x	x					x	x							x								x	x
Trim and paneling, int.					x	x							x				x	x						x	x	x				x	x	x		x
Masonry																																		
Brick	x	x	x		x	x	x	x	x		x	x		x	x		x	x						x				x						
Cement and cinder block	x		x		x	x	x	x	x		x	x		x	x		x	x						x				x						
Cement porch floors	x										x											x						x						
Ceramic tile flooring				x					x						x													x						
Concrete	x				x	x	x	x	x					x	x	x	x	x				x	x					x						
Drywall			x		x	x			x						x		x	x						x				x						
Plaster			x		x	x			x						x		x	x						x				x						
Stucco							x	x						x	x			x				x	x	x				x						
Metal																																		
Aluminum			x		x	x	x		x								x	x	x										x	x	x			
Galvanized surfaces			x		x	x	x		x								x	x	x			x	x	x	x					x	x			
Iron and steel			x		x	x	x		x								x	x	x			x	x	x	x					x	x			
Siding (metal, ext.)							x				x	x							x										x					
Steel windows and doors, ext.							x				x	x	x						x															

over an already painted surface. The lucky ones will be working with a surface that is intact. The paint is sound, and only a thorough washing is needed to prepare the surface for a coat of new paint. In most cases, you are painting because the old paint does not look good, and it has deteriorated to the point where it is not protecting the surface properly. The paint may be *alligatoring*—an indication that old paint has built up excessively. It may be *peeling* and *flaking*—an indication that the current paint is not sticking to the substrate. The paint may have some other defect necessitating removal before refinishing. The only way to insure that the new paint you apply stays put for the maximum amount of time is to remove the old paint. There are several methods of paint removal, and the one you choose depends largely on the paint problem and the size of the affected area.

Chemical Removers

Chemical removers soften paint so it can be scraped off easily (Fig. 1). Chemical removers are especially useful on inside woodwork where you want the finish to be as smooth as possible.

Commercial paint removers are available at all paint stores. Water-base or thinner-base paint removers soften and loosen paint chemi-

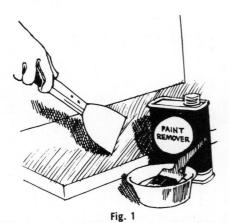

Fig. 1

Paint, Removing. Chemical paint removers work best inside where you want as smooth a surface as possible (courtesy Hyde Tools).

cally for easy removal. Do not use the water-base paint removers on veneer or plywood, as the water in them will make the top layer of wood buckle and crack. Always wear protective clothing, goggles, and rubber gloves when working with chemical paint removers. Always work in a well-ventilated room, because the remover's fumes are toxic.

Use a clean nylon brush to apply the paint remover. Spread a thick coating over the surface to be cleaned, and then allow the material to set until paint begins to blister or wrinkle. Do not try to work with more than 2 or 3 square feet of surface at a time. When paint begins to wrinkle, scrape off with a *putty knife* or taping blade. Wipe the blade frequently and try to get as much of the paint remover and peeling paint off as possible between coats. If all the paint does not come off with the first application, a common occurrence on old thick paint, reapply and rescrape. Follow the directions on the can for treating the stripped wood before sanding and applying a coat of primer or wood sealer.

Heat

Heat is an efficient paint remover on the exterior of your home (Fig. 2). Paint that has built up to such an extent that alligatoring is present requires complete removal, and heat is the best method for removing this excess paint. Many manufacturers make electric heating elements designed specifically for removing paint. Some have a scraper built right in; others require two-handed operation. The element heats up a small area and causes the paint to soften. Scrape the soft paint away with a putty or taping knife.

Many professionals use a blowtorch to remove paint, but this is a dangerous practice. You should never attempt to use an open flame to remove old paint. Although the flame may appear to be under control, it can ignite material beneath the surface through cracks and crevices. By the time you smell the smoke or see the flames, it is usually too late to prevent major damage. If you are removing the paint, use an electric paint remover or one of the other methods outlined in this section. If you are having the job done by a professional, insist that he not use open flame to remove paint. Your house is worth more than the extra expense involved.

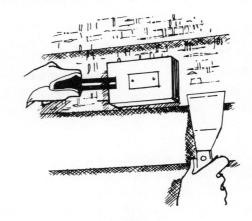

Fig. 2

Paint, Removing. Old paint can be removed with an electric heat element and a scraper (courtesy Hyde Tools).

Sanding

On many larger outside paint removal jobs, you may wish to speed up the process with a power sander. The best power tool for this job is an orbital sander. Unlike disk or belt sanders, an orbital sander does not raise a nap on clapboard, thereby reducing your preparation time. On extremely rough surfaces, you may want to start out with a coarse paper and move to a finer grade for the finishing pass.

Inside, a sanding block holding medium to fine sandpaper is all you need to smooth trim, woodwork, walls, and ceilings before applying paint. Sand with a circular motion to prevent the possibility of creating parallel grooves in the sanded surface.

Scraping

Scraping is usually the first step in removing flaking or peeling paint. A hook scraper, available at any paint store, works better than a putty knife (Fig. 3). The scraper should be

Fig. 3
Paint, Removing. A heavy-duty hooked scraper removes a lot of paint quickly.

dragged across the affected area in all directions to make sure that the edges of the paint that remain are soundly stuck to the substrate. The scraper damages wood if pulled across the grain with excess force.

Inside, a flexible putty knife or taping blade works on most jobs, because the area to be scraped is not usually large. You need less pressure to remove the paint than if you were scraping outside. Work the blade under all loose edges of paint and push gently until the loose paint flakes off. Scraping normally leaves a barely noticeable edge where the old paint has been removed. You can eliminate these edges by feathering with sandpaper before painting. On deeper, more obvious depressions, you need to fill the spot with a *spackling compound*. A 6-inch taping knife works well for applying the patching material. When the patch has dried, sand smooth and prime before topcoating.

Wire Brushes

In many cases you discover that a power sander just does not reach all the cracks and crevices in a wall. For these places, a wire brush does the job. Try to brush in the direction of the wood's grain. Apply light pressure so you do not gouge the wood. On masonry and metal surfaces, a wire brush attachment for a power drill saves time and reduces the probability of gouging the surface. A cup-type accessory brush works well on large flat areas, while a disk attachment gets down into grooves, cracks, and narrow openings along guttering and masonry surfaces.

See *Preparation, Rust Removal, Sanding,* and *Scrapers, Paint.*

PAINTING, EXTERIOR

Painting the exterior of your house is a chore. With a little prior planning and by following the tips offered in this section, you should be able to do the work efficiently.

The exterior of a house can be divided into two sections: the body and the trim. The body is the major area of walls—*clapboard* or another material. The trim includes *windows, doors*, porches, *downspouts and gutters*, steps, and other small parts of the house that are painted a separate color or with a paint different from the coating applied to the body of the house.

Most people paint the body of their house before the trim. This gets the biggest piece of work out of the way early. It allows you the luxury of coming back in shorter work periods to paint the various pieces of trim. Because you are using larger tools on the body than the trim, painting the body first allows you to speed up. You later cover any body paint you get on the trim with trim paint. It is also easier to cut in straight lines with a smaller trim brush.

Whether you decide to use a roller, brush, applicator, or a spray unit for the body, follow the general rule of getting the most difficult areas painted first. This usually translates into working from the top to bottom of the house.

The best temperatures to paint range between 50 and 90 degrees Fahrenheit. Spring and early fall are usually the best seasons in which to paint. To reduce *moisture* related problems, you should not paint within 24 hours after a rain, even when using latex paints.

Sun dodging is an important consideration. Always try to paint a wall that is not in direct sunlight. The period from 11.30 A.M. to 3:30 P.M is normally too hot on the south side of your house for both you and your paint. Work on this side first thing in the morning or later in the afternoon. Professional painters are unsure whether it is better to apply paint in the morning and have it baked dry by the sun, or to apply paint on a hot wall in the afternoon. Most suggest painting a south wall on an overcast day. They also recommend working on the west side of the house in the morning and moving to the east side in the afternoon.

Cut limbs and branches away from your house before you start preparing the house for painting. This may reveal trouble spots, and the removal of extra vegetation gives you more room to maneuver.

Always cover bushes, porches, railings, roofs, and driveways to prevent splattering. It is easier to lay out a *drop cloth* than to stop after every trip down the ladder to wipe up spills. Latex paints, with their fast-drying time, make it nearly impossible to wipe up drips more than a few minutes after you make them.

Plan your work so that you make the fewest trips possible up and down the ladder. Starting at the highest place on your home is a smart move. By the end of the day you begin to tire, and it may not be safe to climb too high. If your house has dormers, these should be painted first. Then work down to the remainder of the house's body. Skip the windows, trim, and overhang. Leave them for later, unless they are high, then paint them after painting the body and before you move the ladder.

On extremely high gables, reduced ladder handling and climbing may make painting both the body and trim an attractive option. Although you have to be careful not to mix the two paints where they meet, choosing a quick-drying latex for the body allows the body paint to set before you begin the trim work. Even if a little mixing does occur, and all your trim/body paint lines are not razor sharp, do not worry. Few people notice them from the ground.

To further reduce the number of times you have to move the ladder, paint in horizontal strips. This reduces the number of times needed to adjust the ladder's height. If you have a lot of area that requires a ladder to reach, you may want to rent a pair of *ladder jacks* and fashion a walk board from which to work.

Change the widths of your reach on the primer and topcoating, so *lap marks* do not show up. The best place to lap different areas of paint is at natural breaks such as windows, doors, corners, and downspouts. These features disguise lap marks caused by starting and stopping.

If you are applying two coats of paint to your house, and the trim and body are the same color, use the body paint as a first coat on the trim. Switch to trim enamel for the finishing coat.

When the body and trim are different colors, you want to paint the siding up to the trim, including the edge of the trim. This strategy becomes a necessity if your house has clapboard siding. At the corners and along the edges of other trim, there is a saw-toothed effect where the siding meets the trim. Painting the side of the trim with trim paint is a tedious and time-consuming chore. Avoid it by painting the side of the trim with body paint.

Trim on the exterior of a house is painted in much the same way as interior trim. You work from top to bottom, inside to outside. On windows, this means painting the muntins, sash, and casings. Regarding doors, the jambs, the door, and then the door edges are painted. The same trim tools you use inside work outside as well.

When bringing the trim paint out to the body paint, make the two meet at the corner of the trim. You get a straight line every time. Keep a rag handy just in case the trim paint slops onto the body paint.

Porch ceilings are generally painted with trim paint instead of flat wall paint. The reason is that porch ceilings tend to collect plenty of dust and dirt. A glossy surface makes cleaning easier. On overhangs where you plan to use trim paint, rolling the paint on may save considerable time and energy.

Paint porch railings, floors, steps, and the foundation of your house last. If your house has both a front and back porch, paint one on one day and the other the next. This eliminates the possibility of painting yourself into or out of the house. On steps, try painting all the risers and every other step. This way you can still use the steps. Come back the next day and finish the unpainted steps.

The foundation of the house is usually painted last. You can make it blend in by painting it the same color as the walls, or you can make it stand out by using a trim-colored paint.

Varnish the wooden thresholds on your doors. Others then know that you have put some effort into keeping your home looking its best.

See *Brushing Techniques; Colors; Estimating Quantity of Paint; Exterior Paint; Paint, Choosing;* and *Preparation*.

PAINTING, INTERIOR

Whether you are painting a single room or the entire interior of your house, you achieve the best appearance and longest lasting job if you plan the work carefully. The very first step for painting a room is moving as much furniture as possible—including drapes, lamps, and *electrical fixtures*—out of the room. Cover the entire floor with *drop cloths*. Wash the surfaces you plan to paint with a detergent and water solution before *patching walls*. After you have completed all these preparations, the most difficult part of the job is finished. It is time to paint.

Interior painting follows a few general rules that sound familiar if you have already read the section on exterior painting. Start

Painting, Interior. An extension handle speeds up rolling those hard-to-reach places.

with the largest, most difficult areas first. This usually means working from the top to bottom of the room. Paint the *ceilings* first, then work on the walls and trim.

When you paint the ceiling in a room, begin by *cutting in* a 2-inch border around the entire edge of the ceiling. Using a roller or brush, begin in a corner and work across the narrowest width of the room. Continue zigzagging back and forth until the ceiling is completed. There is no time for breaks while painting the ceiling, because *lap marks* that form when fresh paint is applied over dry paint will be exposed.

The walls are painted in much the same way as ceilings, except that you are working on a vertical rather than horizontal surface. Begin by cutting in where the wall meets the ceiling, corners, then around windows and doors, and along the *baseboard*. Using a brush or roller,

start in the upper left- or right-hand corner of the wall. Work in 3-foot square sections. Always work from dry to wet paint. This reduces lapping. Begin in a confined area, say a corner with a window, so you are not boxed in by wet paint.

If you are using a roller on a tall wall, an extension handle comes in handy. See the illustration. Work across the top section of the wall, remove the handle, and then paint another horizontal strip in the opposite direction. If you can reach from floor to ceiling with your roller or brush, work in vertical strips from the ceiling to the floor. When you reach the baseboard on the first strip, begin the next section at the floor and work your way up to the ceiling. Both of these methods speed up the job and reduce the chances of lapping, especially when applying an alkyd or latex semigloss or glossy paint. When you finish the wall, step back and take a careful look at it. Did you miss any spots? Do you see any *sags* or *runs*? Touch them up while the paint is still wet, so lap marks do not show. Move on to the next wall.

When you come to a window, paint halfway across the wall above the window, switch to the wall below the window, and paint it halfway across. Return to the area above the opening and paint it parallel with the edge of the window casing. Drop back down to the bottom section and paint it out, too, before continuing with the wall. This method prevents lapping.

Like outside trim, interior trim is painted from top to bottom after the wall paint has dried. As a rule, ceiling molding is painted with the wall paint, unless you are painting it to match the remainder of the room's trim. Paint the windows, working inside to outside—muntins, sash, casing, and sill. Paint the doors, again working from the inside out. Paint the panels of the door first, then the edges, and finish up with the jamb. Complete the room by painting the baseboards. Once the baseboards have been painted, let the room sit until this paint has dried. Walking around or folding drop cloths in a room with freshly painted baseboards is an invitation for dirt and dust to get into the sticky paint.

Often you run into special problems when painting inside. Stairwells are an example. Start at the top in the most difficult place, usually the headwall that faces the stairs. Lean a ladder against the wall by resting the feet of the ladder on a stair tread. Push the foot of the ladder against the riser for security. Climb the ladder and cut in all the wall you can reach. Brush or roll the wall. You may want to do as much area as possible, including the sidewalls, with this setup so that when you take down the ladder, it is down for good. You can construct crude scaffolding to reach most of the high area. Stand a section of an extension ladder in the stairwell, so it leans against the headwall. Place a plank on the rung parallel with the top step of the stairs. This setup should allow you to reach most of the high area in one set.

Another difficult area to paint is the inside of a small closet. As with a regular size room, paint the ceiling first. Paint the walls at the ends of the closet. Paint the back wall. Now comes the most difficult part of the chore—the wall with the door. You will probably have to paint with half your body out of the closet and only your head, shoulders, and arms inside. By saving this wall for last, any skips or runs you make because of limited working area are impossible to see from the door of the closet. Finish the job by painting the door.

Closet shelving is usually painted with a glossy or semigloss trim enamel, because these paints stand up to the wear and tear suffered by often used shelves. Take out *shelves* that are removable and set them on sawhorses for painting. Replace the shelves when they have dried.

See *Brushing Techniques, Ceilings, Colors, Drywall, Estimating Quantity of Paint, Interior Paint,* and *Paint, Choosing.*

PAINTS

See *Acoustic Paint, Alkyd Paints, Aluminum Paint, Antifouling Paint, Barn Paints, Cement Paint, Epoxy Paints, Exterior Paint, Fire-Retardant Paints, Flat Finish Paints, Interior Paint, Latex Paint, Marine Paint, Oil-Base Paint, One-Coat Paint, Porch and Floor Paints, Quick-Drying Paint, Rubber-Base Paint, Sand Paint, Texture Paints,* and *Urethane Paint.*

PEELING PAINT

Paint that comes off in sheets or scales. This is one of the most common paint failures you encounter during painting chores. See the illustration. Peeling occurs in one form or another on painted surfaces, except areas coated with a penetrating stain.

Peeling paint can tell you several things about the condition of your wall. Paint that peels all the way to bare wood indicates that the primer is not doing its job. Primers fail because they were not selected correctly, were improperly applied, or because they were applied over wood containing *moisture.* The peeling areas have to be scraped to bare wood and allowed to dry thoroughly before priming to cure the latter problem. The former problems can be corrected by following the application instructions on the can's label carefully.

When only the topcoating peels and the primer remains intact, the peeling is caused by improper *adhesion* between the two coats of paint. Known as *intercoat peeling,* this defect results from applying a topcoating to a dirty

Peeling Paint. Look closely at peeling paint to determine what is causing the problem.

Even if you applied paint to a perfectly dry wall, moisture may be leaking into the wall. Water from inside the wall attacks paint by soaking through the wall. This water can come from such faulty conditions as leaks in plumbing, overflow of sinks and bathtubs, leaky roofs and guttering, or improper *caulking* of cracks in the wall. The cause of the leak must be determined and corrected before you can end the peeling problem.

Another form of moisture is water vapor that slowly works its way through the walls to the exterior. Humidifiers can be a cause of excess moisture, along with washing machines and showers. To prevent this vapor from traveling through the walls and peeling off exterior paint, you need to create a vapor barrier. Painting interior surfaces with glossy or semigloss enamel seals in most moisture, reducing the peeling induced by this vapor. Painting the outside walls with porous latex primers and topcoatings helps to reduce the problem.

Dirt, grease, and loose paint are also causes of peeling. These substances act as a barrier between topcoatings and primers, preventing the topcoating from adhering to the primer. Scraping surfaces with loose paint and washing all others is necessary to prevent this type of peeling.

Eaves and overhangs present a special kind of peeling problem. The snowflake or tissue paper peeling associated with eaves is usually due to a lack of moisture. Exterior paints are designed to receive a rainwater bath occasionally to prevent dirt and old paint from building up. When they do not get exposed to these conditions, they fail. This failure is due to the buildup of salts that would normally be washed away by rain between paintings.

To correct this problem, scrape and sand the peeling surface thoroughly. Wash the area

primer, or to a primer that has stood exposed to the weather for an extended time. To repair, scrape loose paint to the primer, reprime to establish a sound substrate, and top-coat.

Paint that peels and leaves behind a mottled gray surface indicates that *mildew* is at work. No paint sticks to mildew, so it must be removed. Wash with a solution of bleach and water, then paint with a mildew-resistant paint.

Another cause of peeling is moisture. Peeling results because the wood was not totally dry when painted. After the paint has dried, the moisture tries to work its way toward the air, pushing the paint off the surface and causing it to *blister, crack*, and then peel.

with a strong solution of detergent and water. Rinse with clear water and allow it to dry. When dry, apply a coat of primer. When the primer has dried, top-coat with a nonchalking paint. Trim paints are generally good on these troublesome areas.

Peeling paint on metal surfaces like *downspouts and guttering* is normally caused by improperly preparing the metal before painting. To correct the problem, remove all old paint with a paint scraper, wire brush, or sandpaper. If you are planning to use a latex paint on the surface, prepare the metal with a coat of *solvent*. When the solvent has evaporated, apply the latex paint. Two coats are better than one. For oil-base topcoatings, prime the sanded area with a metal primer. When the primer has dried, apply a metal paint. Finish the job with a coat of house or trim paint.

Paint peels from *masonry* surfaces for the reasons it peels from other surfaces. Chemical compounds called *alkali*, inherent in cement products, react with paint to push it off the wall. Alkali compounds are drawn to the surface by moisture. These powdery formations on the wall's surface are called *efflorescence*.

To repaint peeling masonry, scrape, wire brush or sandblast all loose paint from the wall. Wash the problem areas with a solution of *muriatic acid* and water, rinse with clear water, and allow for drying. Seal with a masonry sealer, allow for drying, then paint with an alkali-resistant paint.

See *Alligatoring, Preparation, and Spot Peeling.*

PERMEABILITY

A characteristic in some paints that allows *moisture* to pass through the paint film. Most flat *latex paints* are permeable in that they allow moisture vapor in the wall to evaporate without *blistering* or *peeling*, while preventing the intrusion of liquid water such as rain. This permeability gives latex house paint a big advantage over *alkyd paints* on walls, but not on metals where moisture must be repelled totally to prevent rust.

See *Breather Film* and *Paint Choosing.*

PHENOLIC VARNISH

A clear *varnish* that contains phenolic resins. This type of varnish produces a warm glowing finish; however, it is the least durable of the available varnishes. Used mostly on fine furniture, phenolic varnishes are being replaced by the more durable alkyd and epoxy varnishes.

PIGMENTS

The finely ground substances that make paints opaque. Pigments are made from a variety of metals, chemicals, and earth minerals that are combined to produce distinct *colors* of paint. Some coatings like varnish and shellac are really pigmentless paints.

Pigments for coloring paint are sold in paint stores under the name universal colorants. By using these colorants, you can custom mix paint colors to your preference.

See *Vehicle.*

PIGMENT VOLUME

A term used to describe the amount of pigment in the *solid* part of the paint. Usually expressed as a percentage, pigment volume is higher in *one-coat paint* and dark-colored exterior paints than in other paints. *Stain* has a low pigment volume that gives it its ability to show grain. *Varnish, shellac*, and *natural finishes* contain few, if any, pigments.

See *Vehicle.*

PILING

An excessive buildup of paint on one area of the wall. It can be caused by not thoroughly brushing out a load of paint or by improper spraying techniques. In extreme cases, piling leads to *sags* or *runs* on the paint surface.

PINHOLING

Tiny holes in a paint film that reduce the ability of the paint to withstand weathering by allowing water to penetrate the film. Pinholes are produced when air bubbles in the paint pop after application. Air bubbles are caused when a paint is mixed too vigorously or applied too rapidly, especially with a roller. To avoid pinholing, allow paint to set half an hour after stirring. Do not roll or brush too fast during application. Pinholing is more common in quick-drying finishes such as *shellac* or *varnish* than in regular paints.

PLASTER

A pasty composition that hardens on drying and is used on walls, ceilings, and partitions. Although *drywall* is the preferred choice for construction of interior walls in today's houses, most houses built before 1950 were made with plaster interior walls. Some builders still use plaster for interior walls. You may have some of the following problems in your plaster walls.

New Plaster

Dry-out is a problem produced when plaster dries too rapidly, and the gypsum crystals in the material do not have a chance to form properly. Dry-out can be remedied by spraying the affected area with a solution of 2 pounds of alum dissolved in a gallon of water. Allow the area to dry thoroughly before priming.

Sweat-outs are large spongy areas that do not hold paint. These form when plaster dries during prolonged periods of high humidity. The best remedy for these sections of wall is replacing the plaster. The problem may be larger than you can handle, and professional help may be required.

Uneven troweling results in plaster of varying density. Different density plasters soak up paints at unique rates, preventing a uniform finish coat. Several coats of primer applied to the thirsty sections should cure the problem.

Unpainted new plaster picks up and absorbs dirt easily, which makes it difficult to clean. To protect uncured plaster, apply one coat of a latex wall paint or primer. Latex paint is not affected by the *alkali* in the new plaster, and this paint allows the moisture within the plaster to escape as it dries. Subsequent coats of paint, either oil-base or latex, can be applied when the plaster has had time to cure. Curing takes several weeks to several months depending on humidity and temperature conditions.

Old Plaster

Cracks, holes, and stains are common problems on old walls. These must be corrected before painting to achieve a professional looking paint job.

Staining through indicates that water is seeping through the wall. The source of the water should be determined and corrected before repainting the stain. Repairing the stain is relatively simple. Seal it with a coat of *shellac* or an opaque oil-base *sealer* such as Loc Tite. Allow the sealer to dry, then spot prime before top-coating the entire wall.

Cracks in plaster come in two varieties—small and large. Small cracks are generally less than ⅛ inch across and can be repaired rather easily. An important step in repairing small cracks is widening the crack, so the patching plaster has an adequate surface to hold onto. A can opener works well for this job. Make sure to extend the ends of the crack into the sound plaster on both ends of the problem. Then vacuum or blow out the dust. Smooth in a patching plaster or vinyl *spackling compound* with a putty knife. Allow the patch to dry, then smooth by *sanding*. Spot prime before top-coating.

For larger cracks, generally ¼ inch wide or wider, you need to give the patching plaster a footing under which to key. This can be accomplished by undercutting the sides of the crack so that an inverted "V" is formed. Undercutting sound plaster in this way prevents the patch from losing its footing and falling out. Vacuum or blow out all dirt and dust.

The next step is mixing a batch of patching plaster to a pastelike consistency. You can buy a more expensive premixed material such as drywall joint compound. Wet the entire length of the crack with a clean paintbrush dipped in water. This step prevents the plaster from absorbing the water from the patch, causing it to dry improperly. Spread the patching material over the crack, pushing it well down into the defect. Apply the patching material in a long smooth ribbon that extends at least an inch over the edges of the crack. Allow the patch to dry. If it shrinks, add another layer. Work the second application beyond the edges of the first. When this layer has dried, sand smooth with a fine grit sandpaper fastened to a sanding block.

Small holes, less than an inch in diameter, are patched by chipping away all loose material around their edges. Wet the edges with water and work the patching material into the depression. Allow for drying. If shrinking occurs, reapply patching material. When dry, sand smooth with fine grit sandpaper.

Larger holes, where the lath is visible, require more work. First, chip away all loose plaster until only sound plaster surrounds the hole. Undercut the edges with a putty knife or can opener in order to give the patch a footing. Vacuum or blow out dirt and dust.

Mix enough patching material to fill the hole. Brush water around the edge of the hole and on the lath with a clean paintbrush. Work the patching material into the hole, pushing it hard so that it keys behind the lath and under the edges of the hole. Smooth the patch just below the surface of the wall and allow it to set a short time. Before the first application of patching material dries, score the patch with the edge of a putty knife or can opener. Roughing up the surface in this manner allows the final patch to grip the first patch tightly. Allow the first application to set up.

Mix a new batch of plaster for the next layer. Dampen the previous patch and the area around the hole. Spread the new patching material into the hole and extend it well beyond the edges of the hole. Level the patch surface with the wall. A wide blade taping knife comes in handy here. Allow this second application to set completely.

A finish layer of spackling compound or joint cement should be applied to the patch. Using a taping knife to spread the material over the entire patch and extend it beyond the edges of the previous application. Let the patched area dry several days until it no longer feels the least bit damp. Smooth the area with sandpaper, feathering the edges into the surrounding wall.

All patches should be primed before top-coating. Walls that have undergone an extensive amount of patching should be painted with primer over the entire surface before topcoating. This priming insures a uniform finish on the wall. Use only latex paints for the primer coat. The patches are thus able to dry thoroughly. Application of an alkyd or oil-base primer over a new plaster patch is asking for trouble. The moisture in the patch causes these paints to peel and blister. After the patches have had sufficient time to dry, usually two or three weeks, a latex, oil-base, or alkyd paint can be applied without worry of moisture-induced problems.

See *Interior Paint, Painting, Interior; and Walls, Patching*.

POLYURETHANE RESINS

Synthetic resins made from isocyanate. Polyurethane coatings have good *abrasion resistance*, approaching that of the *epoxy paints*. The most common use of polyurethane resins is in certain varnish coatings. Polyurethane varnishes are resistant to alcohol and are commonly used for bar and tabletops.

POLYURETHANE VARNISH

This varnish dries to a hard tough finish because of the *synthetic resins* in it. Some polyurethane varnish approaches the durability of epoxy varnish. Polyurethane varnishes are resistant to alcohol and water and are often used as bar and tabletop finishes. Polyurethanes come in ready-to-use formulas or two-component mixes. The two-component systems are the most durable, but they require more careful handling and application.

See *Varnishes*.

PORCH AND FLOOR PAINTS

These paints include *alkyd, latex, urethane, rubber-base* and *epoxy paints*. The paints are made to withstand weather and heavy traffic and come in many colors to match or contrast the reminder of a paint job.

The most commonly used porch and floor paints are glossy alkyd or latex enamels and urethane paints that are designed for use on bare or previously painted wooden floors and previously painted or primed concrete floors.

Rubber-base paints provide a nonskid flat or semigloss surface that stands up well to repeated washing with detergents. Rubber-base paints are commonly used on masonry floors. Epoxy paints are the most durable of the porch and floor paints and can be used to coat any smooth bare floor, or floor previously painted with epoxy finishes. Epoxy paints should not be applied over other types of paint, as they may cause the previous paint to soften, ruining the epoxy's performance.

Porch and floor paints are applied like other paints. Brushing or rolling are the two most common methods of application.

Porches and floors should be scraped free of loose paint and debris, then vacuumed or swept carefully before application of paint (Fig. 1). Grease and oil should be removed with a *degreaser*. All holes and cracks should be

Fig. 1

Porch and Floor Paints. Use an old brush to dust dirt and debris from porch steps prior to painting.

patched and allowed to dry before further work.

When painting a large floor surface, the fastest method is to divide the floor into 3-by-3-foot sections, pour a little paint into the middle of a section, and then roll or brush it out (Fig. 2). Remember that two coats of thin paint last longer than a single thick coating. Work from a dry area to a wet one, blending successive patches together into a smooth continuous coating.

High traffic areas benefit from three or more coats of paint. You can keep these alleys of wear in good shape by periodically spot painting thin or worn spots.

Smart painters plan to paint the front and back porch floors of a house on different days. This way they leave an access into and out of the house during the entire porch painting procedure.

See *Floors, Wood*.

Fig. 2

Porch and Floor Paints. Porch and floor paints can be brushed or rolled. Work in small areas to reduce lapping.

POROSITY

A trait built into certain paints, most notably flat latex house paint and cement paints, that allows *moisture* to pass through the paint film. This porosity gives these paints a characteristic known as breathability or *permeability*. Although porous paints normally do not blister or peel from moisture within the wall trying to work its way out, they are susceptible to *bleeding* and *staining through*.

See *Breather Film*.

PREPARATION

Before a brush is dipped into paint, including primer paint, the surfaces you plan to paint must be properly prepared for the job. The idea behind preparation is to produce a smooth clean surface that holds the paint. Preparation may seem to be a needless time-consuming chore, but without it your paint job suffers. Even the best paints deteriorate rapidly when applied to a surface that has not been properly prepared. By following the general guidelines for interior and exterior preparation, adopting them, and altering them where needed for your specific job, you should be pleased with the result.

Interior Preparation

There are three steps to interior preparation. The first is removing obstructions from the area you plan to paint and covering everything that cannot be moved. The second is insuring that the walls are clean. The third is repairing physical damage.

Although removing all the furniture from a room may seem like wasted effort, this simple procedure saves both time and effort in the long run. If you are planning to paint only the walls of a room, remove the smaller pieces of furniture from the room and move the larger ones to the middle of the floor. Cover these pieces, as well as the floor, with *drop cloths*. If you are planning to paint the ceiling, try to remove all the furniture from the room. If you cannot remove all the furniture, stack the left-over pieces at one end of the room. Begin painting the ceiling at the end opposite the furniture. By the time you reach these obstructions, most of the ceiling has been painted. You can move the furniture to the center of the room to finish the job.

Remove all curtains and draperies, pictures, and other wall decorations. If you are planning to rearrange these objects after the job, pull the hangers from the wall and fill them while *patching walls*.

Remove all electrical switch plates, even if you plan to paint them the same color as the walls. This prevents a buildup of paint around their edges, which is likely to ruin the paint when the switch plates are removed later.

The hardware on doors and windows should be removed. It is much easier to unscrew and replace these pieces than to paint around each of them. You also save the extra work of using steel wool on paint splatters and drips from these pieces.

The next step in your preparation is inspecting the walls to make sure they are clean and ready to accept a fresh coat of paint. Dust the wall thoroughly with a dry dust mop. Dirt prevents even the best paints from sticking to an otherwise suitable wall. In extreme cases, especially with the greasy dirt found in kitchens and bathrooms, wash the walls with a detergent and water solution. If you encounter mildew, this condition can be remedied by washing with a bleach and water solution. Wear rubber gloves and keep the room ventilated.

Try to determine the type of old paint on your walls. If it is a flat latex or oil-base, just

about any new paint sticks to it. If the old paint is a glossy enamel, you have to dull it with a *deglosser* or fine sandpaper. Loose paint should be scraped off and the edges sanded smooth.

If the wall contains wallpaper and you are switching to a painted wall, remove the wallpaper or paint over it with a primer before top-coating. If the paper is stuck on tight in all areas and the seams are butted, it looks good after painting. Test the primer you plan to use on a smaller, out-of-the-way section to make sure that the ink in the paper does not bleed through. Occasionally the wallpaper is too rough or slick to paint. It must be removed before painting in both cases. You may want to consider wallpapering instead of painting.

Masonry surfaces should be inspected for *alkali*, cracks, and deterioration. Loose and flaking paint should be removed. An alkali or *efflorescence* problem should be treated with a solution of *muriatic acid* and water before painting.

Trim that has been painted with a glossy, semigloss, or clear shiny finish should be wiped with a *solvent*-soaked rag or sanded lightly. This is a necessary precaution to prevent later coats of trim paint from peeling off the woodwork. The final step before painting is to perform physical repairs.

Exterior Preparation

Before the first bristles of a brush are wetted with paint, you should perform the following preparations. Walk around the house and inspect the structure, so you can decide which tools and materials are needed for the job. Cut away all tree branches or bushes that rub the house. These impediments get in the way while you work, and they may be hiding serious paint damage. They also ruin your new paint job if left in contact with the paint.

Downspouts and gutters should also be inspected. When left to leak on your house, these defects weather and stain your new paint in no time.

The next step in preparing your house for painting is removing all loose paint and cleaning sound paint, so fresh paint adheres properly. Paint that appears sound may need no more than a thorough washing to make it ready for a new coat of paint. In the best of circumstances, you can wash dirt off the house with a garden hose. In extreme cases, you may want to rent a high pressure sprayer to cut through dirt and *chalking* surfaces. Spray with a mixture of detergent and water, then rinse with clear water. The surface should not leave fingers dirty when you rub the wall.

Occasionally you encounter mildew when washing the house. This can be treated with a solution of bleach and water. Some professionals add bleach to the detergent solution during the wash as an added deterent to mildew.

Blistering, peeling, flaking, and *scaling* paint should be scraped off or removed with heat, chemical paint removers, wire brushes, or sanding. Make sure that all the loose paint is removed and that the edges of the damaged areas have been sanded smooth.

If you are planning to apply a flat finish paint over a semigloss or glossy paint, you need to remove the gloss. This can be accomplished by scrubbing with a detergent, deglosser, or by sanding with a fine sandpaper.

The final step in preparing your house for paint is repairing physical damage to the structure. All holes and cracks should be filled with *caulking, spackling,* or *wood filler*. Remember that any place in which water can penetrate the wall encourages peeling or flaking of the paint later.

Loose boards should be renailed. Drive new nonrusting nails into the siding, counter-sink, spot prime, and then fill the hole with putty or spackling. Deteriorating wood should be removed and replaced with sound material. Rusting nailheads should be sanded to shiny metal and sealed with an oil-base primer.

Knots and pitch runs should be sealed with *shellac* or an oil-base *sealer*. If this precaution is not taken, the spots continue to exude their resins, ruining the new coat of paint. Broken asbestos or wood *shingles* and *shakes* should be replaced prior to painting.

Windows should be glazed and caulked where their casings meet the siding. In extreme cases, where bare wood is showing, sills and lower reaches of the casing should be treated with a *wood preservative*. Windowsills are notorious for holding water for extended periods of time and beginning the deterioration of the remainder of the paint job.

See *Cleaning; Finish Maintenance; Paint, Choosing;* and *Primers*.

PRIMARY COLORS

Red, blue, and yellow. All other colors are combinations of these three tints.

See *Colors*.

PRIMERS

The proper choice of a primer or first coating, whether painting inside or out, does much to insure a long lasting, trouble-free paint job. The miracles of modern paint chemistry have produced oil-base, alkyd, and latex primers with remarkable characteristics. In all cases primers are used to form a bridge between the surface they are applied to and the topcoating. Primers form this bridge by penetrating the material they are applied over and then drying to a flat finish suitable for the application of a finish coat. Always choose a primer that is compatible with both the topcoating you plan to use and the surface material. If the primer and topcoating are *incompatible, intercoat adhesion* is affected, which leads to *intercoat peeling*.

Primer coats should be used when painting a previously unfinished material such as siding or trim, when switching from one type of paint to another (alkyd semigloss to flat latex, for example), and when refinishing varnished or shellacked surfaces with an opaque paint.

Although primers are less expensive than topcoatings, buy the best primer you can afford. Many paint-related problems are associated with an inadequate primer and improper application techniques. Primers are made with less expensive *pigments*, but there is more emphasis on the *vehicle* in these paints. Primers condition porous surfaces by filling in the holes, so less topcoating is required to complete the job. Although some paints, especially latex house paints, are advertised as self-priming, the use of a good primer reduces the amount of topcoating needed. For the best results, choose a topcoating and then match the primer to the recommendations of the topcoating's label.

Topcoatings and primers are manufactured with different ingredients to match the various requirements of interior and exterior conditions. The following discussion of primers, first interior and then exterior, will help you select a primer suitable for the job at hand.

Interior Alkyd Primer

Although most paint salesmen steer you toward latex primers for interior jobs, alkyd primers still have their uses inside. Alkyd primers are recommended for raw wood, because they afford good penetration and do not raise the grain of the wood as water-base primers do. Alkyd primers are also recommended for priming metal, because they do not

promote rust as water-base paints do. Alkyd primers are not suggested for use on *masonry*, because the *alkali* in cement products attacks the oil-base vehicle of this type of paint. Most finishing coats, including latex, adhere to alkyd primers. One major drawback of alkyd primers is that they must be cleaned with expensive thinners. Use them only when you have to or when the topcoating's label recommends them.

Interior Latex Primer

Latex primers have the same advantages as other latex paints. They can be cleaned and thinned with water, dry quickly, and are free from odors. Latex primers are especially useful on masonry, *drywall*, and *plaster*. They breathe more than their alkyd counterparts. Alkali does not attack latex primers as it does alkyd primers. Latex primers adhere to almost any surface, and they are used for switching from an alkyd or oil-base paint system to a latex paint system. On semigloss or glossy alkyd paint, latex primers do not adhere unless the *sheen* has been cut with a *deglosser* or by *sanding*. One place where latex primers cannot be used is on raw wood, because the water in them tends to raise the grain of the wood—an undesirable trait for interior surfaces.

Sealers

Although not really primers, sealers are used to prevent the pores in wood and masonry from soaking up an undue amount of the finish coating. Wood sealers are usually clear and bind the surface fibers of wood together, producing a solid surface on which topcoatings can build up a protective layer. Masonry sealers are used on concrete, cinder block, or plaster to prevent water penetration. They should be used only when a compatible topcoating is to be applied.

Exterior Alkyd Primer

Alkyd and oil-base exterior primers have been the choice among professionals as primers for wood for a long time. They have been losing ground recently to the easier-to-use latex primers. Alkyd primers still have their place on exterior surfaces. Latex paint does not adhere to *chalking* surfaces, and these substrates should be coated with an alkyd primer before top-coating with latex. Alkyd primers also provide better penetration of raw wood, thereby reducing the chances of moisture-induced rot. Alkyd primers are not recommended for masonry or brick, because they are attacked by alkali.

Exterior Latex Primer

Latex primers have become the top choice among do-it-yourselfers due to their easy handling and cleanup. Although latex primers tend to raise the grain on wood siding, this is not nearly as critical outside as inside where a smooth finish is desired. Latex primers are recommended for masonry, because their breathability allows moisture to escape and they can withstand attack by alkali.

Exterior Metal Primer

Metal primers are usually alkyd-base coatings that contain zinc or another rust-inhibiting chemical. These alkyd primers also form an impervious film through which water cannot penetrate. Although there are latex metal primers on the market, these coatings tend to work best on metals that have not rusted or corroded. Latex metal primers have a higher rate of failure when applied to metals that have rusted previously. In all cases, metal primers must be applied to surfaces that have been cleaned of grease, corrosion, and rust.

Wood Preservatives

Technically not primers, *wood preserva-* *tives* are used to protect bare wood against fungus, insects, and water-induced damage. Although they do not work on wood that has been sealed or painted, any finish coat can be used over these materials.

Primers can be applied with brushes, rollers, pad applicators, or sprayers. Brushes work the best, because the bristles work the paint into the small cracks and crevices usually present in unpainted surfaces. Spraying is the least effective method, because rarely is enough material applied to insure proper absorption by the substrate. Regardless of the application method, primers should not be allowed to weather before application of a topcoat. In most cases, the topcoating should be applied within two weeks after the primer has dried.

See *Alkyd Paints; Latex Paint; Oil-Base Paint; Exterior Paint; Interior Paint; Paint, Choosing;* and *Preparation*.

PROBLEMS WITH PAINT

See *Agglomeration, Alkali, Alligatoring, Bleeding, Blistering, Bloom, Blushing, Bubbles, Chalking, Checking, Coagulation, Cracking, Crawling, Crazing, Crocking, Curdling, Curtains, Efflorescence, Fading, Flaking, Flashing, Floating, Fungi, Grain Checking, Grain Raising, Hairline Cracks, Hot Spots, Intercoat Peeling, Lap Marks, Lifting, Mildew, Moisture, Peeling Paint, Piling, Pinholing, Rain Spots, Runs, Sags, Scaling, Settling, Spot Peeling, Staining Through,* and *Yellowing*.

PUTTY

The generic term used for patching materials of a doughy consistency. Putties are used for sealing holes and cracks and for holding window glass in place.

Oil-base glazing, used to hold glass in place, sets up hard on the outside. Its inner

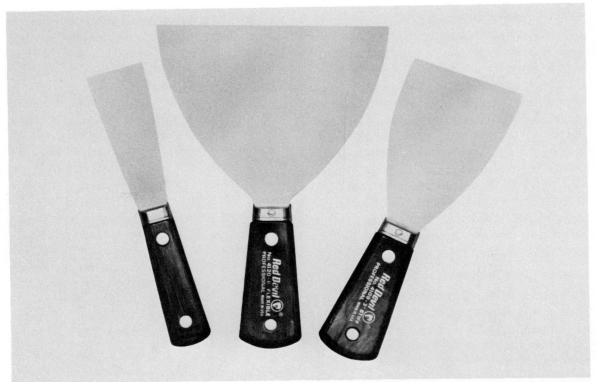

Putty Knife. Three common size putty knifes are the 1-inch scraper (left), 6-inch taping knife (center), and 3-inch knife (courtesy Red Devil, Inc.).

core remains moist for several years. This characteristic allows easy removal of the putty if the glass needs to be replaced. Putty for repairing holes and cracks comes in a powder that is mixed with water to form a paste. After application, these putties air-dry to a rock-hard consistency. Because of this hardness, water-mixed putties should not be used where a flexible patch is needed, say in a crack between two different materials.

See *Caulking and Glazing.*

PUTTY KNIFE

A tool that is used in almost every operation associated with painting. See the illustration. Putty knives come in handy for everything from scraping loose paint and opening paint cans to prying open stuck windows.

The most common and useful size putty knives are 1 to 2 inches wide. They come in both flexible and stiff blades. The size and type putty knife you choose depends on your preference and the job at hand. A 3-inch-wide flexible blade is useful for scraping loose paint. A 6-inch-wide taping knife is useful for smoothing patching materials such as *spackling* and joint compound. Stiff blade putty knives are useful for prying loose *plaster* or *drywall* from the edges of holes and cracks or for working *glazing* into a window frame. The use of putty knives is not limited to these activities, so keep one in your pocket while painting.

QUICK-DRYING PAINT

Many coatings are advertised as quick-drying. Quick-drying coatings dry enough for a second coating in four hours or less. Latex paints, shellac, and lacquer are the best known quick-drying coatings.

At times a quick-drying paint can be advantageous, such as when you have to double-coat a room and have only one day set aside for the chore. Quick-drying flat latex wall paint dries so quickly, in a well-ventilated room, that by the time you have finished the first coat you can probably begin the second. At other times a quick-drying paint can be a disadvantage— for example, when painting a ceiling. Most weekend painters cannot work fast enough to keep the entire leading edge of their paint wet when working on a ceiling. This results in *lap marks* that could have been avoided by using a slower drying paint.

R

RADIATORS

If your house has steam or hot water heat, you should paint the radiators to make them look as good as your just painted room. Although radiators may appear difficult to paint because of their hot dry surfaces, they are no more difficult to paint than other metal surfaces.

Remove any rust and loose flaking paint with a scraper, wire brush, or sandpaper. Vacuum or dust with a brush before painting. If rusting is a problem, the best type of primer is a heat-resistant red lead primer. When the primer has dried, paint the visible parts of the radiator. If the paint on the radiator is sound, it can be painted over with regular interior paint. Latex should be used only where no rust is present.

Flat, light-colored paints work best on radiators. Flat paints radiate more heat than shiny ones, although glossy or semigloss finishes are easier to clean. The radiator can be painted to match the walls or set off with a contrasting color. Thin paint films radiate more heat than thick ones. Do not use *aluminum paint* on radiators, because this type of paint cuts heat output by up to 15 percent.

Paint can be brushed or sprayed onto a radiator. Spraying is preferred, because it applies the thinnest coating possible. Use cardboard to keep *overspray* from reaching the wall. If you plan to brush the radiator, use a long-bristled, trim brush 1½ inches wide. Paint the hard-to-reach areas first to make the job easier.

See *Metals*.

RAIN SPOTS

The dull places left on a paint finish when the paint has been moistened by rain or dew before the paint film has thoroughly dried. Oil-base paints tend to suffer from rain spots more often than latex paints. To avoid rain spots, do not paint when precipitation is in the forecast. See *Blushing*.

REDUCE

Painter's slang for thinning a paint. A liquid *solvent* or *thinner* is stirred into the paint to make it less viscous.

RELATIVE HUMIDITY

The amount of humidity in the air compared with the maximum amount that the air can hold at the same temperature. This term is usually expressed as a percentage.

Painting on excessively humid days slows a coating's drying time. Some of the clear finishes, lacquer in particular, get *cloudy* when applied under high humidity conditions.

RESINS

One of the main ingredients of paint. Originally resins were extracted from certain plants and insects. Nowadays most resins used in paint products are man-made. Common resins used in paints are alkyds, acrylics, polyvinyls, and urethanes. Resins give paint the ability to form tough, shiny films. Glossy or semigloss enamel paints and varnishes contain a higher percentage of resins than flat wall paints. This is one of the reasons that enamels wash better than wall paints. Resin is also the sticky secretion that exudes from wood knots.

See also: *Knots in Wood* and *Synthetic Resins*.

RICH

When related to paint, the term refers to warm, dark colors.

ROLLERS, PAINT

A paint roller covers twice as much area in less time and with less effort than a paintbrush. Rollers have put weekend do-it-yourselfers on an equal footing with most professionals. Cheap, inferior tools result in a shoddy job. Take the advice of the pros and spend a little extra money on your rolling equipment. The quality of the finished job makes the money you spend worth it.

Roller frames are made with a handle, a bent piece of stiff wire, and a cage over which the roller cover or nap fits. The roller frame should have a spring cage that supports the entire length of the cover (Fig. 1). This prevents the cover from caving in at the center, causing skips in the paint application. Ball bearings in the end caps of the spring cage keep the cover turning smoothly to prevent runs and smears while promoting even paint application. The handle on the roller frame should be threaded, so it accepts an extension handle. The most widely used paint rollers have 7 to 9-inch-long cages. Although the wider 9-inch rollers cover more area on smooth surfaces, the 7-inch size is easier to handle and does a better job in confined areas such as closets or on rough walls.

Covers

The most important part of the roller is the cover. The cover should be cylindrical with beveled ends (Fig. 2). The beveling of the nap prevents the fibers at the ends of the cover from matting together and producing a paint buildup along the edge of each stroke that painters call railroad tracks.

Roller naps come in a variety of materials—everything from foam rubber to ram's wool wrapped around the core of roller covers. Nowadays most paint salesmen recommend the new synthetic fibers used for nap making. Synthetic fibers retain their shape and resilience even in latex paints. These charac-

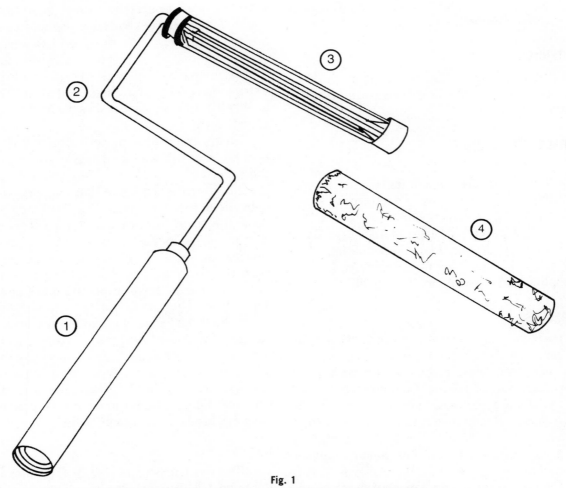

Fig. 1

Rollers, Paint. The basic parts of a roller are: (1) handle, (2) wire support, (3) cage, and (4) cover.

teristics insure that the roller acts the same on the last stroke of a job as on the first. Ram's wool naps are not recommended for latex paint, because their fibers absorb water, swell, and go limp. The wool's ability to hold paint is reduced by its tendency to mat and flop over. This problem is not present when ram's wool is used in alkyd or oil-base paints.

Look closely at any cover you plan to buy and check for these features. The nap should wrap in a spiral around the core. This config-uration prevents ridges from forming in the paint film. The core should be plastic or plastic-coated cardboard, so washing does not destroy the cover's shape and rigidity.

Roller covers come in three nap lengths: short, medium, and long (Fig. 3). Although the nap length has much to do with the amount of paint a roller cover holds, it is not the only factor. Fiber thickness and density of the fibers on the cover also play an important part in determining how much paint the cover holds.

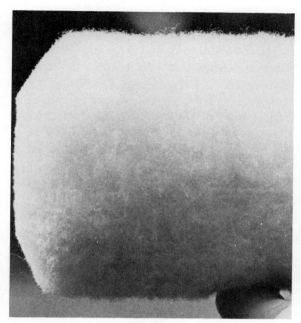

Fig. 2
Rollers, Paint. The beveled end of a roller cover prevents matting of the fibers during use.

Fibers that are too dense and thick on the cover leave little room for paint. Sparsely spaced fibers do not hold much paint. Check the cover you plan to buy by pulling the nap apart. Can you see the cardboard core? If you can barely see it, the nap thickness should be about right.

Short naps, ¼ inch or less, are useful for applying a glossy or semigloss paint to smooth surfaces such as metal or flat doors. These naps apply a thin smooth coating of paint. Unfortunately, these covers do not hold much paint, and you have to reload the roller quite often. The foam rubber and carpet-covered rollers fall into this short nap category. These naps apply paint very smoothlyoam rubber naps should not be used with alkyd or oil-base materials, because these paints may cause the foam rubber to melt.

Medium naps, ½ to ¾ inch long, hold paint well and produce a soft-textured finish perfect for flat walls and ceilings. The longer naps in this range are useful on masonry and other rough-textured surfaces, because they work paint deep into holes and crevices.

Long naps, 1 to 1¼ inches in length, carry lots of paint and apply it in a generous thick coating. Long naps are especially useful for special cases such as chain-link fences where the nap has to work the paint around each wire.

Another type of roller cover is the plastic texture naps. These covers resemble plastic honeycombs. They are used with *texture paints* to add a random texture to walls and ceilings. With these naps, the deeper the pile, the more pronounced the texture effect is.

In addition to the regular rollers for flat surfaces, many manufacturers are making unique-shaped rollers that paint many irregularly-shaped surfaces. A doughnut-shaped roller paints the inside surfaces of corners and in the grooves of paneling (Fig. 4). Narrow rollers, 2 or 3 inches wide, are useful on trim and woodwork (Fig. 5). Skinny rollers reach behind radiators and other close-to-the-wall fixtures.

If you are planning to paint many rooms in your house at one time, you might check into the possibility of renting a pressurized paint roller. A special lid fits over a gallon paint can. Air is pumped in, forcing paint through a flexi-

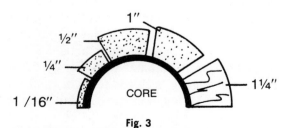

Fig. 3
Rollers, Paint. Some common nap thicknesses.

Fig. 4

Rollers, Paint. A doughnut roller paints inside corners quickly and effectively.

ble tube attached to the handle of the roller. The paint travels up the hollow handle until it is forced out of the roller cover and into the nap. This device saves much dipping time on large jobs.

Dipping Containers

There are two containers to dip from when loading a roller. One is a roller tray; another is a 5-gallon bucket. The choice of a container depends on the size of the job. Painting the bathroom ceiling out of a 5-gallon bucket is overdoing it. A tray holds enough paint for this small job. Line the tray with heavy-duty aluminum foil to make cleanup easier. Removing excess paint from your roller is much easier if you buy a screen to lay in the tray. Outside, on the body of your house, a tray would hold so little paint that you would be constantly running back to the paint can for a fresh supply. A 5-gallon bucket with a roller screen inside holds enough paint to make headway on large expanses of exterior siding.

Before you dip a brand new cover into the paint, dampen the nap with the thinner recommended for the paint you are using—water for latex and paint thinner for alkyd or oil-base paints. Roll out the excess thinner on a dry newspaper. This thinner treatment helps the nap pick up the first load of paint and makes cleanup easier.

Before painting a wall with a roller, cut in around the entire perimeter of the wall with a paintbrush. Bring the paint out about 3 or 4 inches onto the wall.

Dip the roller into the paint, so about half the diameter of the cover is submerged. Roll the roller back and forth on the slanting bed of the tray or on the screen in a 5-gallon bucket.

Fig. 5

Rollers, Paint. Narrow rollers will reach where regular rollers cannot.

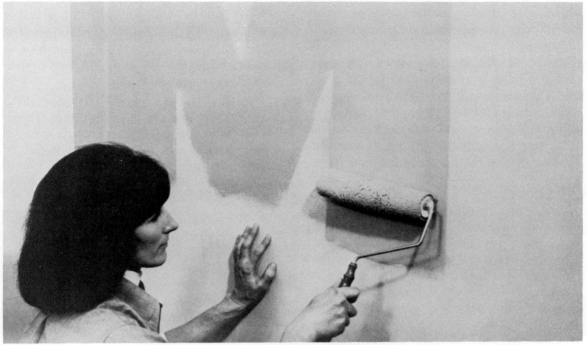

Fig. 6

Rollers, Paint. The first strokes with a roller should resemble an "M." This will keep drips and runs within the immediate working area (courtesy National Paint and Coatings Association).

Work the paint well into the nap, redipping as necessary.

Painting Techniques

To paint with the roller, make the first stroke up so the paint does not dribble down the wall. Pull the roller back down at an angle, push up again, and pull down so that you make a "M" motion and work the paint coating uniform. The roller should be fairly dry by the time you get this area covered. Finish the section with light finishing strokes. Move on to the next section, either horizontally or vertically, and repeat the process.

After the first few strokes with a roller, the nap tends to lay over in one direction along the entire length of the cover. When you roll in that direction, the smoothest finish is ob-tained. Look at the end of the roller to deter-mine the direction of the nap, then flop the roller so you make the finishing strokes with the lay of the nap.

When rolling ceilings, follow the same basic pattern as used on walls. Work across the shortest width of the room and from a dry area into a wet one. An extension pole screwed into the handle of the roller frame helps you reach all of the ceiling from the floor. These handles also make reaching the entire height of a wall possible.

Do not overlook the possibility of painting floors with a roller. Pour a small amount of paint into the center of a 3 by 3-foot area and then roll it out with slow, smooth strokes.

Outside, clapboarding can be rolled to speed up the paint job. There are two methods.

The first is painting the bottom edges of the boards with a brush and then rolling horizontally along the lengths of the boards. The second method is using a long nap cover and running the roller vertically over the clapboarding. The long nap helps work paint onto the bottom edges of the clapboards. Touch up skips with a brush while the paint is still wet. Experiment with both methods to determine the one that works best for you.

Cleaning and Storing Equipment

By cleaning roller frames and covers immediately after each use, you can keep them in shape for many jobs. Begin by rinsing away most of the excess paint from the roller and pan. Place a little detergent in the pan and add water. Dunk the roller in this solution and agitate so the detergent solution is worked well into the nap. Remove the cover from the frame and squeeze the soapy water through the nap. Work out as much color as possible.

Dump the soapy water and rinse equipment in clean water. When no more color washes from the nap and the frame has been thoroughly cleaned—best accomplished with a strong spray from a garden hose—slide the cover back on the frame. Run the roller quickly down a flat surface to spin excess water out of the nap. This spinning fluffs up the nap close to its original shape. Hang the roller up so it dries with no pressure on the cover's fiber.

To store, work the cover back into its plastic wrapper or wrap in aluminum foil, brown paper, or plastic wrap. You can leave the cover on the roller frame and hang the unit up until the next use, or remove the cover and stand it on end. Do not store the cover so that it rests on its side, or a flat spot develops in the nap.

See *Cutting-In; Painting, Exterior;* and *Painting, Interior*.

ROSINS

Rosins and *resins* have similar properties. The difference between the two is their source. Rosins are generally regarded as plant derivatives. Resins are man-made.

Rosins remain when the oil of *turpentine* is distilled from crude turpentine. These light-yellow to almost black materials are used in the manufacture of some varnishes.

RUBBER-BASE PAINT

Made from liquefied rubber or synthetic rubberlike compounds. These paints should not be confused with *latex paint*, which does not contain rubber. Rubber-base paints are expensive and come in a limited selection of colors with flat or low-gloss finishes. Because these paints are waterproof, more durable than all paints except epoxies, and *alkali*-resistant, they are often used in basements and on porch floors, steps, and patios. These paints are strong smelling and require special *solvents* for thinning and cleanup. Latex, oil-base, or alkyd paints can be applied over rubber-base paints.

RUNS

Runs and sags occur in paint that has been applied in too thick of a coating. See the illustration. This paint failure happens most frequently with slick, runny paints like trim enamel, lacquer, varnish, and shellac. Excessive runs may indicate a paint that has been thinned too much.

If runs are noticed before the paint has dried, they can be brushed out with an unloaded brush. If not noticed until the paint has dried, runs should be sanded smooth with fine sandpaper and repainted.

See *Curtains* and *Sags*.

Runs. Runs should be brushed out before they have a chance to dry.

RUST REMOVAL

Paint sticks best to bare shiny metal, but metal that needs painting is probably rusty. This necessitates removing rust and *corrosion* from metal surfaces by wire brushing, *sanding*, or using steel wool before painting. Removing rust can be a difficult and tedious process; however, there are several wire brush attachments for electric drills that make the job easier. Use a cup-shaped attachment for flat surfaces and a wheel attachment for surfaces with grooves or awkward angles.

All freshly cleaned metal should be coated immediately with an alkyd or oil-base primer containing zinc to keep rust from forming again. As a general rule, oil-base and alkyd paints with glossy or semigloss finishes are good for preventing rust. Several manufacturers also make metal paints that are especially good at preventing the return of rust to metals. Flat latex paints have two drawbacks against them for use on metals: they are water-base, and their porosity may give moisture a chance to penetrate to the metal, renewing the rusting process.

See *Downspouts and Gutters, Metals, Nails,* and *Wrought Iron*.

SAFETY

Although some of the following recommendations sound like common sense, you would be surprised at the number of people who ignore safety when painting. There is more to painting safely than using a ladder correctly. Even though modern paints do not contain lead, they are dangerous when handled improperly.

Never paint in a completely closed room. Good cross-ventilation not only helps to remove fumes and odors, but it shortens the paint's drying time. Paint fumes are especially harmful to young children and pets. Avoid sleeping in a freshly painted room until the paint has dried and fumes no longer persist.

The fumes from some solvent-thinned paints can be very dangerous if you are drinking. Alcoholic drinks can so reduce your body's resistance to certain fumes that breathing a small amount of them can be harmful or fatal. Alcohol can also make climbing on ladders a dangerous activity.

Do not paint in a room where there is an open flame or fire (including pilot lights). Solvent paints give off flammable fumes.

Although latex paints are safer to use than oil-base paints, they are made of powerful chemicals that can cause illness when ingested. Like all poisons, paint should be kept out of the reach of children at all times. Keep the label from the paint can handy, because it lists specific first aid and antidotes for the paint.

When painting above your head, work carefully to prevent dripping paint into your eyes. You should wear safety goggles.

Do not leave paint in contact with your skin very long. Wash it off each time you take a break.

When paint gets into your hair or on the hair of a pet, wash it out immediately. To remove latex paint, use soapy water and a rag. Use a rag soaked in mineral or cooking oil for cleaning out oil-base or alkyd paints. Do not use petroleum-based solvents or turpentine, because these materials are skin irritants. Petroleum-based solvents may cause sickness if licked by a pet.

When you finish painting, dispose of oily rags by placing in an airtight can. When left lying around, oily rags can catch fire by spontaneous combustion.

Always store paint in a safe, well-ventilated place that is out of the reach of children. Store it well away from furnaces and other sources of heat that may cause an explosion. It is best not to store painting materials within the house. Some paints may be ruined by freezing. Small quantities of paint may not be worth saving unless they are needed for touching up. Dangerous clutter can be avoided by throwing worthless odds and ends away.

See *Ladders*.

SAFFLOWER OIL

A *vegetable oil* pressed from the seeds of the safflower plant. This oil is one of the best nonyellowing paint vehicles around. The oil is slower to dry than *linseed oil*, but faster to dry than *soybean oil*.

SAGS

Occur on vertical surfaces when there is a too thick layer of paint, or paint that has been thinned excessively is applied carelessly. To prevent sags, do not overthin paint and brush or roll it out thoroughly. Sagging is often encountered when using oil-base or alkyd trim enamels or varnish on doors and other large, smooth surfaces. Brush out sags in wet coatings with an unloaded brush. Sags in dry paint can be corrected by sanding smooth and recoating.

See also *Curtains* and *Runs*.

SANDBLASTING

An effective but difficult method of removing paint and corrosion from masonry or metal surfaces. Sandblasting involves applying a jet of air carrying sand across the surface being cleaned. The sand particles blast away loose paint, rust, and corrosion. The process requires lots of cumbersome equipment and extreme caution.

Although many rental stores carry sandblasters, most sandblasting chores are beyond the skill of homeowners. If you feel that you must have a wall sandblasted, check into having it done commercially. If that proves to be beyond your resources, paint or corrosion can be removed from the surface by scraping or using a chemical paint remover.

See *Paint, Removing* and *Preparation*.

SANDING

For almost every home painting job, you must smooth the surface some to be painted. Refinishing a floor may require you to spend a whole day sanding, while finishing a spackled interior wall may not require more than a few quick strokes to smooth the patches. Regardless of the size of the job, remembering the following tips will make sanding jobs easier and faster.

Sandpaper comes in several grit sizes and materials. The one you choose depends on how much you are willing to spend and the requirements of the job. Flint papers are cheapest and can be discarded when you finish the job. Because flint paper cuts slowly and dulls rapidly, it is suitable for use on small jobs.

Garnet papers cost slightly more than flint papers, but they are worth the extra price when much sanding is to be done. This paper outlasts flint paper.

Table. Sanding. Sandpaper Information.

Word Description	Grit Number	Grade Number	Use
Very Fine	400 to 600	8/0 to 6/0	Sanding between coats of varnish, paint and lacquer. Extra smooth final sanding.
Fine	100 to 300	2/0 to 6/0	Final sanding before primer or sealer on metal and for removing light rust.
Medium	100 to 80	1/0	For removing light stock and rust stains and preparing walls prior to painting.
Coarse	80 to 40	0/0 to 2	For rough stock removal and smoothing deep scratches and imperfections.
Very Coarse	40 to 12	2 to 4	For removing heavy coats of paint, enamel or varnish and heavy rust deposits.

Man-made grits such a aluminum oxide or silicon carbide (Carborundum) papers are the most expensive and the longest lasting papers you can buy. Big sanding jobs, like wood floors, are hastened by the long lasting cutting power of these synthetic grit papers.

Sandpaper is graded according to the size of the grit. The larger the grit, the quicker the cut, but the rougher the finished surface is. Fine sandpaper is slow to remove old paint and wood, but it produces a very smooth finish. See the table for suggestions about the sandpaper to use for a particular job.

When sanding flat surfaces, wrap the paper around a sanding block. See the illustration. A simple sanding block can be made by taking a piece of wood about 3 inches wide and 4 or 5 inches long and wrapping the paper, rough side out, around it. Commercially available sanding blocks come in many sizes and shapes. These blocks are available in metal, plastic, or rubber and use clamps or nails to hold the paper in place. The rubber blocks have

a tendency to round corners more than metal or plastic blocks.

When sanding flat wood and metal surfaces or patches in plaster and drywall, grasp the block firmly while holding the sandpaper securely in place around it. Bear down lightly on the block and move it in a gentle circular motion. On patches, *feather* the edges of the patch into the surrounding wall, so there is no

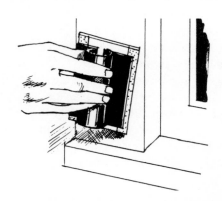

Sanding. Sanding blocks make sanding flat surfaces easier and save your fingers (courtesy Hyde Tools).

seam between the patch and wall. Be careful when sanding drywall to not raise a nap on the wall's paper finish.

While sanding, stop occasionally to tap the paper on a hard surface to remove dirt buildup in the grit. Vacuum the sanded area when finished or wipe with a *tack cloth* before painting.

When sanding previously painted surfaces, start with a medium paper and finish with a fine or extra fine grit. On virgin wood, use only fine paper and sand with the grain— usually along the length of the board. If across the grain sanding is necessary, use steel wool instead of sandpaper.

Use fine paper on woodwork such as door jambs and baseboards and for *deglossing* enamels and varnish prior to painting. The new nylon fiber pads coated with fine abrasives also work well on delicate trim work. These pads also produce less dust than sandpaper.

To cut sandpaper, turn it rough side down and score the back with an awl or other sharp instrument. Turn the rough side up, lay the scored line along the edge of a table or other straightedge, then tear the paper along the mark.

The inside corners of window trim and indentations in moldings can be reached by folding sandpaper into quarters and then using the folded edge to sand the corner. When the paper wears out along the fold, refold and continue working.

Curved surfaces such as stairway balustrades can be sanded quickly and easily by cutting the sandpaper into strips and working the paper back and forth around the wood like a shoeshine cloth. For the inside curve on trim pieces, you can use an appropriately sized dowel as a sanding block.

You may want to use a power sander on larger sanding jobs. There are several sanders to choose from: disk, vibrating, belt, and drum. Each has its advantages and drawbacks.

Disk sanders are not recommended for use with flat wood surfaces, because their circular motion leaves a swirl pattern where they cut across the grain. Their ability to get close in corners makes them useful for sanding the edges of a wooden floor. Use light pressure to reduce the chances of gouging the wood. Disk sanders are highly recommended for metal surfaces where grain is not a problem.

Vibrating sanders are available in two types—straight line and orbital. The orbital sander is subject to the same restrictions as the disk sander, although it is not as powerful. The danger of damaging wood with cross-grain sanding is less. The straight line vibrating sander is useful for sanding all types of wood. It is the preferred power tool for working on clapboard siding. Keep the sanding surface moving along the length of the boards. Do not use a disk or disk attachment for a power drill when sanding clapboard, because across the grain sanding makes the surface too rough for good paint adhesion.

Belt sanders are also useful for smoothing clapboard, because they are capable of removing a lot of wood and paint quickly. Always sand with the grain when using this type of power sander.

Drum sanders are designed for use on floors. If you are going to sand a floor, renting one of these machines is a must. Although drum sanders are big and heavy, they are easy to use because the drum rotates in such a way that it propels the machine. You control the speed and bite of the sander by the amount of pressure applied to the handle. Sand with the grain, working from a coarse to a fine paper for the final pass.

See *Drywall; Floors, Wood; Preparation; Spackling Compounds;* and *Walls, Patching.*

SAND PAINT

This paint is no more than regular latex wall paint with a fine-grained sand or sandlike synthetic grit mixed in. The grit causes the paint to dry rougher than flat wall paints and adds a texture to walls and ceilings that reduces glare and hides flaws inherent in the wall. Because of the gritty feel of sand paint, its use is normally limited to ceilings and out-of-the-way walls.

Sand paint is applied with a long nap roller or a wide stiff bristle synthetic brush. Tip off the paint in all directions, so an unpleasant pattern is not established. Keep this paint stirred well so that sand does not settle. Painting over walls already coated with a sand paint requires about 25 percent more paint than an area of equal size finished with a smooth surface paint.

See *Texture Paints*.

SASH

The movable part of a window that holds the glass. The molding on a door into which a window is set is often called a sash. Because sashes receive much wear and tear, they should be painted with semigloss or glossy trim enamels.

See *Casement Windows, Double-Hung Windows, Glazing,* and *Putty*.

SCALING

The act of paint coming off in thin layers. Scaling paint can be an indication of many paint problems. The chief problem is intrusion of water through cracks or holes in the paint film on the wall. The water swells the wood beneath the paint and forces it to curl, edge first, from the surface. Occasionally the cause of the scaling is applying a coat of paint when the wood is damp. Advanced stages of *blistering* may also produce scaling.

Localized scaling can be corrected by eliminating the source of *moisture* from the wall. External sources of water can be corrected by repairing leaky roofs, *downspouts and gutters*, and *caulking* cracks before working on the defective paint. Scaling that appears on the wall outside a kitchen or bathroom may indicate moisture seeping through the wall from these high-humidity rooms. Creating a moisture barrier by painting the interior walls with a semigloss or glossy enamel should reduce or cure the problem.

Another common cause of scaling is applying a coat of paint over a surface that is dirty or chalking. Wash all surfaces thoroughly before painting. A solution of detergent and water should do the trick in most cases.

After moisture leaks have been corrected, remove all loose paint with a scraper or an electrical heat element. Smooth the edges of the old paint with sandpaper and then prime all bare wood. Top-coating the surface with a breathable latex paint helps reduce the chances of scaling reoccurring.

See *Peeling Paint*.

SCRAPERS, PAINT

There are four common types of hand paint scrapers. Hook scrapers, wall scrapers, putty knives, and razor blade scrapers are useful for paint scraping needs.

The hook scraper is a metal, wood, or fiberglass-handled scraper with a double or single-hooked steel blade. See the illustration. On some models the blades are replaceable; on others the blade can be sharpened many times with a file.

A hook scraper is useful for scraping down large areas of rough surface on the exterior of a house. Although it is best to scrape with the grain when using a hook-type scraper, this

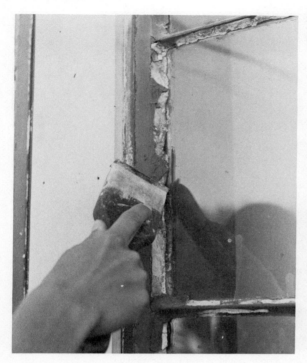

Scrapers, Paint. Hook scrapers are useful for many purposes—from removing peeling paint to working old putty from a window sash.

does not always remove all the loose paint. It is okay to scrape across the grain of wood siding, but do not push down too hard. It is easy to gouge the soft wood.

Wall scrapers resemble the taping knives used for hanging drywall and are generally available in widths from 1 to 6 inches, with either stiff or flexible blades. These tools are useful inside where delicate walls would be damaged by a hook scraper. Outside, their width allows them to take off substantial amounts of paint with one pass.

The leading edge of this tool is worked under the loose edge of *flaking* or *scaling* paint and pushed toward sound paint. This effectively removes the loose paint while leaving the sound paint on the surface. You may have to

attack a bad spot from several directions to remove all the loose paint.

Putty knives work well as paint scrapers in confined areas. These knives are used in the same manner as wall scrapers, although they do not cover as much area with each pass. A stiff knife 1 to 1½ inches wide works best for scraping outside . The same size knife, with a flexible blade, works well on interior surfaces.

A razor blade scraper is basically a handle designed to hold a razor blade. These tools are especially useful for removing dried paint from glass. Because of the weakness of the razor blade, a razor blade scraper is not satisfactory for use on walls. A razor blade scraper cuts quickly and deeply; handle carefully.

See *Paint, Removing* and *Preparation*.

SCREENS AND STORM WINDOWS

These items should be removed from a house before painting. See the illustration. Setting screens and storm windows on a sawhorse or similar support makes the job of painting them quicker and easier. Additionally, painting them while still in the window may seal them in place when the paint dries. When the time comes to remove the screens or storm windows, you have to pry them loose, damaging the paint and reducing its resistance to weathering.

As with other windows, work from the inside out on screens and storm windows. Scrape and sand the frames as necessary, then spot prime bare wood. Allow for drying and then paint with a trim enamel that matches the paint on the window and casing. As a general rule, the edges of screens and storm windows should not be painted unless bare wood is showing. An excessively thick paint buildup on the edges of screens and storm windows prevents them from fitting into their assigned space. If you want to paint the edges, remove

Screens and Storm Windows. Removing storm windows is the first step in painting an exterior window.

all old paint with sandpaper or a plane, so a paint film does not buildup.

If you decide to paint the actual screen, the best method for this is spraying, either from a can or a spray unit. Use a metal paint or screen enamel compatible with the screen material. Coat bronze or copper screens with shellac or varnish to prevent corrosion of these materials. There is no need to paint plastic screens, because a thorough washing should remove dirt. When spraying, mask off the screen's wooden frame and spray both the screen's sides. Allow the paint to dry then paint the frame in the normal manner.

To paint a screen with a brush, wash or dust the mesh thoroughly. Paint one side of the screen wire and turn the window over. Without filling your brush, spread the excess paint over the screen. This works paint out of the open-

ings and spreads the paint as needed. Allow to dry thoroughly before painting the frame.

Wait several days after screens and storm windows and the window openings on the house have been painted before replacing. This allows the paint to dry thoroughly, so the screens and storm windows do not get stuck in place.

See *Casement Windows, Double-Hung Windows* and *Windows*.

SEALER

A coating which forms an impervious film that prevents topcoatings from penetrating to the substrate of a wall. Sealers also prevent materials in the substrate from migrating to the surface where they can destroy the topcoating. Shellac, special oil-base paint sealers, clear wood sealers, and masonry sealers form impervious films on the surfaces to which they are applied.

Shellac is a commonly used sealer for stains on interior walls and ceilings. Two coats are usually enough to seal in water stains and prevent them from *bleeding* through and disfiguring the topcoat.

Oil-base paint sealers are white primer materials that lock in stains and provide a sound flat finish surface over which topcoatings may be applied. There are several brands and types of these sealers on the market. Different ones are capable of handling everything from water stains to creosote. Ask your paint dealer to help select a sealer suitable for the problem at hand.

Masonry sealers vary in their composition and intended use. Clear sealers are used mainly to prevent *chalking* where the natural look of the masonry is desired. Opaque sealers are normally used to stop the seepage of water, which causes *alkali* or *efflorescence* problems, and to provide a sound base for application of opaque or colored topcoatings.

Wood sealers are generally clear. They soak into the wood binding the fibers together, thereby protecting the wood against dirt and moisture. In addition to making sanding easier, these sealers provide a flat finish over which clear finishes or opaque paints can be applied.

See *Staining Through*.

SELF-CLEANING

This term describes a characteristic of some alkyd and oil-base paints to form a chalk on their surface. The chalk allows rain or a well-aimed hose to wash away oil paint, dirt, and debris. The removal of old paint is important, because too thick of a buildup may lead to *alligatoring* or cross-grain *cracking*.

SEMIGLOSS FINISH

Semigloss paints have a finish that is less glossy than *glossy finish* paints, but shinier than *flat finish* wall paints. The subdued *sheen* of semigloss paints makes them a good choice for woodwork and trim where you want a paint that can be cleaned easily, but does not stand out too much. Semigloss enamels are also useful on bathroom and kitchen walls where a flat paint would be impossible to keep clean, and a glossy paint would be too gaudy. Semigloss paints are available in *oil-base, alkyd*, and *latex* materials.

See *Paint, Choosing*.

SETTLING

The separation of the *solids* from the *vehicle* in a paint. The solids normally migrate toward the bottom of the can. Paints that have set for extended periods of time on paint store shelves often suffer settling. Settling can be an indication of an old paint. A thorough shaking on the paint store's mechanical mixer should eliminate the problem. Stains are especially subject to settling and should be stirred frequently during use.

SHAKES AND SHINGLES

Popular exterior siding for houses. Most wooden shakes or shingles are made from western red cedar or redwood. Asbestos shingles are found on many older houses. Although the procedure for preparing and painting shakes and shingles is similar to other sidings, the rough texture and porosity of these materials allow two basic types of finishes—those that penetrate the wood (*stain*) and those that lay on top (paints). The type of finish you apply depends largely on the previous finish.

If your shake or shingle house has been coated previously with a nonpenetrating paint, finishing with a penetrating stain is impossible. The siding should be painted again after it has been properly prepared.

When you are going to apply a penetrating finish, there are two choices—penetrating shingle stain or a *wood preservative*. Shingle stains are made from a penetrating liquid that has been left uncolored or colored with varying amounts of different *pigments*. Some of the pigments remain near the surface of the shakes or shingles, while the stain's *vehicle* is absorbed by the wood.

Because stains penetrate into the wood, there is no coating left on the surface that can peel or flake off later. Penetrating stains are ideal finishes for the rough wood surfaces of shakes and shingles that are considered difficult for paint to adhere to. Stains are also recommended for surfaces exposed to high moisture conditions.

Wood preservatives soak completely into the wood. They leave sidings with a natural look while affording excellent protection against mold, mildew, and decay.

Before painting or staining shakes and shingles, damaged pieces should be replaced. With asbestos shingles, break away as much of the damaged shingle as possible with a hammer. Be careful not to damage surrounding shingles. Work a hacksaw blade up under the broken shingle and cut off the nails holding the damaged shingle in place. Fit a new shingle into the empty space, then drill two holes just below the bottom edge of the shingle above the new one. Insert two noncorrosive nails and tap the nails into place. Use a nail set to prevent breaking the shingle. Prime the new piece with paint or stain before top-coating.

To replace wood shakes, remove the broken or rotten piece with a chisel and mallet. Work a new shake into place and secure it with a nonrusting nail. Prime the shake with paint or stain before the finish coating.

Coating shakes and shingles follows the method for treating most types of wood siding. Scrape or wire brush loose material from the surface, then wash with a solution of detergent and water to remove dirt and grease. If mildew is present, treat with a commercial *mildewcide* or with a solution of bleach and water. The bleach solution may lighten the wood, but subsequent staining brings it back in line with surrounding surfaces.

Work stain or paint into the rough grooves of shakes and shingles with a brush, spray unit, roller, or one of the pad *applicators* designed especially for this surface. Sprays and rollers have a few drawbacks that may make them less desirable than brushes and pads. Spraying usually does not apply enough stain to thoroughly soak in. Rolling also does not normally apply enough material. Additionally, rolling usually leaves numerous skips that have to be touched up with a brush.

When brushing shakes and shingles, coat the bottom edge of each shingle. Coat the top by brushing in the direction of the grain or grooves in the surface. Finish each shingle before moving on to the next one. A pad applicator is used in the same manner as a brush. After several hours of work, you may notice that the pile on your pad is laying down. Remove the pile and reverse it, so the pile lays in the opposite direction. This makes the pad last longer and insures uniform coverage.

Under normal conditions two coats of stain last up to 10 years before the stain fades enough to need recoating. Paint does not last quite as long, because the rough surface of shakes and shingles makes the paint's job of adhering to the surface more difficult than on flat surfaces.

See *Brushing Techniques* and *Painting, Exterior*.

SHEEN

The word painters use to describe the brightness or luster of a dried paint. Shine and luster are measures of the amount of light reflected from the painted surface. The more light that is reflected, the shinier the surface appears.

The description of a paint's sheen has evolved into several categories: ceiling flat, flat, eggshell, semigloss, glossy, and high or extra glossy finishes. The flat paints reflect little light and are used on surfaces that should not attract attention. The glossy paints reflect a lot of light and make the surface they are on more noticeable.

Selection of a sheen is an important part of choosing a paint. For example, the tough nonporous semigloss sheen of trim paints makes them easier to clean while drawing little attention. Using a porous flat paint would create a difficult to clean and not very durable coating for this heavily used part of the house. When choosing a sheen, consult your paint dealer.

See *Eggshell; Flat Finish Paints; Glossy Finishes; Paint, Choosing;* and *Semigloss Finish.*

SHELLAC

A coating made from lac resins dissolved in alcohol. Lac resins are secreted by various scale insects. This secretion is melted, strained, and hardened to form shellac. Although shellac is basically a clear finish, it also comes in an orange tint.

Shellac has many qualities that make it an attractive choice for finishing woodwork and floors. It is easy to use. It dries quickly, and brush marks disappear as it dries. Shellac is also inexpensive, has good *abrasion resistance*, and is easy to repair when damaged.

Shellac also has a few characteristics that limit its use. It is highly susceptible to water and alcohol damage, and it cannot be used over other coatings as the alcohol in it tends to dissolve them. Another disadvantage of shellac is its short shelf life. When buying shellac, check the manufacturer's date to insure that it is not more than one or two months old. If there is no date, an extra long drying time, several hours instead of the usual 30 to 40 minutes, is an indication that the shellac is old.

Shellac can be purchased in varying "cuts." A cut is the amount of lac resin dissolved in a gallon of alcohol. A 5-pound cut has 5 pounds of resin dissolved in a gallon of alcohol. This mixture is usually too thick to work with, and it should be thinned. To reduce a 5-pound cut to 4 pounds, add enough alcohol to increase the shellac's volume by one-quarter. Floors normally require a 3-pound cut; fine furniture needs a thinner cut. When thinning shellac, remember that the thinner the cut, the deeper it penetrates into wood and the smoother it flattens out. Remember, too, that thinner cuts require more coats to build a sufficient finish.

When finishing wood with shellac, brush it on with short light strokes over stains or raw wood. The first coat should be applied freely, so it soaks well into the wood. The first coat may raise a little grain on the wood, but these rough spots are smoothed during the sanding necessary between coats. The second coat should be thinner than the first and applied with brush strokes that match the direction of the grain.

Shellac is one of the most popular materials for finishing wood floors. This is due to its ability to be patched without showing *lap marks*. Patching is difficult when a varnish has been used. To patch a shellacked floor, sand and clean the bad spot well beyond the edges of the blemish. *Feather* a new coat of shellac into the area, allow it to dry, then sand and recoat.

Allow the patch to dry overnight before waxing or walking on it.

Some professional painters use a 3 or 4-pound cut of shellac to seal water spots in ceilings and walls. After the source of the *moisture* has been cured and the area has dried thoroughly, paint over the stain with shellac. The shellac soaks into the wall or ceiling and then dries to an impervious film. The idea is not so much to keep the stain from coming through as to prevent the next coat of paint from soaking into the stain, causing a new round of *bleeding*. Shellac is also used to seal knots in wood and prevent them from bleeding through and ruining the topcoating.

Regular paint *thinner* and *solvent* do not cut shellac. Therefore, they are useless for cleaning shellac from brushes. Using alcohol for cleanup can get expensive, so try ammonia. This cleaner cuts shellac easily and keeps your cleanup bill low.

Shellac is hard on brushes, so select a good natural bristle brush and use it only with shellac. This prevents excessive wear to other brushes and insures that other oil-base coatings do not contaminate your shellac jobs.

See *Floors, Wood* and *Knots in Wood*.

SHELVES

These pieces should be painted with a durable semigloss or glossy trim enamel. Choosing a tough paint helps keep shelving look good through heavy use and reduces the frequency with which the shelving needs to be painted.

Bracketed shelves should be taken apart and placed across sawhorses to make painting easier. Scrape and sand all damaged areas, then paint one side and all the edges of each piece. Allow for thorough drying, usually overnight, then flip over and paint the remaining side.

When refinishing built-in shelves, work on one compartment at a time. Paint the most difficult-to-reach areas first—the bottom of the shelves and the back wall. Paint the sidewalls, then the top of the shelf. Paint the outside edges last. Check your work frequently for drips and *runs*.

As an aid to painting in the close quarters of a shelving unit, cut off several inches of a sash tool's handle. This allows you to keep the brush perpendicular to the surface without marring fresh paint with the end of the brush.

Shelves can also be stained. Wipe stain onto bare wood after sanding. Remove excess stain with a clean rag, allow for drying, then coat with several coats of *varnish*. Sand varnish with fine sandpaper between coats.

Metal shelves can be painted with a metal paint. Paint after removing rust and dirt. Choose a glossy or semigloss finish. The job can be completed quickly and efficiently by *spraying* paint *with a can*.

SHUTTERS

Whether functional or decorative, these covers or screens should be removed from the house before painting. Functional shutters are removed by lifting them off their hinges. Decorative shutters are normally bolted or screwed directly to the body of the house.

Removing the shutters during preparation prevents dripping and splattering paint on them as the body of the house is painted. Removal also allows you to work on them in a garage or workshop at your leisure. Be careful when removing shutters, because wasps like to build nests behind them.

Shutters are usually painted with a semigloss or glossy trim paint—black and white being the two most common colors. Although preparations for painting shutters include scraping, sanding, and spot priming, a thorough washing with a solution of detergent and water may be all that is required. Most people paint their shutters every other time the body of the house is painted.

Spraying paint is the easiest way to coat louvered shutters. Paint the backside first. When it has dried, finish the front. Because you are working inside, you can control *overspray* and work during rainy weather or at night.

To paint shutters with a brush, lay them out on sawhorses and paint the backside first. Check frequently for drips and runs. When the backside is dry, flip them over and inspect for drips and runs. Sand these defects smooth before painting the front. Painting the front last keeps any drips and runs on the backside of the shutter out of view. Metal shutters should be painted with a metal paint or a glossy or semi-gloss oil-base trim enamel.

See *Louvers*.

SIENNA

A yellowish-brown or reddish-brown *pigment* used for coloring paint. It is one of the most common tint colors and is available as a universal colorant.

See *Colors*.

SILICONE WATER REPELLENTS

Used to preserve the natural look of exterior wood surfaces. The silicone in these repellents prevents water from penetrating wood surfaces. These repellents also prevent topcoatings from adhering to the wood and should be used only where you want wood to show.

See *Natural Finishes, Water Repellents,* and *Wood Preservatives*.

SKIN

The layer of rubbery, dried material that forms on the top of open paint containers. The paint beneath the paint skin is usually still applicable. When removing the skin, make sure that no pieces fall into the paint. These pieces show up as lumps in the paint during application.

A skin forms on paint and varnish when these coatings are exposed to air during storage. In most cases the skin can be fished out of the paint, leaving the material underneath ready to use. Be aware, however, that skin formation is a sign of age. The paint may not perform at new paint standards.

SOFFITS

The visible underside of structural members such as staircases, cornices, beams and roof overhangs or *eaves*. Because soffits are usually protected against the effects of weathering, they may not need to be painted each time the body of the house gets refinished. Because soffits do not weather, they should not be painted with *chalking* paints designed to be washed by rain. Instead, use a *latex* or *alkyd* enamel.

See *Exterior Paint*.

SOLIDS

The nonvolatile *pigments* and fillers in a coating that remain on the surface after the *vehicle* has evaporated. Measured by weight or volume, solids are found in varying amounts in different paints. *One-coat paint* tends to contain the most solids, while penetrating stains contain few solids. As a general rule, the more solids in a coating, the thicker the film that material builds on the surface to which it is applied.

See *Specifications*.

SOLVENTS

Liquids that will thin or cut a paint. They are used when making a coating to dissolve the solids and to keep them in suspension.

Solvents are volatile or capable of evaporation and are listed in two categories: oil-base and water-base. Oil-base solvents are *resin, vegetable oil, turpentine,* petroleum-base *thinner,* benzene, or *mineral spirits* that are used to *clean up* or dilute oil-base paints. Water is the solvent used to clean or thin water-base paints. Because all water-base paints can be thinned and cleaned up with water, many homeowners are switching to these convenient paints for all their painting needs.

When using oil-base paints, always use the solvent recommended on the paint can by the manufacturer. Although oil-base paints cover a wide category of coatings, some solvents do not work on different coatings in the category. For example, mineral spirits do not cut *shellac.* When using oil-base solvents, remember that these materials are toxic and flammable. They should be used in a well-ventilated area away from open flames.

SOYBEAN OIL

The oil pressed from soybeans and commonly used by paint manufacturers as a *vehicle* for *alkyd paints.* Soybean oil is slower to dry than both *tung oil* and *linseed oil*, although its excellent nonyellowing characteristic is useful for white paint.

See *Vegetable Oils*.

SPACKLING COMPOUNDS

Used both inside and outside the house to patch cracks, holes, and other depressions in walls and ceilings. Spackling compound comes in two forms: ready-mixed vinyl paste and powder, which is mixed with water to form a paste just before use.

Ready-mixed vinyl spackling compound is convenient, easy to use, and offers excellent adhesion to *plaster*, wood, *masonry,* and *drywall* surfaces. The vinyl in this material

makes it slightly flexible, so it is especially suited for use on cracks and joints between dissimilar materials such as brick and wood. Vinyl spackling compound dries quickly and can be painted over as soon as it has dried. This material shrinks little, and most cracks less than ½ inch in width do not need repeated coats to build up a level surface. The material can be applied with fingers or a *putty knife*. Like powdered spackling compound, vinyl spackling compound is easily cleaned from tools and hands with soap and water. Do not wash extra spackling compound down the drain, or it may harden and clog the plumbing.

Powdered spackling compound is considerably cheaper than vinyl spackling compound. It is most often used when extensive patching must be done. Powdered spackling compound tends to shrink somewhat as the water evaporates from the material; therefore, two applications are usually necessary to build a smooth surface. Most powdered spackling compound cures instead of dries and needs adequate time to set up completely before painting. If the patch is painted before thoroughly cured, the paint peels from the patch.

Both types of spackling compound should be sanded prior to painting. The first coat of paint should be a primer or sealer to prevent the patch from showing up as a dull spot when top-coated.

See *Walls, Patching* and *Wood Fillers*.

SPAR VARNISH

Originally developed to protect wooden boat parts against weather and salt spray. Spar varnish has, however, gained popularity as an exterior *varnish* for protecting wood against weather while retaining the natural appearance and color of the wood. Spar varnish is widely used on doors, lawn furniture, porch ceilings, and other trim. Although spar varnish is the most weather-resistant varnish, it does not last as long as trim enamel or house paint. It must be renewed every 12 to 18 months and is not widely used where beauty of the wood is not important. As with other clear finishes, several coats are better than one heavy one. Sand between coats with fine sandpaper. Spar varnish is best applied with a natural bristle brush. It can be thinned and cleaned with a suitable *thinner* or *solvent*.

See *Natural Finishes*.

SPECIFICATIONS

The specifications of a paint product, listed on the can by the manufacturer, tell the user what materials were used to make the coating, under what conditions it can be applied, how it should be applied, where it lasts the longest, the rate of coverage, what *solvents* thin it, and the appropriate antidotes for accidental ingestion. Always read the specifications on a coating's label at the paint store before you buy it to insure that it is the best material for your particular job, and that you have the proper *thinners* on hand.

SPIRIT VARNISH

This varnish is made by dissolving a gum or *resin* in a *solvent*. These varnishes tend to penetrate the surface of the *substrate* and require several coats to build up a sufficient *film thickness*.

SPLINTERING

A wood failure related more closely to improper sawing of siding at the mill than improper painting. When the flat or wide grain of the wood is exposed, the varying rates of expansion and contraction of the wood cause long cracks and splinters parallel to the length of the board to form. Once this deterioration has started, there is very little cure outside of replacing the board with a properly cut one. If you cannot afford the expense of replacing the defective piece, sand the deteriorating wood smooth and coat with a *wood preservative* before priming. Use an alkyd or oil-base primer, because the water in latex primers may cause the grain to start cracking immediately. The wood preservative reduces the intrusion of water and slows down the rate at which the cracks and splinters reappear.

SPOT PEELING

Peeling paint confined to a small area of a house indicates a localized *moisture* problem. As with other peeling problems, the source of the moisture should be located and corrected. The loose paint should be scraped off, sanded, and primed before applying a topcoat.

See *Peeling Paint*.

SPRAYING PAINT

Modern technology has produced many tools for spraying paint. The range includes everything from *spray painting with a can* to the commercially rented *airless sprayers*. Practically any paint that can be brushed or rolled can be sprayed. You gain a considerable amount of time when spray painting large areas, but you lose time and money by spraying small areas.

Some sprayers apply the equivalent of two coats of paint at once. This saves considerable time and numerous trips up and down ladders when working on large areas such as the body of a house. Inside, when planning to paint several rooms at one time with the same color, spraying reduces the time spent by one-fourth to one-third. Although spraying may cut actual painting time, cleanup is lengthened in most cases. The extra time necessary for setting up equipment and the expense of buying solvents for cleanup make spraying prohibitive for small jobs. On large jobs, the cost of thin-

Fig. 1
Spraying Paint. Airless spray units shoot nothing but paint, allowing excellent control of the spray.

ners and solvents more than make up for the time saved. Choosing a spray unit depends on the size of the job at hand.

Spray Equipment

Aerosol spray cans are self-contained spray units made of a container, valve, propellant, and paint. Aerosol spray paints are handy for small jobs like furniture and are available in a variety of colors, finishes, and chemical compositions.

When painting with an aerosol spray paint, use rapid smooth strokes parallel to the surface being painted. Keep the nozzle 10 to 12 inches away from the surface. Press the button after movement has started and release before movement has stopped. Spray slightly beyond the edges of the object. Do not hold the spray in one place too long or *runs,* drips, and *sags*

develop.

The manufacturers of many vacuums now market spray painting attachments powered by their units. These weak sprayers are suited for small jobs like cabinets and furniture. They may not be able to handle heavier paints, and painting the walls in a single room may be pushing the equipment beyond its capabilities.

Electric or vibrator sprays are very convenient in that you can plug them into an ac outlet and spray without trailing hoses across the room or leaving cans of open paint sitting around. These units have a paint canister right under the gun. They are useful for louvers, furniture, and may be used successfully for painting interior rooms.

Air compressor spray units are more powerful than the first units and are suited to jobs beyond the scope of vacuum or electric spray outfits. Air compressor sprays are complicated, and you should ask for operating instructions when renting or buying one. Air compressor sprays come with a gasoline or electric-powered compressor unit. When using the unit, make sure the compressor is beyond the spraying area to prevent fire. Gasoline engines also need a continuous stream of fresh air for cooling and combustion. One of the hazards of an air compressor sprayer is its excessive *overspray*. Make sure to mask hardware and other objects not to be painted as part of the preparation. Paint on windless days.

Airless sprayers produce less overspray than their air compressor counterparts, although they are more powerful (Fig. 1). These machines pump nothing but paint and are suitable for the big jobs. Although not widely used by weekend painters, airless sprays can be rented at rental or paint stores.

Operation

Although most paints can be sprayed as they are when they come from the can, some of the heavier paints require thinning. Consult the manufacturer's *specifications* on the can's label for recommended thinning ratios. Strain all paint, whether thinned or not, through a fine mesh material such as nylon hose before pouring into a spray machine (Fig. 2).

Test the spray equipment on a surface made of material similar to that which you plan to paint. Regulate the size and pattern of the paint fan at the gun. For small articles such as furniture, a narrow fan is best. A wider fan is good for walls. Try for a horizontal or vertical fan that gives good coverage with a minimum of overspray.

As a general rule, spray nozzles should be held from 8 to 12 inches from the surface to be painted. Keep the spray head perpendicular to the area being sprayed. Do not move in a

sweeping arc, because this motion produces a paint film that is heavy in the middle, but excessively thin at the ends (Fig. 3). Make decisive vertical or horizontal strokes when painting with a spray gun. The spray should be moving perpendicular to the surface before the trigger is depressed, and the trigger should be released before the stroke has stopped. Do not jiggle the trigger during the stroke, and each stroke should overlap the previous one by 30 to 50 percent. Several thin coats are better than one thick one.

Before spray painting walls, mask all areas not to be painted and cover surrounding areas with *drop cloths* to protect against overspray. Overspray is the biggest concern when painting with a spray unit. To reduce the overspray at corners, run a vertical strip of paint down the corner before painting the rest of the wall. This strip of paint gives you several inches of cushion to lap into when beginning or ending a horizontal movement.

When painting inside corners, do not aim the gun directly at the corner. You end up with

Fig. 2

Spraying Paint. All paints should be strained through a fine mesh, such as nylon hose, before being poured into a spray unit.

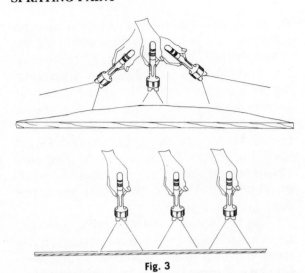

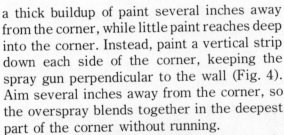

Fig. 3

Spraying Paint. Moving spray gun in an arc (top) produces an uneven coating. Keeping the nozzle parallel (bottom) results in even paint application.

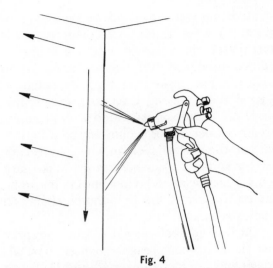

Fig. 4

Spraying Paint. When painting an inside corner, make a vertical pass with the spray gun parallel to the corner. Then make horizontal strokes away from the corner.

a thick buildup of paint several inches away from the corner, while little paint reaches deep into the corner. Instead, paint a vertical strip down each side of the corner, keeping the spray gun perpendicular to the wall (Fig. 4). Aim several inches away from the corner, so the overspray blends together in the deepest part of the corner without running.

When painting a horizontal surface, apply two thin coats—one horizontally and one vertically. This is especially necessary on rough surfaces, where spraying in only one direction may result in shadows of unpainted surface.

When painting overhead, expect lots of overspray to drift down on you. Stand as far back from the surface being painted as possible. Wear long sleeves, goggles, and a respirator to protect yourself as much as possible from the overspray. When working with a spray gun with the paint cup attached to the nozzle, tilt the spray at a 45 to 60-degree angle. Attempting to keep the spray perpendicular to the surface prevents paint from feeding prop-

erly. Airless sprays can be held perpendicular to the surface, since the paint is picked up at the compressor unit and not at the nozzle.

If the tip of your spray should become clogged during use, clean it with a straw or copper wire. Do not use stiff steel wire or a nail, because the precision diameter and shape of the tip may be altered.

Spray equipment should be cleaned immediately after use. Although cleaning is no more complicated than running the correct solvent through the machine, cleanup can be expensive. When choosing a paint, consider the thinner needed for cleaning. Alkyd and oil-base paints may need several gallons of an expensive solvent. Latex paints need only warm water.

Clean valves and nozzles of spray cans by turning them upside down. Press the valve until aerosol spray comes out clear.

Remember that spray painting requires extreme caution. Always paint in an adequately ventilated room. Do not paint near open flames or sparks with alkyd, oil-base, or aerosol paints.

SPRAYING WITH A CAN

A variety of paints are available in easy-to-use aerosol spray cans. These paints are expensive, making them especially suited for small jobs, but prohibitively costly for use on large surfaces. The two most prominent advantages of painting with an aerosol is that it produces a paint film free of *lap marks*, and there is minimal cleanup. Simply throw the can away when it is empty.

Before buying an aerosol paint, read the label to make sure to check its *compatibility* with the surface you intend to cover. Look, too, for the *covering power* you can expect from a single can. You can buy as many cans as necessary for the job at hand during one trip to the store.

Before painting with an aerosol, thoroughly prepare the surface to be painted. Remove all loose paint, rust, and corrosion. Make sure no dirt or grease remains on the surface. Shake the can for a minute or two to make sure the *pigments* are thoroughly mixed with the *vehicle*.

When spraying, hold the nozzle 10 to 12 inches from the object being painted. Keep the nozzle parallel to the work and avoid swinging the spray in an arc, which results in an uneven application of paint. Press the button to start the spray after the can is in motion. Release it before the can's motion has stopped. This prevents runs and *sags*. Spraying beyond the edges of the object also reduces the chance of runs. When spraying outside, work only on a windless day. When spraying inside, make sure the room is well-ventilated. There should be no open flames or sparks in the room. The propellants in aerosol sprays are extremely flammable.

The best job is achieved by applying several thin coats of paint instead of one thick one. Apply the first coat, then wait until the paint is *tacky*. If a third coat is necessary, allow the surface to dry thoroughly before application.

When finished, clean the nozzle by turning the can upside down. Depress the button. Allow the propellant to spray out until it comes out clear. Replace the cap and store in an area where temperatures do not rise above 120 degrees Fahrenheit, and the can is out of the reach of children.

SPREADING RATE

The spreading rate of a paint depends on its viscosity and the type of surface to which it is being applied. Most paints cover from 350 to 450 square feet of surface per gallon (assuming a standard film thickness of 3 to 4 mils). Read the can for an estimate of the spreading rate for the surface you plan to cover.

One-coat paint has a lower spreading rate than regular paint, because it builds a thicker film. Stains also have a lower spreading rate, because they are designed to soak into the surface over which they are applied. The same paint has a different spreading rate on painted siding and concrete block. A porous surface like concrete block reduces a paint's spreading rate by about 20 percent. When using *shellac* and *varnish*, the second and third coats spread considerably farther than the first coat. The first coat has sealed the surface.

If you are unsure about the spreading rate of a particular paint, discuss it with your paint dealer. He is familiar with the way different paints spread on various surfaces.

See *Covering Power, Estimating Quantity of Paint,* and *Paint, Choosing*.

STAINING THROUGH

Staining or *bleeding* problems occur when

water or resins seep out of a substrate and through the topcoating to leave discoloration on a painted surface. Staining can occur both inside and outside a house. Inside, it usually reveals itself by producing a brown watermark where the *moisture* is seeping through the wall or ceiling. Outside, natural pigments in redwood or cedar siding are usually the problem.

The first step in curing interior water stains is eliminating the moisture source. Check plumbing and roofs for leaks. The source of the water must be stopped before the problem can be halted. Once you have stopped the leak, let the affected area dry. Seal the stain with shellac or an oil-base spot sealer. When the sealer has dried, coat with a *primer* and topcoating.

Outside, stains on redwood and cedar siding indicate that moisture is working its way through the topcoating. This can be caused by either internal or external moisture. External moisture is a problem where the paint is too thin and porous, allowing rain and dew to pass through the coating and dissolving the extractives in the wood. This failure can usually be corrected by priming the surface with a good nonporous oil-base or alkyd primer prior to top-coating with a nonporous glossy or semi-gloss house paint. Staining the surface with a pigmented *stain* is also a good solution, although it requires stripping all old paint from the surface.

The first step in curing internally caused moisture stains is eliminating the source of moisture. If it is water vapor coming from inside the house, you may need to create a moisture barrier on the interior walls by painting them with a nonporous alkyd or oil-base paint. Installing vents in the exterior wall reduces the amount of moisture penetrating the wall. A leaky roof needs to be patched as do cracks in the siding, which may be allowing

water to enter. When the leaks have been corrected and the wall has dried, prime with a nonporous alkyd primer before top-coating.

See *Alkali, Efflorescence, Knots in Wood* and *Water Repellents.*

STAINS

Finishes designed to accent the natural color and grain of wood or to darken and color the wood without hiding the grain. Stains contain varying amounts of *pigment* suspended in an oil, water, or alcohol *vehicle* that soaks into wood, providing both color and protection. The major difference between a stain and a paint is that paints lay on the surface, while stains penetrate into the top layer of the wood and leave little or no coating on the surface.

Stains can be applied in any manner that other paint products are applied: brushing rolling, spraying, or with an applicator. Additionally, many stains are applied to furniture and other small objects with a cotton rag. Brushing and pad applicators are preferred for applying stains to rough surfaces, because they work the coating into cracks and crevices the best. Rollers tend to leave cracks and fissures untouched, while spraying doesn't usually apply enough stain to soak in thoroughly.

Stains work best when applied to raw woods or wood treated with a bleach or *wood preservative.* Stains cannot be applied over nonporous coatings like shellac, varnish, or sealers. Stains can be applied over previously painted surfaces, provided the paint has weathered almost completely away.

All woods take stain differently, so test the stain on a small, inconspicuous area before tackling the whole area. It is always better to apply a stain that is too light instead of one that is too dark. Too light a stain can be darkened by applying a second coat. If a dark stain is applied, bleaching or sanding is required to lighten it.

The second coat of stain should be applied while the first is still wet—usually within an hour—so that both coats penetrate. If the first is allowed to dry, it acts as a sealer, and the second coat does not penetrate. Stain that has not penetrated should be wiped from the surface with a rag to prevent shiny areas from appearing.

Although most paints can be used over stains, beware of *bleeding*. Test the paint on a small section of the stained material first.

Inside the house, stain is used on furniture, floors, paneling, woodwork, doors, and cabinets. Old finishes, except other stains, must be removed with heat, a chemical remover, or sanding before staining. Patch and fill any nail holes or scratches with a *wood filler*, allow for drying, then sand the patch smooth before staining. Sanding before staining is important, because it removes raised wood fibers and opens up the wood to accept the stain.

After applying the stain, wipe it or allow it to soak in, depending on the type of stain being used. When the stain has dried, usually overnight, it should be sealed with a varnish, shellac, or wood sealer to preserve its appearance. Because stains do not form a surface coating, the topcoating is necessary to reduce nicking, gouging, and to facilitate washing later. Interior stains last a lifetime if their protective coating is kept in good repair.

There are two basic types of stain for wood floors: pigmented wiping stains and penetrating stains. Pigmented wiping stains should be applied immediately after sanding. They are brushed on and then wiped off. The darkness or depth of the stain depends on how long you leave the stain on the surface. These stains must be wiped off for grain to show.

Lacquer and shellac are not recommended for use over these stains; however, varnish works fine.

Penetrating stains produce the most permanent colors. No wiping is involved, because the stain is designed to soak into the wood and produce a deep, pleasing tone. The stain can be finished with shellac, varnish, or lacquer.

Exterior stains range anywhere from nearly clear to almost opaque. They contain more pigment than interior stains and need to be mixed thoroughly and often during use. One coat of stain should last three to four years on a smooth surface, while a double coat applied to a rough surface often lasts up to 10 years. Stains have an advantage over paint on rough surfaces. They allow the wood to breathe. The problems of *peeling, cracking,* and *blistering* are reduced, which usually plague paints on other than smooth surfaces.

Stains lap—specially on the front edge of shingles and shakes—so work one or two courses of shingles at a time. Complete the entire row (both coats if double coating) before moving on to the next row. Stop at natural breaks such as windows, doors, and corners where *lap marks* will be less noticeable.

Exterior stains penetrate into wood and preserve it from weathering by repelling water and reducing mold, *mildew*, rot, and other bacterial growth. Stains that contain pentachlorophenal are highly toxic to wood bacteria. They are also toxic to humans, so wear long sleeves and gloves when applying stains containing these materials. Additionally, cover all nearby plants to prevent damaging them.

Alcohol Stains

Alcohol stains are transparent stains that penetrate and dry fast, making them one of the most difficult stains to use. These stains should be brushed on a small area and then wiped off immediately to prevent streaking and lapping. They dry quickly and can be coated with a clear finish within hours. This type of stain is most often used under lacquers on fine furniture and woodwork.

Stains. Latex stains have all the advantages of oil-base stains, but cleanup is easy with soap and water.

Latex Stains

Many manufacturers have recently introduced latex stains into the marketplace. See the illustration. These stains have all the advantages of latex paint—easy cleanup, odorless, and quick-drying time. They also have a couple of disadvantages. The water in stains makes them raise a grain when applied to wood. The roughness must be sanded smooth after staining and before top-coating to produce a smooth surface. Latex stains are also a little more difficult to use than oil-base stains, because they dry so quickly. Work in small areas. Wipe up leftover stain frequently to prevent lap marks. Latex stains can be top-

coated after 12 hours of drying.

Oil-Base Stains

Oil-base stains come in two varieties: penetrating and pigmented. The pentrating stains contain pigment, but not enough to hide the grain in the wood. These stains are designed to be applied and allowed to soak in for a short time before being wiped off the surface with a clean rag. They are especially suited to fine interior work where the characteristics of the wood are desirable.

Pigmented stains contain enough pigment to fully mask the grain of the wood to which they are applied. Most often used on exterior siding where they color the wood, these stains are designed to be applied and allowed to soak into the wood without being wiped off. These stains are especially useful for hiding defects in walls that would be accented by penetrating stains.

Varnish Stains

These stains are a combination of varnish and a pigmented stain. They are designed to both soak into the wood and form a protective topcoating with only one application. Unfortunately, these coatings do not last as long, or look as nice, as the traditional stain/topcoating system. They should be avoided except where speed of application is the only consideration.

See *Natural Finishes, Shakes and Shingles,* and *Wood Preservatives*.

SUBSTRATE

A term used to describe the material to which you are adding a new coating. The substrate can be in one of two conditions: uncoated or covered with an old coating. There are specific ways of treating previously painted and unpainted substrates.

See *Preparation*.

SURFACE TENSION

A measure of the molecular cohesive force on the surface of a liquid. This property is responsible for the rate of evaporation.

SWIMMING POOLS

At first glance, painting a backyard swimming pool may appear to be a job beyond your capability. It is not. Coating manufacturers have created modern materials for use on swimming pools. The total surface area of your pool is considerably less than the exterior of your house. Before running off to a contractor, talk with the salesman at your paint store or at a local swimming pool supply outlet. He can introduce you to the available materials and give you the confidence to do the job yourself.

As with painting any surface, the first step is determining the type of pool you have. Most are concrete, aluminum, steel, or fiberglass. If the pool is fiberglass, a thorough scrubbing is generally all that is necessary to bring this type pool up to par. Painting the other three pools involves the same basic procedures as painting these materials when they are found elsewhere around your home: preparation, selecting a coating, and applying the material.

Preparations

As a general rule, contractors are responsible for applying the initial finish coatings on a pool. If finishing was not included in your contract, you need to do it yourself or hire the job to be done. If you decide to finish a concrete pool yourself, the first step is to wait at least two weeks so the concrete has a chance to cure. The longer you wait, the better. Etch all surfaces with a solution of *muriatic acid* (20 percent). Apply the acid with a stiff brush on a long handle. Allow the acid to remain on the surface until it stops bubbling. Wash thoroughly with clear water. After the rinse, allow for drying. You are ready to prime and finish the pool.

On metal pools, do not wait. The longer you delay sealing the pool against air and water, the more the metal corrodes and the harder the job is. Aluminum pools should be cleaned with a strong detergent and then etched with a solution of phosphoric acid, rinsed thoroughly, and allowed to dry before priming. Steel pools are usually primed by the contractor, but if your pool was not, remove any rust or corrosion with chemical rust remover or by *sandblasting*. Immediately after the bare metal is exposed, apply a metal conditioner and primer.

The choice of primer you use on the pool is determined by the material and the system you plan on applying. Consult the label of the material you plan to use for a topcoating, then select the primer recommended by the manufacturer.

On old pools, the preparations are a little more involved. Because pools are exposed to harsh weather conditions, strong chemicals, and extreme water pressure, preparations and repairs must be correct and thorough for optimum results.

Old concrete pools that have extensive chipping, cracking, and fading of paint should be sandblasted to remove the old material. After this step, treat as if you were working with new concrete, except that allowing the concrete to cure is not necessary.

On concrete pools with minor chipping and cracking, the first step is washing the entire pool with detergent to remove suntan oil and grease. This is necessary because paint, *caulking*, concrete patches, and muriatic acid are inhibited by these materials. Scrape off all bad paint with a *putty knife*, paint scraper, or wire brush. Smooth rough paint edges with sandpaper, then etch all exposed concrete with a 10 percent solution of muriatic acid. All new concrete patches should also be etched after the patch has had time to cure properly. All cracks should be filled with a caulking type sealant designed for swimming pools. Regular caulking does not work, because the water pressure and the chemicals in the water cause rapid deterioration of these materials. As with all caulking jobs, cracks should be cleaned thoroughly before application of the material to insure proper adhesion.

On previously painted metal pools, the extent of preparation depends on the condition of the pool. Painting the pool every year, or every other year, before the problem gets worse is the best way to prevent extensive repairs when painting time comes.

Aluminum pools usually require scraping and sanding to remove loose and flaking paint. Follow this by scrubbing with a detergent and water solution to remove oil and grease and to dull the previous finish. Make necessary caulking repairs in cracks, then prime and top-coat.

Steel pools require removal of all loose and flaking paint with a wire brush or scraper. Sand rusting metal until shiny and immediately apply a primer. Wash sound paint with a detergent to remove grease and oil and to degloss

the surface. Caulk as necessary. When caulking is dry, seal with primer and then top-coat the entire pool.

Pool Paints

There are several pool paints available. The one you choose depends largely on your experience in handling tricky paints and the material of your pool.

Solvent-thinned and chlorinated *rubber-base* paints are the most popular and widely used paints for concrete pools. These paints resist *alkali* damage and are easier to handle than two-component *epoxy paints*.

Vinyl-base solvent-thinned paints are difficult to handle and should not be used if it is your first pool painting job. Phenolic or vinyl-base paints are the best bet for metal pools, although two-component or catalytic coatings also work well.

Two-component paints require careful mixing and have a short pot life, usually less than eight hours. On a large job, you may want to mix only enough paint to do one or two walls. Save the remaining paint for finishing the job the following day.

When painting over old paint, make sure that the coating you have chosen is *compatible*, with the paint already on the pool. To test for compatibility, cover a small area and let it dry. Check for wrinkling, *blistering,* and *lifting* of the previous coat.

Estimating Amount of Paint

Estimating the amount of paint necessary for coating a pool is done in a manner similiar to that of figuring the paint requirements for painting the siding on your house. Multiply the width and height of each of the sides. Add an extra foot or two to the height on curve-sided pools. Measure the length and width of the bottom and multiply these figures. Add the

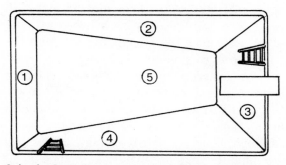

Swimming Pools. The sequence for painting a swimming pool is to paint (1-4) the walls and then finish with the bottom (5), beginning at the end opposite the ladder.

areas of walls and bottom, and you have the total square footage of your pool. Remember this number when you go to buy paint. Divide this number by the coverage per gallon of the paint you select to arrive at the number of gallons of paint needed for the job. If there is any doubt in your mind, buy an extra gallon just to be safe.

Applying Pool Paints

Pool paints can be applied in the standard coating methods: spraying, brushing, and rolling. Most professionals prefer rolling, because it works the paint into cracks and crevices effectively while speeding up the job. Spraying may not penetrate all the imperfections in a pool's surface, and brushing takes an extremely long time. When in doubt, consult the label for the manufacturer's application recommendations.

Pools should be painted during dry weather. Avoid windy days, because dirt and grit will be blown into the pool, leaving a rough texture to the finish. Most manufacturers advise applying paint when the temperature is above 45 degrees Fahrenheit, and all suggest following the shade around your pool. Paint the

walls first, beginning and ending at the corners to avoid *lap marks*. Paint the bottom last. Work from the end opposite the ladder toward the ladder. See the illustration. Allow the paint to cure the length of time recommended by the manufacturer before filling the pool.

The trim, decking, and fences around pools should be painted with the recommended exterior trim enamels for best results. On areas where you want a rough nonskid surface, add texture sand to the final coat.

See *Masonry* and *Metals*.

SYNTHETIC RESINS

As alkyd and latex paints replace oil-base paints, the natural resins once used in paint are being replaced by synthetic resins. Synthetic resins are man-made, usually petroleum-based materials that have a more uniform color, texture, and appearance in paint than their natural counterparts. Synthetic resins adhere better, are more flexible, and retain their color longer than natural resins. They are found in almost all paints. *Shellac* with its lac resin is one notable exception.

See *Acrylic Resins* and *Resins*.

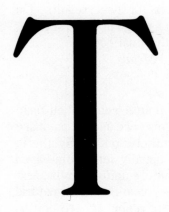

TACK CLOTH

A cloth impregnated with a sticky substance. It is used for picking up dirt and dust left behind by sanding. Tack cloths do a much better job than water-dampened cloths, which tend to leave behind a dust film. Although tack cloths are inexpensive and can be purchased at the paint store, you can make your own quite easily.

To make a tack cloth, dampen a clean cotton cloth with water. Work equal parts of *turpentine* and *varnish* into the cloth. Roll the cloth back and forth, or wad and unwad it between your hands until the cloth is barely damp, but slightly sticky. A tack cloth that has lost its stickiness can be rejuvenated with a fresh application of the varnish/turpentine mixture. Tack cloths should be stored in an airtight container to prevent the possibility of fire.

TACKY

A condition of paint during the drying process. Following application, but before the paint has dried thoroughly, the paint is in a state where your fingers stick to it. This condition makes it susceptible to flying insects and blowing dirt. Latex paints have a shorter period of tackiness than alkyd or oil-base paints. If insect and dirt contamination may be a problem during drying, choose latex instead of oil-base paints for the job.

TEXTURE PAINTS

Heavy-bodied flat latex or alkyd paints designed to dry to a rough, rather than smooth, surface. Some people like texture paints simply because they are a contrast to flat wall paints. Texture paints can also be used to hide flaws on walls and ceilings that are nearly impossible to correct by other means.

Texture Paint. A series of overlapping arcs made with a whisk broom is a popular texture paint finish.

Texture paints can be applied over any surface *compatible* with standard latex or alkyd flat wall paints. Occasionally texture paints are applied to drywall as a combination primer/finish coat. Once a texture coat has been applied, it is more or less permanent. The uneven surface may prevent the use of rollers for repainting, and painting over a texture paint usually requires 25 percent more paint than a similiarly sized flat surface. Texture paints are more fragile and harder to wash than flat wall paints, so they should not be applied on surfaces that get heavy use.

Texture paints can be applied in many ways. Many manufacturers now make texture finish roller covers for use with texture paint. These durable plastic pile naps apply texture paint and create a texture finish in one easy application. The depth of the texture is determined by how hard you press down on the roller during the finishing strokes. Light pressure creates a shallow pattern, heavy pressure

creates a deep pattern. When applying texture paints, work in 3 by 3-foot sections. Build a paint film ⅛ to ¼ inch thick. Finish the texture pattern in each area before moving on to the next section.

Although texture paints can be brushed on, it is best to use a pad *applicator* to build a film thickness of sufficient depth to accept a pattern. The process is more like troweling on the paint than brushing. Again, create a texture pattern in each area before moving on.

A common texture pattern is the stipple effect, which can be made with a pad applicator, sponge, or crumpled newspaper. Pat the paint with the flat of the applicator, the flat of the sponge, or the paper so that little points are created. The more pressure you apply, the deeper the pattern is.

Another popular pattern involves the use of a whisk broom. After applying the paint, wavy or straight lines can be created by drawing the broom lightly over the surface. A series of overlapping arcs is a good choice for this type of finish. See the illustration.

See *Sand Paint.*

THINNERS

Liquids with which the thickness of a paint's body can be reduced, or with which tools, spills, and drips can be cleaned up. Although various types of paint demand different thinners, two or three basic thinners should handle all your home painting needs.

All thinners, except water, are flammable and should not be used near open flame or in enclosed areas. Read paint labels and thinner labels carefully to insure that the paint and thinner are *compatible* prior to mixing. Thinners are designed to evaporate in a way compatible with the paint product that they are used with. When choosing a thinner for altering the consistency of a coating, buy the best you can afford. This eliminates thinner-related problems later on.

Epoxies

When using the two-component epoxies and *urethane paints*, note that the manufacturer recommends specific thinners on the label. Use only these thinners, because the chemistry involved in the coatings is complex. The addition of a foreign substance destroys their effectiveness.

Lacquer

Lacquer thinner, just as its name implies, is used for cutting and cleaning up lacquer finishes. Although it is classed under the general heading of oil-base thinners, it is a powerful material that will not mix with alkyd or oil-base materials. Lacquer thinner causes these materials to wrinkle and remain soft when mixed with them. Lacquer thinner should be used only with lacquer finishes. This material is highly flammable and should be used in a well-ventilated room away from flames and sparks.

Latex

Water is becoming the most widely used paint thinner, because latex paints are becoming the preferred paint among weekend painters. For thinning latex paints, clear room-temperature tap water is best. Tools used in latex materials can be cleaned with warm, soapy water.

Oil-Base

Most oil-base and alkyd paints and varnishes can be thinned with a petroleum-base paint thinner. Many contain benzene or other hydrocarbon combinations. *Turpentine* and *mineral spirits* can be used for thinning these paints, but these materials cost more than petroleum-base thinners. Turpentine is the best thinner for use with varnish and quality furniture stain.

Inexpensive and odorless petroleum-base thinners cut paint quite well. They can be used for cleanup and keep for many years when stored in an airtight container. *Pigments* and paint *solids* settle out of these thinners. By pouring off the clear liquid, you can recycle thinner many times. You should use only fresh thinner for thinning paints. Thinner that has been used to clean brushes alters the characteristics of the paint to which it is added.

Shellac

Alcohol is a useful thinner for shellac. Although alcohol is expensive, its quick-drying and odorless qualities make it the only material really suited to thinning shellac. Because alcohol is expensive, you may not want to clean your shellac brushes in it; instead, use ammonia. Alcohol is flammable and should be handled like lacquer thinner.

See *Cleanup, Solvents,* and *Vegetable Oils.*

TILE PAINTING

Painting the ceramic tiles in your home is a tricky proposition. Most people choose not to paint over tiles. If you decide to paint ceramic tiles, use an *epoxy* or *urethane* two-component paint. For a clear finish, the moisture-cured *urethane varnishes* are the best. To add color and keep a slick surface, use a two-part urethane or *epoxy paint*.

TINT

A term used to describe the process of changing the color or tone of a paint. Most manufacturers make enough colors, so you can obtain the color of paint you want ready-mixed.

TOOTH

A term used by painters to describe the light roughness necessary on a surface for adequate paint *adhesion*. A tooth can be cut in a shiny surface by washing with a strong detergent, *sanding*, or by using a commercial deglosser. The flat finish produced by primer paints and flat wall paints has adequate tooth to allow subsequent coats of paint to adhere tightly.

See *Deglossing, Intercoat Adhesion,* and *Intercoat Peeling.*

TOUGHNESS

A term used to describe how well different paints resist wear and tear, scratches, washing, and chipping. As a general rule, the more *resins* in a material, the tougher it is. Because trim enamels and semigloss or glossy paints contain a higher percentage of resin than flat finish paints, they are considered tougher and are more often used in high traffic and heavy-use areas.

See *Abrasion Resistance, Durability*, and *Hardness.*

TRIM

Although the lighter woodwork on your house may not cover much painting area, it often requires more time than the large expanses of walls, ceilings, and floors. Painting trim right involves the most patience and skill of any painting job around the house. Trim is a transition from wall to window, wall to floor, or wall to door. Do not let this seemingly simple function fool you. Trim takes a beating from the weather and the wear and tear of everyday use. To make your paint job last the longest and look its best, do a good job on the trim.

Outside, windows collect water on their sills more readily than the wall. The sun beats down on this trim more than the wall, meaning

Fig. 1

Trim. Use a waterproof trim enamel on interior windows (courtesy National Paint and Coatings Association).

that the meeting of putty, glass, and wood presents a special paint problem. The opening and closing of doors has its effect on the *durability* of the paint on the door and jamb. Additionally, doors receive more than their share of handprints and scuff marks that are difficult to wash off.

Inside, *baseboards*, door jambs, and windows get dirty with grime and grease through normal use. They are washed often, but they are expected to last as long as the less heavily used wall surfaces. Painting them so that they last requires careful preparation in addition to choosing the right paint for the job.

Preparing Previously Painted Interior and Exterior Trim

The first step in preparing previously painted interior trim is a thorough washing with detergent and water. Any dirt or grease that remains should be removed with a rag soaked in *turpentine,* paint *thinner*, or a similiar commercial *solvent*. If the paint remains shiny, sand it with medium or fine paper to cut a *tooth* for the next coat of paint.

While sanding, inspect the woodwork for worn spots, chips, gouges, and water damage. Prime worn spots. Make sure to *feather* edges of paint well into the previous paint. The sharp edges of chips should be sanded smooth, then any bare wood should be spot primed. Gouges should be filled with *wood filler*. Check for cracks and fill any that appear between woodwork and walls or between pieces of trim.

Reset all nails that have worked their way above flush. Fill holes with putty or wood filler.

Moisture-related problems on trim should be corrected by curing the water source. This often involves repairing leaky roofs, plumbing, and moisture barriers. Make the necessary repairs before refinishing woodwork, because even the best paints cannot protect wood that is repeatedly soaked from within the wall.

The inside surfaces of windows often sweat during the winter, causing water to run down onto the trim paint and ruin it. Treat such

Fig. 2

Trim. Paint trim after walls and ceilings have dried (courtesy National Paint and Coatings Association).

areas with a *wood preservative* to reduce the amount of damage. Check into installing storm windows or improving the effectiveness of storm windows to reduce sweating. Use a glossy paint on such windows, because this finish has the best water-resisting characteristics (Fig. 1).

Outside, any areas of trim that have weathered to bare wood should be treated with a wood preservative and then primed before top-coating. Chipping and flaking paint should be removed with scraping and sanding. All bare wood should be primed prior to top-coating. Putty or *glazing* should be replaced after priming and allowed to dry a day or two before top-coating. Make sure to *caulk* around the edges of trim to prevent water from working its way beneath the woodwork.

Painting Over Newly Installed Trim

You may have to paint over newly installed trim. Here are a few steps that insure a good job.

After thoroughly sanding the woodwork, wipe it with a *tack cloth* or a rag soaked in one of the commercial wiping solvents. This removes all dirt and prepares the surface for priming. Prime the surface. Use only the primer needed by the topcoating you plan on using. Enamel primers do more than color the wood. They also seal it and build a surface to which the topcoating adheres. In problem areas such as windows where moisture is prevalent, you may find that a deep penetrating alkyd primer works the best.

After priming, it is time to patch and fill any holes or cracks in the trim. Waiting until after priming to patch prevents the oils in the patching materials from soaking into the wood and becoming excessively dry. Sand patches smooth were necessary, then top-coat.

Many people prefer the look of natural or stained woodwork inside their homes. If your trim has been painted, it is impossible to achieve this look. If your trim has not been finished yet, you can create this look by using a wiping or penetrating stain to color the wood. Staining follows the sanding sequence and is followed by the application of a sealer such as varnish or shellac. On woodwork that has already been stained and varnished, simply sand the varnish to raise a tooth and reapply a coat of varnish.

You can apply an opaque paint over stained and varnished woodwork. Most trim paints stick to varnish, provided it has been thoroughly roughened with sandpaper or a deglossing chemical. A first application of primer both covers the surface with an opaque film and provides a suitable substrate for later topcoats.

The next important step in insuring that trim keeps looking good is choosing the right paint for top-coating. Most manufacturers make what they call trim paint. Really no more than a latex, alkyd, or oil-base glossy or semigloss enamel, this paint is wear and moisture-resistant because of the high percentage of *resin* found in it. When the *vehicle* of trim paint evaporates, a tough shell is left on the surface. The glossy paints have the highest percentage of resins, and this makes them especially suitable for areas where heavy use and frequent washing are necessary considerations for choosing a finish. The semigloss and eggshell paints provide a combination of durability and nonobtrusiveness. In most cases, the less shiny trim paints are preferable, because they do not show irregularities and mistakes as well as glossy paints.

Flat, Semigloss, and Glossy Finishes

Here is a short review of how three types of paint—*flat, semigloss,* and *glossy finishes*—

work on trim. Flat wall paint makes your trim disappear by blending it in with the walls. This can be especially useful in rooms such as the living room where the woodwork does not get much abuse, and you do not want it to stand out. Remember, however, that flat paints are porous. When they get dirty or greasy, it is difficult to remove the dirt, even with scrubbing.

Outside, flat wall paints can be used to make irregularly-shaped windows disappear. You may touch up trim painted with flat paints more often than trim painted with a semigloss or glossy finish.

Semigloss enamels are the most widely used paints for trim, because they combine the unobtrusiveness of flat wall paints and the durability of glossy paints. Semigloss enamels are available in latex, alkyd, and oil-base materials and are colored to match or contrast with almost any wall paint. As with other paints, latex trim enamels are easier to clean up. Alkyd enamels generally provide longer lasting protection, especially in high moisture conditions.

Glossy enamel trim paints make trim really stand out, adding emphasis to a room. Unfortunately, glossy paints do a poor job of hiding imperfections in woodwork. Glossy enamel is a good choice for exterior trim, because it is the most moisture-resistant paint around. It is also the best choice for interior woodwork that takes a lot of physical abuse. Glossy enamels are available in latex, alkyd, and oil-base materials and in many colors. Latex glossy paint, however, is not as shiny as the other two materials.

Painting Techniques

When painting trim, inside or out, it is best to follow the sequence generally used on the remainder of your house. Paint trim after the wall or ceiling paint has dried (Fig. 2). The brushes used for trim painting are smaller, more accurate, and easier to handle than large wall brushes. This reduces the chance of slopping paint onto completed work.

Paint from top to bottom when working on trim. Trim around ceilings and overhangs gets painted first. Windows, doors, *radiators*, and baseboards are then painted. When you have finished the baseboards in a room, keep pets and other family members out of the room. This prevents dust from settling into the fresh paint.

When working outside on ladders, many painters coat the trim during the same set that they coat the walls. When you use a quick-drying latex paint for the walls, it dries by the time you have finished all the area you can reach from the ladder. Climb back to the top and paint the trim. This saves many ladder movements.

When applying trim paints, use slow brush strokes. Check often for skips and sags and cross-brush to insure thorough coverage. Cross-brushing involves putting on the paint with strokes across the width of the board and then smoothing out the paint with strokes along the length of the board.

The size of the trim determines what size brush or pad applicator is necessary for the job. As a rule, you should choose a trim brush or applicator ½ inch narrower than the trim. The natural spreading of the brush or pad does not cause you to get paint beyond the edges of the trim. Keep a rag handy just in case.

See *Brushing Techniques, Casement Windows, Doors, Double-Hung Windows,* and *Paint, Choosing.*

TUNG OIL

A fast drying *vegetable oil* extracted from the seeds of the tung tree. Tung oil is used primarily in varnish and marine paints, because it possesses a greater resistance to water than other vegetable oils. Additionally, this oil has a greater reactivity with varnish resins than other vegetable oils.

TURPENTINE

A colorless, volatile essential oil distilled from pine and other coniferous trees. This strong smelling liquid is used as a solvent in some oil-base paints and varnishes. Because it is expensive, turpentine is used mostly for thinning varnish. Turpentine has been largely replaced by petroleum or benzene *thinner*.

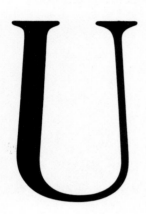

UMBER

A common color used for tinting paints. Reddish-brown to brown in tone, it is available as a universal colorant.

See *Colors*.

URETHANE PAINT

Made from polyurethane or urethane (a crystalline compound used as a solvent) resins. These resins have a tremendous resistance to abrasion, moisture, chemicals, and deterioration caused by the stress associated with the flexing of the surface to which they are applied. Urethane paints come in two forms—those that are ready-mixed and two-component systems. The two-component systems are the most durable of the two types, nearly matching *epoxy paints* for toughness and longevity.

Urethane paints are used widely as industrial coatings for floors and walls that receive much chemical and physical abuse. Around the home, they are often used on porch floors and in utility rooms and workshops where *durability* and moisture resistance are important considerations.

Urethane paints can be applied to bare wood or over latex, alkyd, and oil-base paints. Conversely, alkyd and oil-base paints can be applied over urethane paints, although the surface must be thoroughly roughened with sandpaper before painting. Urethane paints require expensive special solvents for thinning and cleanup. Read the label carefully and follow the directions, because these paints are among the hardest to use.

URETHANE VARNISH

Like urethane paints, urethane varnishes contain urethane resins. These varnishes are the toughest around. Moisture-cured urethane is the toughest varnish.

Urethane varnishes are used on exterior surfaces where a natural look is desired. They can also be used over difficult surfaces such as ceramic tile. Despite their toughness, these varnishes need to be reapplied every 18 to 24 months.

Urethane varnishes require special *solvents* and harden best under ideal temperature and moisture conditions. Read the label carefully. They can be applied with a fine natural bristle brush and require 24 hours of drying time between coats.

See *Polyurethane Varnish* and *Varnishes*.

VARNISHES

Clear finishes made of resinous materials dissolved in an oil-base *solvent*. Basically an on the wood finish, varnish is used to produce a smooth glossy and semigloss surface on wood trim, paneling, furniture, and other decorative wood. There are several types of varnish on the market. Each has a varying degree of moisture and wear resistance. Unfortunately, there is no all-purpose varnish. The one you choose for a particular job depends on the environment in which it exists and the surface material to which it is applied.

Types of Varnish

Acrylic varnish is the best varnish for use on metals. It must be reapplied every year or two for maximum protection.

Alkyd varnish is slightly longer lasting than spar varnish in conditions where salt or salt spray is not present. This varnish is a good choice for use on exterior surfaces.

Epoxy varnish can be applied to raw or painted wood and nonporous materials such as ceramic tile. These varnishes are expensive, difficult to handle, and available in two forms—ready-to-use and two-component mixtures. The two-component system lasts longer than the ready-to-use variety, but is more difficult to handle.

Phenolic varnish is not very durable and should be used only on interior wood surfaces. This varnish has a warm glowing tone and is most suitable for furniture.

Polyurethane varnish is a tough finish commonly used on wood floors. This varnish is resistant to water and alcohol, which makes it a suitable choice for finishing bars and tabletops.

Spar varnish is the most commonly used exterior varnish. It contains added resins that make it resistant to the effects of salt water and weathering. Although spar varnish is widely used on exterior surfaces, it does not last much longer than 18 months. Frequent revarnishing is necessary to keep the surface looking good.

Stain varnish is a combination of stain and

varnish. This coating stains and seals wood in one application; however, it does not last as long or look as good as a stain covered by a separate application of varnish.

Urethane varnishes are the toughest. They are often used on wooden floors. Moisture-cured urethane varnish is the longest lasting type of varnish, but it is expensive and must be applied when conditions are right for proper curing.

Application

Although varnish is a surface coating like paint, unlike paint it requires several coats to build a sufficient thickness for adequate protection. Varnish should be applied following these basic guidelines.

The surface to which varnish is applied must be sanded smooth and wiped free of all dust. Ignoring this fact results in small bumps in the finish. Dust floating in the air also causes bumps in the finish. Clean all surfaces with a *tack cloth* or vacuum before varnishing. Work in as dust-free an area as possible. A further complication of varnish is that it is relatively slow drying. This allows dust and dirt extra time to settle into the work.

Varnish should be applied in several thin coats, with adequate drying and sanding between each coat. Therefore, a varnish job may take several days.

When applying the first coat of varnish to bare wood, thin the varnish with 1 part *turpentine* to 6 parts varnish. This allows the varnish to penetrate the wood and act as a *sealer*. When the first coat is thoroughly dry, sand lightly and brush on a second coat at full strength.

Brushing on varnish requires a slightly different technique than paint. Use only a natural fiber brush—china bristles are the most common choice—and load the brush with more material than if you were using a stan-

dard paint. Make long, smooth strokes with the brush. Repeated short strokes cause bubbles in the coating. These bubbles are difficult to sand out. When using varnish, unlike paint, set the loaded brush down on the wet area and stroke toward the dry surface. This prevents *lap marks* and insures adequate coverage.

To check for skips, look at the varnished surface from a low angle. Dull spots indicate skips. Puddles of varnish should be brushed out immediately before the material becomes tacky.

Sand between coats with fine to very fine sandpaper. Dust carefully with a tack cloth and repeat the application for third and subsequent coats. It is always best to varnish on horizontal surfaces to reduce the chance of runs and *sags*. Final coats of varnish should be applied with the direction of the grain, usually along the length of the wood.

Unfortunately, varnishes are not easy to patch. When damage occurs, it exposes bare wood. When this area is sanded out and recoated, the varnish soaks into the wood and causes a slight dullness. The varnish feathered onto the surrounding varnish dries to a shiny finish. The best thing to do with varnish is to protect it with wax. When it deteriorates to the point of no longer looking good, recoat the whole surface, or at least make the edges of the patched area correspond with natural breaks in the surface. Cracks between floorboards, or joints between door panels and cross members, are examples of natural breaks.

Clean your tools immediately after use in a suitable *thinner*. Some varnishes, notably the epoxies and urethanes, require special solvents for cleanup. Check the can to make sure you have the appropriate thinner before beginning the job.

See *Floors, Wood; Lacquer; Natural Finishes; Shellac;* and *Stains.*

VEGETABLE OILS

The oils pressed from the seeds of castor, linseed, safflower, soybeans, and tung plants are widely used in the *vehicle* of oil-base varnishes, stains, and paints. These *drying oils* bind paint *solids* and *pigments* together before evaporating. They are being replaced by man-made oils in alkyd and latex paints.

See *Linseed Oil, Safflower Oil, Soybean Oil,* and *Tung Oil.*

VEHICLE

The term used for the liquid part of a coating. During the manufacturing process, *binders, resins,* and pigments are suspended or dissolved in the coating's vehicle. When the coating is applied to a surface, the vehicle evaporates, leaving behind a film of paint. When you add *thinner* or *solvent* to a paint, you are adding more vehicle.

The type of vehicle in a paint determines what type of paint it is. For example, oil-base paints contain *vegetable oils*, latex paints contain water-base vehicles, and shellac has an alcohol vehicle. The specialized vehicles in *epoxy paints, lacquers,* and *wood preservatives* require special solvents for thinning and cleanup. Read the label carefully on special vehicle coatings to make sure you do not mix an incompatible solvent or thinner into the coating that will destroy its effectiveness.

VISCOSITY

The ability of the coating to resist flow. *One-coat paints* have a high viscosity (some are so thick that you can stand a stirring stick up in them). Stains are not very viscous and run like water.

The viscosity of a paint is related to its function. Surface coatings, like exterior house paint, are thicker than coatings designed to soak into a surface. Most paints are manufactured and canned at the proper viscosity for their intended use. In most cases they should not be thinned, because thinning alters their characteristics and may cause problems with durability.

VOLATILE

When used in painting, the term means that the liquid evaporates. Volatile fluids are used as the *vehicle* for all coatings and thinners. They evaporate after application, leaving behind a paint film.

VOLUME SOLIDS

A reference found on paint can labels giving the amount of *solids, pigments, resins* and *extenders* in the coating. It is usually expressed as a percentage of the total paint volume. The volume of solids is directly related to the film thickness a material builds. One-coat exterior house paints have the highest volume of solids and build a thick paint film. Stains have very few solids and leave little material on the surfaces to which they are applied.

See *Binders.*

WAINSCOTING

When the lower 3 or 4 feet of an interior wall is lined with paneling, tile, or other material that is different from the rest of the wall, the bottom section is called wainscot. Most wood wainscoting is finished with a stain and then top-coated with a varnish. Wainscoting can also be painted. Enamel trim paint is the most common choice.

See *Trim*.

WALLS, PATCHING

An important part of every interior paint job is patching the cracks, holes, and gouges that accumulate in walls and ceilings through normal wear and tear. Cracks normally occur as the house settles on its foundation, or because of the uneven expansion and contraction of two sections of wall. Gouges and holes result from such physical abuses as hitting the walls with furniture while it is being moved. Damaged walls must be repaired in all cases, because even the best paints do not hide such imperfections.

Repairing walls has been made much easier by the introduction of ready-mixed vinyl *spackling compounds*. These pastes have excellent adhesion to wood, plaster, masonry, drywall, and other wall materials. Spackling can be used on all but the largest holes. Vinyl spackling is particularly useful when patching cracks between two dissimiliar materials like wood and masonry. Vinyl spackles have a low rate of shrinkage and can be painted over with latex paint as soon as their surface is dry to the touch. These obvious advantages make vinyl spackles the most popular choice of both professionals and amateurs for repairing small cracks, holes, and gouges in walls.

Vinyl spackling is not the only material available for repairing walls. Vinyl does not work on holes several inches in diameter.

187

Drywall joint cement, plaster of paris, and water-mixed putty all have uses when repairing walls. If you are repairing many walls in your home, buying vinyl spackling may be prohibitively expensive. A good substitute in this case is drywall joint cement.

The first step in patching large holes is chipping away loose plaster, drywall, or old patches with a putty knife or chisel. Hairline cracks hold a patch better if they are widened first with the corner of your putty knife or a can opener. See the illustration.

Cracks about ⅛ inch wide do not need to be widened. They can be filled satisfactorily with spackling compound and smoothed over with a putty knife or taping blade. Many professionals like to prepare the crack by brushing it with a water-wetted brush before applying the patching material. This reduces the tendency of the wall material from absorbing too much moisture from the patching material, thereby allowing it to set up properly.

Larger cracks, ¼ inch or more, should have an inverted "V" cut under the edges so the patching material has a lip of sound material to key under. Use the edge of a putty knife or a utility knife to make this undercut. The reasoning behind this procedure is to give the patching material a footing, so it does not fall out of the crack. Holes an inch or more across should be treated with this undercutting.

Very large cracks should be repaired in two stages, because patching material shrinks when applied in substantial amounts. Work the first application into the crack and smooth somewhat, leaving a little roughness on the surface so the next application has something to hold onto. When the first application is dry, apply a second layer, build it up level with the wall surface, and smooth with a putty knife or taping knife.

For all these methods, allow the patches

to dry thoroughly, then sand smooth with circular motions. The patches need to be primed and then coated with at least one layer of topcoating, so they blend in with the rest of the wall.

When using patching compounds, do not wash excess material down the drain. The material is likely to harden and clog the plumbing.

When patching textured surfaces, try to match the surface with your patch. On stippled surfaces, lay the flat of your putty knife on the

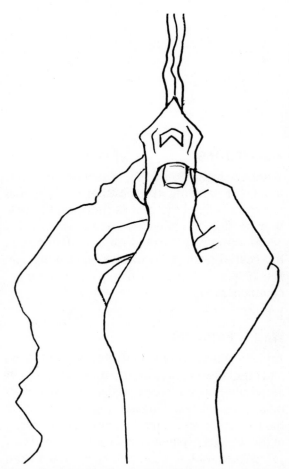

Walls, Patching. Hairline cracks hold spackling compound better when widened with a can opener.

patch and pull away to raise little stipples that match the surrounding area. On surfaces, especially ceilings, that have been sand finished, you can add a little fine sand or texture additive to the skin, or topcoating, of the patch. With a little practice, you can match the surface texture of your walls rather closely.

WATER REPELLENTS

There are two types of water repellents—those designed for wood surfaces and those designed for *masonry*. Both seal the pores in the material to which they are applied, so *moisture* cannot penetrate the surface. They can be applied with brush, roller, or spray. Brushing works best, because it works the material into cracks and holes effectively. Rolling and spraying speed up the job considerably.

Water repellents for wood usually contain paraffin or wax dissolved in a *drying oil* or *solvent* such as *turpentine* or *mineral spirits*. Many contain mildewcides and *fungicides* such as pentachlorophenol. Because these finishes resist the *adhesion* of paint, they are normally used on siding where a *natural finish* is desired. They are especially effective on redwood and cedar where paints are subject to *staining through* and penetrating stains hide the beauty of the wood.

In most cases, an initial application of two coats of water repellent is necessary to effectively reduce warping and cracking associated with weathering. Additional coats can be applied when the wood begins to darken.

Water repellents that contain mildewcides and fungicides are toxic and should only be applied outside. Wear gloves, goggles, and long sleeves when applying them. Cover all nearby plants to prevent defoliation.

Water repellents for masonry usually contain a silicone resin. These materials build a film on the surface, preventing the intrusion of water that reduces the effects of *alkali* and *efflorescence*. Water repellents usually do not stop moisture problems or plug leaky walls. They also resist paint and are most suited for use on brickwork where the natural look of the wall is desired.

See *Sealer* and *Wood Preservatives*.

WAX REMOVAL

Removing wax from trim before refinishing can be accomplished through two methods—chemical or mechanical.

Chemical wax removal is accomplished by loosening the wax with *turpentine,* paint *thinner*, or a wax remover. Cover the surface with one of these materials and spread it around. Allow to stand until the wax is soft and can be wiped up easily with a clean rag. Steel wool helps dislodge stubborn patches. A thorough wiping with a *solvent*-soaked rag completes the job. Remember that thinners, turpentine, and solvents are flammable and should not be used near open flames or sparks.

The mechanical method of wax removal involves sanding off the wax and the first layer of the substrate's finish. Begin with a medium sandpaper, but apply light pressure to prevent damage to the wood. Switch to a fine paper for the second pass. Dust thoroughly with a *tack cloth* or vacuum before applying a new finish.

See *Paint, Removing*.

WEATHERING

Weathering of wood involves a change in color, roughening and checking of the surface, loosening of the surface fibers, and warping. Wood is also attacked by microorganisms during the weathering process.

The weathered look of wood has gained popularity in the last several years. Many manufacturers market *stains* and preservatives designed to produce a weathered look while protecting the wood. Some people prefer the stained appearance, while others like the real thing.

Without paint or treatment, wood exposed outdoors changes in appearance. The time required to produce a fully weathered appearance depends on the exposure to sun and rain. Dark-colored woods usually become lighter, and light-colored woods usually become a little darker. Eventually, most woods become gray. After the initial change, wood remains the same color for a long time.

Most homeowners prefer to allow their siding to weather before application of a natural finish. This is a good idea, because weathered wood takes penetrating finishes such as stain much more readily than new wood. Eventually, boards warp and pull loose if not treated with a *water repellent* or other *natural finish*. Nails used in natural-look siding should be rustproof. Stainless steel or aluminum nails are the best.

See *Shakes and Shingles* and *Wood Preservatives*.

WHITEWASHING

This liquid composition for whitening a surface has just about been replaced as a coating by modern latex and alkyd paints. Whitewash is inexpensive and easy to apply. Whitewash is most widely used on the farm. Brightens the interior of barns and service buildings.

To prepare surfaces for whitewashing, remove all dirt, scale, and loose materials by scraping or brushing with a wire brush. For most whitewashing jobs, further surface preparation is not necessary.

Dampen walls before applying whitewash. Unlike most paints, whitewash application and adhesion are improved when the surface is damp. Whitewash may be brushed or sprayed on. When brushing, use a stiff whitewash brush. When spraying, strain the mix through three layers of cheesecloth before pouring into the machine. During application, remember that two coats are better than one coat that is too thick.

The first step in making whitewash is mixing a lime paste. Protect your eyes and skin during mixing. Lime paste is prepared by soaking 50 pounds of hydrated lime in 6 gallons of water. Refined limes such as chemical hydrate, agricultural spray hydrate, finishing lime, and pressure hydrated lime have fewer lumps and make a smoother paste.

Different mixes of whitewash are suggested for various surface materials. For wood, dissolve 15 pounds of salt in 5 gallons of water. Add this solution to 8 gallons of lime paste, stirring constantly. Thin the preparation to desired consistency with fresh water. To reduce *chalking*, use 5 pounds of calcium chloride instead of salt.

For brick, concrete, or stone, add 25 pounds of white portland cement and 25 pounds of hydrated lime to 8 gallons of water. Mix thoroughly to a thick slurry. Thin to the consistency of thick cream. Mix only enough for a few hours use. You can reduce chalking by adding 1 or 2 pounds of calcium chloride, dissolved in a small amount of water, to the mix just before use.

For plaster, soak 5 pounds of *casein* in 2 gallons of water until thoroughly soft—about two hours. Dissolve 3 pounds of trisodium phosphate in 1 gallon of water, add this solution to lime paste, and allow the mixture to dissolve. The mixture will heat. When cool, add the casein solution to the lime paste, stirring constantly.

Because whitewash contains caustic chemicals, gloves, goggles, and long sleeves should be worn while handling the material. Tools can be cleaned with running water.

WHITING

A finely ground chalk. It is used to color *putty*, *whitewash*, and some paints white.

WINDOWS

Whether you are painting on the interior or exterior of your house, windows can be a difficult painting problem. The secret to doing a professional job on windows is to apply the right paint with the correct tool. In most cases, an angular sash tool works best. Some of the new trim pad *applicators* work effectively. *Glossy* or *semigloss finish* trim paints are the most common paints for use on wooden windows. Metal windows last longer if coated with a metal paint.

There are two basic types of windows— *double-hung* and *casement*. Double-hung windows are most common in frame houses. They are made with two sashes that slide up and down within the window's casing. The sashes are held in place by a jamb that is wood in the older windows and aluminum in the newer ones.

Casement windows swing in or out instead of up and down and are often found in stone, brick, and masonry homes. These windows are usually made of a metal such as aluminum or steel.

WOOD ALCOHOL

Also known as methanol or methyl alcohol. It is used as a *vehicle* in *shellac*, alcohol *stains*, and *sealers*. Its primary use in painting is thinning these materials. Wood alcohol is flammable and very toxic. It should be used in areas with adequate ventilation and no exposure to open flame or sparks.

WOOD-BURNING STOVES

Wood-burning stoves, barbecues, stovepipes,

fireplace screens and grates, and furnaces can be painted with special stove or heat-resistant paints. Most heat-resistant paints for home use come in aerosol spray cans. Brushable, heat-resistant metal paints are also available. These paints contain metallic oxides of copper, chrome, or magnesium in combination with silicates, silicone resins, and hydrocarbons. Many of these paints withstand temperatures of up to 1,200 degrees Fahrenheit. None can withstand direct contact with flame, so it is a waste of time and paint to paint surfaces in direct contact with open flame.

The selection of a paint is important, because inferior paints produce shabby jobs subject to blistering, peeling, and flaking. Talk

Wood-Burning Stoves. Special heat-resistant paints can be used to refinish wood stoves, fireplace screens, and barbecues.

with paint salesmen, friends, or wood stove, fireplace, and outdoor grill dealers about choosing a paint.

All surfaces should be cool—room temperature—and clean before painting. Wire brush loose paint and rust from surfaces. On extremely rusty surfaces, a heat-resistant primer does a better job. Grease can be removed with a *solvent*-soaked rag. Dust or vacuum thoroughly. Repair cracks with a furnace cement. Allow the cement to cure several days before painting. When all other preparations are completed, mask hardware and controls not to be painted with *masking tape*.

When using an aerosol paint, shake according to the can's instructions and test the spray on a piece of cardboard before working on the stove. When you begin painting, start with the hard-to-reach surfaces such as around latches and the backs of legs. Paint indentations or seams before finishing with the flat areas. See the illustration. Keep the can moving to prevent runs. When finished spraying, clean the nozzle by holding the can upside down and depressing the button until the spray comes out clear.

The same order should be followed when working with a brush-applied paint. Remember that two thin coats give better and longer lasting results than one thick coat.

Many heat-resistant paints require heat to cure the paint. During this curing process, the paint is likely to give off toxic fumes. Do not wait until the first cold day to cure the paint.

WOOD FILLERS

There are two basic uses of wood fillers. The first is filling nail holes, gouges, cracks, and other obvious defects in wood. The second is sealing the pores in wood surfaces to make sanding and sealing easier.

Wood fillers come in a variety of consistencies—from liquids through pastes to powders. This wide selection of wood fillers permits use on many types of wood. The choice of filler is guided by its intended use.

Liquid

Liquid wood fillers are used on raw wood surfaces to close the pores and make sanding easier. They are especially useful for filling the open pores of walnut, mahogany, and oak.

These fillers can be brushed directly on the surface without thinning. When the filler has dried, it is sanded with a fine sandpaper. Because fillers do not protect the wood, they should be top-coated with a sealer and then varnished or shellacked to produce a durable natural-looking finish.

If you want to stain the wood, it is usually best to apply the stain before filling. You may be able to stain and fill in one operation by mixing the stain with the filler. (Check the manufacturer's suggestions on both products to insure compatibility.)

Paste

Paste fillers are generally reserved for filling wood floors. These fillers are a combination of *resins* and *pigments* that fill the cracks and pores to produce a very smooth surface for the topcoating. Unfortunately, paste fillers should not be used under shellac or lacquer, as these topcoatings may soften the filler and reduce wear resistance.

These type fillers come as a thick paste when purchased. The paste is thinned with *turpentine* or *solvent* recommended by the manufacturer and then applied to a sanded bare wood surface with a brush or trowel. When brushing, apply against the grain and then with it. Allow the filler to dry some until it begins to dull. Wipe the remaining filler off with a clean rag. When troweling, spread the material across the boards with the flat edge of the tool, then stroke along the length of the boards. Wipe up excess with a clean cloth, after the filler has dried to a dull sheen. Rub hard, because you want the filler to remain only in the pores and cracks. After the filler has dried, sand with fine or very fine paper prior to top-coating.

Powders

Powdered wood fillers are mixed with water right before use. This type of filler is inexpensive and most widely used in large cracks and holes in a house's exterior walls. Because the water in this material raises a grain on wood, it is not recommended for use on fine interior work. After the patch has dried, it must be sanded smooth and sealed before application of a primer and topcoat. This material accepts stain readily and can be colored after it is dry, but before sealing, to match the surrounding wood.

Putty

Putty wood fillers are the most widely used. They are a ready-to-use mixture of resins and solvents that stick tight in holes, cracks, and gouges. They are most often used to fill nail holes and small cracks in woodwork, because they do not contain water that might raise a grain.

Putty wood fillers should be worked completely into the defect and left with a little of the material above the surface of the surrounding wood. After the fillers dry, they can be sanded smooth, sealed, and top-coated along with the remainder of the surface. Mix a little stain with these materials to get them to match stained woods.

These materials are also useful for filling the knots in woods such as pine. If the knots

are loose, remove them. Fill the hole with a putty wood filler and leave a slight bulge. When dry, sand smooth and stain to match the surrounding wood. When the stain has dried, seal and finish with an appropriate topcoating.

See *Block Filler, Knots in Wood, Putty, Sealer,* and *Spackling Compounds.*

WOOD PRESERVATIVES

Liquid chemical compounds that soak into wood and protect it against fungus, *mildew*, decay, and insects. This material also slows but does not stop the weathering of the wood. Wood preservatives are especially useful on wood that is exposed to excess *moisture* and near or in contact with the ground. Wood gutters, trellises, door and window frames, and sills are some common places where wood preservatives can be used.

Wood preservatives can be brushed, rolled, or sprayed on. Brushing works the material in more thoroughly, while spraying and rolling save time. Spraying may not apply enough material, and the overspray could damage nearby foliage. The best method for applying a wood preservative is to soak the wood in the liquid for several hours or overnight.

Some wood preservatives, usually the ones with a water or light oil-base, are designed to be painted over or stained. Others, such as those made with creosote and heavy oil bases, cannot be painted over and are used where no further topcoat is desired. Read the preservative's label carefully to make sure it performs the way you want.

Wood preservatives contain powerful chemicals that can be injurious to man, animals, and plants. Keep pets away when using these materials and wear gloves, goggles, and long sleeves. Do not spill these materials on the ground, because many are root-poisonous to plants. The fumes from preservatives are toxic and flammable, so they should be used outside away from flame.

See *Creosote, Natural Finishes, Stains* and *Water Repellents.*

WROUGHT IRON

A commercial form of iron that contains little carbon. Next to aluminum *downspouts and gutters,* wrought iron is probably the most common metal around a house. The secret to attractive wrought iron is keeping the metal coated with a waterproof and airproof coating of paint.

There are two types of paint systems used on wrought iron—a primer followed by a topcoating and a combination primer topcoating metal paint. The latter is used when repairs are small, and it is an effective method of keeping paint defects from spreading. Wire brush all flakes, soft spots, and powdered rust down to sound metal. You do not need to see shiny metal, but it helps. Then spot paint with a metal paint that matches the paint already on the wrought iron.

If the rust on your wrought iron is out of control, use a two-coat system. Remove all rust and flaking paint with sandpaper, scraper, wire brush, or a wire brush attachment for an electric drill. Dust thoroughly. Coat all surfaces with a read lead or zinc-base primer. When the primer has dried, finish with a topcoat of oilbase, alkyd exterior trim paint, or a glossy metal paint.

A trim brush is the easiest to handle when working on wrought iron, especially if it has many ornamental twists and turns. You may find that the convenience of painting wrought iron with a *mitten applicator* is worth the extra pint or two of paint that this method uses. Spraying may also be an option, although most of the paint is lost to *overspray.*

See *Metals* and *Rust Removal.*

YELLOWING

A term used to describe the process of a white paint turning yellow with age. Yellowing is usually a problem only on flat exterior house paints. The paint defect is a natural result of the aging of the small amounts of *vehicle* left in a paint film.

Yellowing can be prevented by using latex paints or by choosing oil-base and alkyd paints that contain nonyellowing vehicles. *Soybean* and *safflower oils* are noted for their resistance to yellowing.

See *Color Retention* and *Fading*.

PART 2
WALLCOVERING

ALL-OVER DESIGN

One of the most popoular styles of wallcovering. Usually of a floral theme, all-over designs reach from ceiling to floor and from one wall to another with a pattern that evenly covers the wallcovering's surface.

See *Patterns*.

B

BASKET WEAVE DESIGN

An embossed or printed effect in wallcoverings that resembles the over-under look of weaving. Some wallcoverings, burlap, and grass cloth contain an actual basket weave.

See *Patterns*.

BOLT

The term used to specify the quantity of material contained in a commercially available package of wallcovering. Commercial packages can be one, two, three, or four-roll bolts. Although the number of rolls in a bolt varies, manufacturers are uniform on the amount of covering in a roll. A single roll contains 36 square feet of material. Rolls are available in varying widths. To keep the area of material in a roll constant, wider rolls are shorter and narrow rolls are longer. Most manufacturers suggest figuring 30 square feet of coverage per roll. Six feet of material are sacrificed to *trimming*, matching patterns, and mistakes.

See *Estimating Quantity of Material*.

BOOKING

The practice of folding pasted surface to pasted surface during the pasting phase of wallcovering hanging. See the illustration. To book a wallcovering, spread paste on the backside of one-half of a strip of wallcovering. Fold the end toward the center so that paste lays on paste. Repeat for the opposite end. The section of the strip that covers the wall's top should overlap considerably more than the end that covers the wall's bottom. This prevents a mix-up later when you hang the covering. Folding the wallcovering in this manner allows you to handle the paper easily without fear of getting paste all over your hands and clothing. It also has the advantage of allowing the covering to relax and loosen up before application.

BORDERS

Narrow strips of decorative wallcovering that are used along the ceiling and around windows and doors. See the illustration. Borders are not sold in bolts. Instead, they are sold by length,

Booking. Booking is the paper hanger's term for folding a strip of wallcovering pasted side to pasted side.

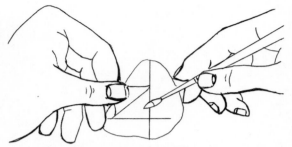

Bubbles. To repair bubbles in a wallcovering, cut an "X" in the defect. Apply paste with an artist's brush. Press flaps back into place.

regardless of width. Most stores offer many pleasing matches for standard wallcoverings.

BUBBLES

Bubbles of air occasionally form under a wallcovering. The most common cause of bubbles is improper pasting. In most cases, a spot is missed during pasting. After the material is hung, air collects in the loose area, forcing the covering from the wall and ruining its flat appearance. Fortunately, these mistakes can be easily corrected.

To repair bubbles, simply cut an "X" in the bubble with a razor knife. See the illustration. It is best to cut along the lines of the covering's pattern whenever possible. On pat-

terns with many curves, make cuts that follow the curves. After cutting, moisten the area with a clean damp sponge to make the material flexible. Carefully lift each flap and apply adhesive to the flap's underside. An artist's brush or cotton swab is handy for this procedure. Take care not to pull the flap back so far that it stretches, folds, or tears. Fold the flaps down one at a time, realigning the pattern as well as possible. Press the flaps into place with a seam roller. After a few minutes, remove excess paste with a sponge. Take care not to pull the flaps loose. As the covering dries, it shrinks slightly, tightening up the patch.

See *Tears*.

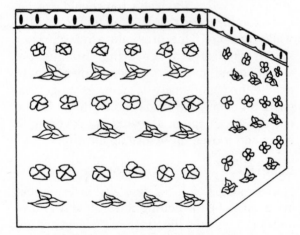

Borders. Borders add an extra touch to wallcoverings.

BUTT JOINT

Formed when the edge of one strip of wallcovering is positioned so that it butts the edge of the previous strip.

The butt joint is the most often used and best looking of all wallcovering seams. Butt joints are best made with coverings that have had their selvages trimmed off at the factory or wallcovering store. Most coverings come pretrimmed, but you may buy one that is not. Ask the salesman to trim the extra paper.

To make butt seams, work the second strip of covering against the first, using pressure applied with the palms of your hands.

Avoid pulling the covering by the edge, as this stretches the covering and ruins the seam. The two pieces should butt as tight as possible. Always roll the joint with a seam roller 10 to 15 minutes after completion of the joint. Sponge off excess paste and move on to the next piece. The butt joint disappears as the wallcovering dries.

See *Lapped Seams* and *Wire Edge*.

CEILINGS

Ceilings are seldom finished with coverings today, because the variety of colored flat paints makes adding color to a ceiling easy. In most cases, it is much easier to paint a ceiling. If you insist on a patterned ceiling, be prepared for a difficult and exacting job, particularly in rooms where the ceiling is not square.

When choosing a covering for a ceiling, select a pattern very carefully. Sometimes the pattern ends up upside down or sideways on three out of four corners where the ceiling meets the wall. This discrepancy is especially noticeable if you decide to cover both ceiling and walls with the same material. To avoid such awkward combinations, choose a different pattern for ceiling and walls when covering both.

When choosing a color for the ceiling, remember the effect different shades have on the apparent height of the room. Selecting a light covering raises the apparent height of low ceilings, while a dark paper lowers the apparent height of the ceiling. Another way of affecting the ceiling's apparent height is choosing vertical patterns on walls for raising low ceilings and horizontal patterns on walls for lowering high ceilings.

Preparation

After selecting a style of covering and *estimating quantity of material* you need to prepare the ceiling for covering in the same manner that you would prepare a wall. The ceiling must be clean, smooth, and have a coat of *sizing* before covering. Remove light fixtures, or at least unfasten them so that they hang away from the ceiling. Protect floors with drop cloths or newspapers. If you have *cornice* trim between the ceiling and wall, this should be painted prior to hanging the covering. In most cases, it is painted the same color as the wall.

You can make the job of working on the ceiling easier by constructing a walk board. Place a 2 by 12-inch plank across the steps of two stepladders. Adjust the height so your head nearly reaches the ceiling (Fig. 1). It is nearly impossible to cover a ceiling by yourself, so enlist a helper for the job.

Plan to work across the shortest width of the ceiling. This reduces the total length of each strip of covering and gives you more frequent stopping points to rest your arms.

Because a plumb bob obviously does not work for marking a starting point on your ceiling, you have to use a different method. Choose the end of the room with the straightest ceiling and wall corner. Measure out from the corner 1 inch less than the total width of your covering. Make a pencil mark. Move to the opposite wall, repeat the measurement, and make another mark. Tack a

chalk line between the two marks. Snap the line to leave a mark, then remove the string. The mark is your reference point. The excess inch of covering laps down off the ceiling, onto the wall, and is trimmed off later.

Hanging Strips

Cut a strip of covering at least 2 inches longer, on each end, than the width of the ceiling. Paste it as you would a wallcovering, but fold it up accordion style to facilitate handling (Fig. 2). An accordion fold alternates back and forth, pasted side to pasted side, instead of folding both ends toward the center as in *booking*. The accordion fold allows you to unfold a small amount of material at a time and

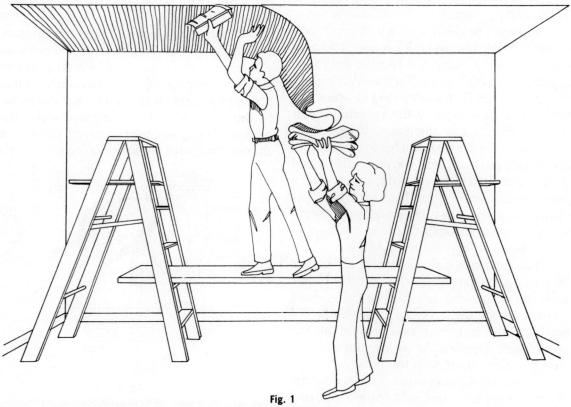

Fig. 1

Ceilings. Construct a scaffold and enlist a helper when covering a ceiling.

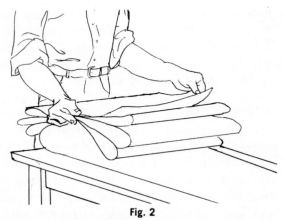

Fig. 2

Ceilings. Fold wallcoverings for ceilings pasted side to pasted side in an accordion fold.

smooth it onto the ceiling. Allow the coverin to relax several minutes before trying to put it on the ceiling.

When you begin, leave a 2-inch overlap on the wall. Work the paper, a section at a time, onto the ceiling. Keep the edge of the paper aligned on the chalk mark. Pat the covering just enough to keep it in place. Do not press too hard, so you can remove the covering if you need to change the alignment. Your helper should stand on the floor and feed you a section of covering at a time, until you reach the far end of the room. When the covering appears to be positioned properly, go back and brush it firmly into place with a *smoothing brush.* Begin at the center of the strip and work toward the edges. Keep an eye out for bubbles.

You can make a clean seam at the corner by pushing the covering well into the corner with the smoothing brush. Mark the exact corner and pull the covering loose. Cut a "V" notch into the corner with the point of the "V" at the mark. Replace the paper, smoothing it well into the corner with the brush.

If you are planning to paper the walls, trim off excess paper on the ends of the strip, so 1 inch of paper laps down onto the wall. Smooth

firmly into place. If you plan to paint the walls, trim the excess off in the crack with a cutting wheel or trimming knife guided by a straight-edge.

When all trimming is completed, smooth the covering with a clean, slightly damp roller or a broom covered with a rag. Work the roller from the center to the edges of the material with short forceful strokes. Be careful not to wrinkle the covering. Finish by running a roller or broom from one end of the strip to the other, making all movements in only one direction.

To hang the second strip, repeat the steps just covered for the first piece. When you encounter fixtures or obstructions, trim the covering to fit with scissors, leaving an inch overlap.

When you approach a light fixture, mark the center of the receptacle on the covering. Cut the material with an "X" just large enough to allow passage of the obstruction. Finish placing the strip on the ceiling and come back to the receptacle. Using a razor knife, trim around the edges of the receptacle and smooth the covering onto the surrounding surface. Re-

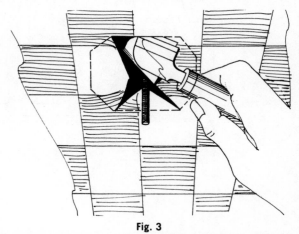

Fig. 3

Ceilings. Trim around ceiling obstructions after the covering is in place.

place the receptacle while you have the equipment set up to reach it.

When you reach an obstruction that cannot be removed, cut into the covering from the nearest edge until you come to a point that corresponds with the fixture's center. Cut out a series of triangular cuts, so the remaining wedges have their points in the center of the fixture and their base around the perimeter of the receptacle. Work the covering over the fixture, so it lies flat on the ceiling. Finish positioning the remainder of the strip before coming back to the receptacle. Use scissors to cut an opening around the fixture that leaves about an inch of overhang. Press the covering in place against the joint formed by the fixture and the ceiling. Trim this joint with a razor knife (Fig. 3). Roll the edges of the cut with a seam roller. Trim the ends of the strip and then roll the entire strip, using firm pressure to secure it in place.

About 10 minutes after each strip is hung, go back and roll the seam between it and the previous strip with a seam roller. After the entire ceiling has dried, roll on a *conditioner*, if the covering calls for it, and the job is completed.

See *Corners, Cove Ceiling,* and *Order of Hanging.*

CELLULOSE PASTE

A nonstaining, odorless adhesive made from plant fibers. It is used chiefly for hanging coverings made of natural materials such as silk and linen.

See *Paste* and *Wheat Paste.*

CHOOSING WALLCOVERINGS

Choosing a wallcovering can be more difficult than choosing a paint. Wallcoverings come in an almost infinite variety of *colors, patterns,* and *materials.* With a little forethought and

prior planning, you can choose a wallcovering that produces professional results. Nearly 60 percent of the wallcoverings bought in America are hung by homeowners.

Wallcoverings are designed to offer an alternative to the monotones of painted walls, but beware of overdoing it. A house that has every room finished with a wallcovering may be too busy. You may suffer from an overabundance of pattern and design without the soothing effect of painted walls. You can choose to cover only certain rooms or cover only a wall or two in each room.

Colors and Patterns

Also, remember that the colors and patterns of a covering affect your mood in the same manner that different hues and colors of paint do. As a general rule, rooms in which you spend little time can stand more patterns than rooms where a large portion of your time is spent. In terms of breaking up monotony, rooms with many windows, doors, shelves, pictures, or a fireplace may be better left painted. These objects provide patterns of varying texture in themselves.

If walls are bumpy, ceiling lines are uneven, or there are other architectural difficulties, stay away from coverings with stripes and straight line designs. These materials and patterns draw attention to the defects. Embossed textures or an *all-over design* can cover up many minor irregularities in the walls.

Colors that contrast—say a light with a dark tone—work together more successfully than those with hues of nearly the same intensity. A unique effect can be achieved with one of the new wall *murals* that are capable of bringing a part of the great outdoors within your home.

Patterns can be used to alter the appearance of a room or hallway. Active patterns brighten a dull room, while a solid texture mellows the mood of active rooms. Strong vertical patterns can be used to make a short room look taller. Conversely, horizontal patterns make narrow rooms look wider. Light colors can enlarge a room, and dark colors shrink a room.

When deciding on a store for buying wallcoverings, choose one with trained sales people. They know decorating tricks that can aid you in blending wallcoverings with the remainder of your decorating scheme. Try to take along a swatch of carpet or drapery material to help make shopping easier. When you look at coverings, inspect them in natural and artificial light.

Always choose a pattern that you like, because the covering is in place many years. If you can, borrow a sample of the covering you intend to buy, so you can look at it while you are home. You can also buy a single roll of the covering, bring it home, and tack it in place. Live with it a couple of weeks to make sure it appeals to you.

When choosing a covering, remember that the pattern and color of the material are not the only factors on which a selection is based. Think also of the use for each room. Does the room get heavy use like a child's playroom? Then choose a washable and tough covering. Is elegance a factor like in the living room? Choose a finer hand-printed paper or a flocked design. In bathrooms and kitchens where moisture is a consideration, choose a waterproof and easy-to-clean material.

Covering Classifications

Remember the following rough classifications of coverings (listed in descending order of durability).

Fabric-backed vinyls are the toughest of the commonly used wallcoverings. Although

expensive and a little difficult for an inexperienced person to hang, vinyl coverings are scuff-resistant and easier to wash than paint. Unbacked vinyl and vinyl-coated papers afford slightly reduced washability and toughness, but are easier to hang. Most vinyl coverings come in prepasted and strippable forms that make hanging and removal easy.

Fabric wallcoverings afford the same basic capabilities as papers, although they are slightly thicker and harder to cut. These coverings should be hung over *lining paper* and can be cleaned with dry cleaning fluids or cleaning powders.

Paper coverings are made in three basic materials—untreated, vinyl-backed, and cloth-backed. The untreated papers are recommended for first time hanging. They are inexpensive and easy to cut, paste, and hang. Wallpaper withstands moderate wear, but it is susceptible to staining even when coated with a *conditioner.* Cloth-backed papers are strippable.

Burlap and grass cloth wallcoverings provide a soft textured finish. Burlap is considerably more durable than the grass cloths. Both need to be hung over a lining paper, so they are protected from excess moisture. Moisture can cause the fibers in these materials to swell and separate from their backing. Both are susceptible to grease stains.

Cork coverings come on a backing of fabric or burlap. They should be hung over lining paper. Little maintenance is required beyond an occasional vacuuming.

Foils and flocks are the most difficult and fragile wallcoverings to hang. Hanging these materials is best left in the hands of a professional. Foils tear easily and show irregularities in the wall. They should be hung over lining papers. The fuzzy surface of flocked papers requires a careful hand with the paste brush to keep the flock from becoming matted. These coverings should be hung over lining papers. Because these coverings are highly susceptible to damage through excessive rubbing and grease, they should be used only where they are not exposed to heavy use.

When choosing a covering, consider purchasing one with a *prepasted* back. This eliminates the job of mixing and applying paste prior to hanging.

Another consideration is the covering's width. As a rule, the narrower width coverings are easier to hang—especially around windows, doors, and other irregularities. Wider papers produce fewer seams and result in a cleaner look.

When choosing among patterns, you find two different methods of production—machine-printed and hand-printed. Machine prints, within the same lot number, have identical colors throughout the pattern, because they are printed in a continuous "run" of the machine. This production method produces a uniform pattern that is easy to match.

Hand-printed designs are produced by silk screening. They are more expensive and fragile than machine-printed coverings. Colors are not closely matched and may require some juggling to get the varying shades and patterns to match. Most hand-printed coverings come with untrimmed edges to protect them during transportation.

Textured patterns like woven grass and burlap, embossed papers, and flocking have subtle changes in shade and intensity from roll to roll. The fibers composing these materials do not respond uniformly to dyes, so changes in shading are present. To avoid abrupt changes where two rolls meet (especially with grass coverings), alternate the top and bottom of each strip as you hang it. The lighter shade on the bottom of a strip more closely matches

the bottom of the next, because they were close together on the roll.

See *Color Run, Stain-Resistant Wallcoverings,* and *Strippable Wallcoverings.*

CLEANING WALLCOVERINGS

You can add years of functional good looks to a wallcovering with periodic cleaning. The method of cleaning wallcoverings depends on the material of the covering and the type of blemish. If you are not sure what to use for cleaning a particular covering, take a sample back to the store and ask the salesman to suggest a cleaning agent.

Vinyl wallcoverings and treated cloths are the most washable and can usually be cleaned with a mild soap and water. Never use abrasive cleaners—even on the toughest wallcoverings. Do not use household wood cleaners, especially those that contain petroleum distillates. Always rinse what you have cleaned with cold, clean water. Although vinyl materials withstand a liberal application of elbow grease, experiment with the cleaning solution in a hidden corner of the room before working on exposed areas. If the cleaner and covering are not compatible, the mistake is not as noticeable.

When cleaning vinyl coverings, keep your sponge as dry as possible and wash only a small area at a time. When working on porous materials such as wallpaper, work from the baseboard to the ceiling. Water does not run down into the dirty covering and cause streaks that are difficult to remove.

Fabric-covered walls can be washed like vinyl coverings, but test a small area first. Grass cloth, burlap, and rice papers are not generally washable, but they can be treated with paper cleaners.

For wallpapers, there are many spot cleaners, putties, spray cleaners, and dry powder cleaners on the market. These materials are easier on the paper than a sponge, detergent, and water. They reduce the chance of moisture-induced peeling. Follow the instructions carefully and test these materials in a hidden spot to make sure they do not cause the paper to bleed or bleach.

Grease and oil stains are best removed with a paste made of powdered chalk or flour and carbon tetrachloride or liquid spot remover. Spread the paste on about ⅛ inch thick, allow it to dry, and then brush off. When working on dirty wallpaper, clean around the spot before applying this paste, or a dirt ring forms around the edges of the paste.

Ink stains are best removed when they are still fresh. Soak up as much of the excess ink as possible with a paper towel or blotting paper. Apply a commercial ink remover or a weak solution of chlorine bleach (on white papers). Rinse immediately with cold water. Reapply as necessary.

When applying wallcoverings, especially porous papers, you can make future cleaning jobs easier by treating the material with a *conditioner*. Conditioners close the surface pores of the paper with a protective film that resists dirt and grease better than untreated paper.

See *Stain-Resistant Wallcoverings*.

COLOR RUN

The color run (or lot number) is printed on the back or selvage of each roll of wallcovering. This number tells you in what batch that roll of covering was printed. Because different machine runs have slightly different variations of ink and background, buy rolls with the same lot number. If the salesman cannot guarantee enough rolls of covering in a specific lot number to complete your job, choose a different pattern. If you get home and find that you have a stray roll with a different lot number, ask the salesman to trade rolls. This assures color uniformity across the entire width of your job.

The mismatching of color between two different color runs is the most frequent complaint received by wallcovering salesmen. Most wallcovering stores do not carry a complete inventory of patterns and colors. Instead, you choose a pattern and color from a catalog. The store then orders from a warehouse. The material eventually ends up in your hands. If you did not order enough material to complete your job, the store has to reorder. You have no guarantee of receiving the same lot number. Order more than enough material the first time.

See *Estimating Quantity of Material* and *Patterns*.

COLORS

When you paint a room, an important consideration for choosing a color is how well it works with the remainder of your decorating scheme. The same holds true for wallcoverings, perhaps more so because of the variety of colors, shades, textures, patterns, and combinations that is available.

Light coverings make small rooms seem larger and airier, while dark coverings make large rooms seem smaller. Colors also have an effect on the mood of the people in the room. Pink is a cheery color and is useful in bedrooms, kitchens, and baths, but unappropriate for the seriousness of a den or study. Greens, blues, light browns, and other natural tones tend to subdue the emotions. These colors work best in serious rooms.

When choosing a wallcovering, consider the trim. Try to envision how the covering will look when matched with the trim. The safest way to match trim and wallcovering is by choosing one of the colors in the pattern and painting the trim with this color. Remember that the brighter colors in the pattern add that much more activity to the room when applied to the woodwork. Matching woodwork to the subdued color of the covering's background mellows the room.

See *Choosing Wallcoverings* and *Trim and Woodwork.*

COLOR WAYS

A technical term used to describe the number of colors in a pattern. Most *patterns* come in two or four colors. As a general rule, the more colors, the more expensive the covering is.

COMPANION WALLCOVERINGS

These wallcoverings are designed to harmonize with another wallcovering. Most wallcovering collections include a variety of *patterns* and *colors* such as stripes, flowers, dots, and checks that can be mixed and matched for pleasing results. For example, you can break up the monotony of a single design in a large room by doing one wall with a companion wallcovering. Generally, stripes go with floral prints, textured materials with plaids, and solid tone coverings can be matched with almost any pattern. When using companion wallcoverings, make the switch from one pattern to another at natural breaks such as corners, bookshelves, or a fireplace. Use two different coverings above and below a *chair rail.*

See *Choosing Wallcoverings.*

CONDITIONERS

Wallpaper conditioners are designed to close the porous surface of papers and render them more durable, scuff-resistant, and easier to clean. Conditioners come as ready-to-use liquids or mix-with-water powders that reduce

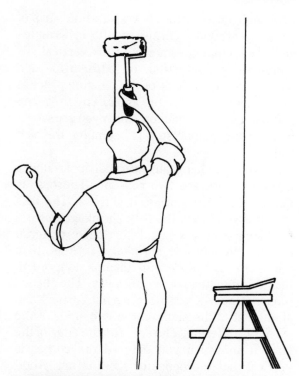

Conditioners. Roll conditioners onto wallpapers after paste has dried. Conditioners keep paper looking good longer and make wiping up smudges easier.

the severity of stains and soil by creating an impervious barrier on the surface of wallpapers. Paper conditioners should be applied at the end of a papering job to insure the longest life possible for your coverings. These coatings can be rolled or sprayed onto newly hung wallpaper as soon as the adhesive is dry and before dirt begins to collect. See the illustration.

CORNERS

Although hanging wallcoverings around corners is a little more difficult than working on flat walls, you can eliminate much worry by thinking of each corner as a fresh starting point for the strips to be hung on the next wall. Because two walls seldom form a precise vertical angle, attempting to wrap a whole strip of covering around a corner results in wrinkles and a seam that does not run truly vertical. To eliminate this situation, on both inside and outside corners, think of the hanging process for corners as a two-step affair. The first step is finishing up the wall on which you are working, and the second step is beginning the new wall.

Why not hang an entire strip around a corner? There are two reasons. The first is that as a covering dries, it shrinks. The less material you have, the less shrinkage occurs. By hanging only a small section of material beyond the corner, shrinkage is kept to a minimum. The covering remains adhered to the corner instead of pulling away. The second reason is because corners are not vertical, the alignment of the strip on the two sides of the corner is different. The seam on the edge of the strip from which you entered the corner is vertical, but the opposite seam is not. Additionally, excessive wrinkling results because of the less than perfect shape of the corner.

When you reach the point where there is less than a full strip of distance between the edge of the last strip hung and the corner, stop and take a few measurements. Measure the distance from the edge of the strip to the corner in three places—ceiling, midway down the wall, and at the baseboard. Add ½ inch to each of these measurements. Return to the strip you are going to hang in the corner. Transfer these measurements to the strip and cut along the line with a straightedge, razor cutter, or scissors. Paste the strip.

When the strip is ready, hang it as you would a strip on a flat wall. Where it enters the corner though, work it into the corner as deeply as possible. You can make the covering work into the corner easier by snipping a vertical cut at the ceiling and baseboard ends of the

strip. Finish by trimming the excess covering from ceiling and floor.

Now that the first strip is in place, measure the width of the remaining section of wallcovering strip, or begin with a new strip. Using the strip's measurement, position a plumb line so that the edge of the new strip overlaps the ½-inch overhang from the previous strip. When the plumb line has been made, paste the new strip and hang it by aligning the factory-cut edge on the plumb line. Try to match the pattern on the overlap as much as possible, but keep the priority of the alignment with the plumb line. Because the pattern mismatch occurs at a corner, it is hardly noticeable.

The same procedure is used on outside corners. You could hang a normal width strip around the corner, and the shrinking action of the drying material would tighten against the corner. Because of the less than true nature of most corners, the final edge of this strip would not be true.

Instead, measure the distance from the edge of the last strip hung to the corner at ceiling, mid-wall and floor. Add 1 inch and cut the strip lengthwise along these measurements. Wrap the overlap around the edge of the corner, make vertical cuts at ceiling and baseboard to release pressure on the strip, and then smooth into place (Fig. 1). Trim as usual at the ceiling and floor.

To properly position the next strip, measure the strip width and add ½ inch. Measure from the corner (not the edge of the overlap) and mark a plumb line on the wall (Fig. 2). Hang the strip, matching patterns as well as possible, but keep the edge of the strip true to the plumb line. Trim at the ceiling and floor and move on to the next strip.

When hanging on an outside corner, try to keep the edge of this last strip, nearest to the

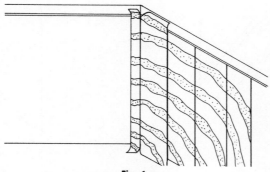

Fig. 1

Corners. The last strip on a wall should wrap an inch or two around an outside corner.

corner, at least ½ inch away from the corner's edge. This small detail prevents the material from being peeled back or frayed through normal wear.

    See *Slanting Walls.*

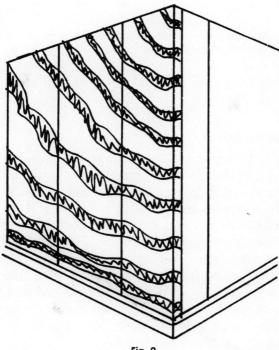

Fig. 2

Corners. Make a new plumb line a little more than one strip width away from the corner. Hang the first strip so it is aligned on the plumb line.

CORNICE

The molding occasionally attached at the corner between ceiling and wall. Paint cornices and other *trim and woodwork* before hanging the covering. Use a semigloss or glossy trim enamel or ceiling paint. Choose *colors* according to whether you want the molding to blend with the ceiling, walls, or to stand on its own.

    A common treatment of the cornice is painting it with the ceiling paint. The molding blends in with the ceiling and more or less disappears.

    Choosing to paint the molding the same color as one of the background colors is also a common practice. This choice makes the cornice a part of the wall. The molding is a little more noticeable than if it was painted to match the ceiling, but it does not stand out.

    Selecting one of the brighter or bolder colors in the covering's pattern and painting the cornice to match result in a vivid separation of ceiling and wall. Some people find this boxing in of the ceiling attractive; others do not.

COVE CEILING

A ceiling that rounds gracefully into the wall. This situation is difficult to cover; however, you can reduce the difficulty substantially by thinking the problem through before beginning the job.

    If the ceiling is to be painted, this task should be completed before beginning the covering job. Bring the paint well down beyond where you want the covering to end.

    When the paint has dried, mark the point on the curve where you want the covering to stop—the nearer the bottom of the curve, the better. Measure the distance between the mark and the baseboard. Go to the opposite end of the wall and measure up from the baseboard the same distance. Make another mark. Stretch a chalk string between the two points and snap it. Go about *hanging wallcovering* up to this line, treating the line as it if were a ceiling/wall corner. Leave the top of the covering untrimmed until the wall is completely covered. Make another chalk line and trim the covering using the new line as a guide.

You can finish the job by adding a *border*, so it extends an inch or more beyond the covering's edge. Press the border firmly into place, as the curved surface makes adhesion difficult.

See *Slanting Walls*.

CUTTING TOOLS

The tools necessary for cutting wallcoverings can be found in most home workshops. Generally, you will need no more than a razor cutter, utility knife, cutting wheel, and scissors. Cer-

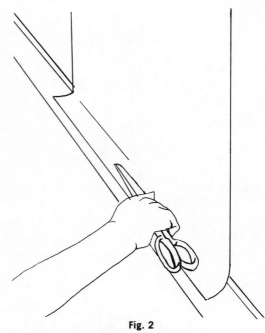

Fig. 2

Cutting Tools. Crease already hung coverings with the back of the scissors prior to cutting.

tain coverings respond better to different tools.

Utility Knives

Utility knives are recommended for cutting and *trimming* medium-weight and heavy-weight coverings and nonbacked vinyls. These knives are used to trim coverings at the baseboard, ceiling, and around windows and doors after they are in place. First, make a crease in the covering with the corner of a *taping knife*. Lay a straightedge along the crease as a guide (Fig. 1). Cut the covering with your knife and peel back the excess covering. Change blades frequently to prevent tearing or stretching the covering.

Utility knives can be used to cut strips to their desired length. Mark a line across the strip at the correct length, line up a straight-

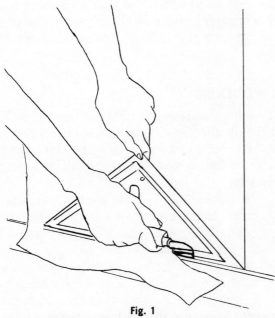

Fig. 1

Cutting Tools. Use a straightedge to guide a utility or razor cutter when trimming a wallcovering.

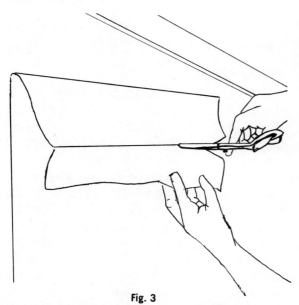

Fig. 3

Cutting Tools. Pull back the covering and trim along the crease with scissors.

edge, and cut along the straightedge with the knife. Utility knives also come in handy when removing selvage from untrimmed coverings. After the strips have been cut to their desired lengths, line a straightedge up exactly on the selvage and pattern edge. Draw the razor knife along the edge with a firm stroke. To prevent ragged cuts and to eliminate the possibility of stretching vinyl materials, change blades frequently. Instead of trying to trim the covering yourself, have the store trim the covering when you buy it. The store cut is more accurate.

Scissors

Scissors—the longer the shear blade, the better—work well on heavy fabrics and cloth-backed vinyls. When cutting strips to length, mark a line with a straightedge and cut with scissors. When cutting already hung coverings, crease the material along baseboard or ceiling joints with the back of the scissors (Fig.

2). Pull the covering back just enough to allow you to cut with the scissors (Fig. 3). Trim along the crease, then reposition the covering and smooth into place.

Scissors also work well on curves and small cuts in tight corners. When cutting around a curve, use small snips. Work slowly and patiently for best results. Scissors can also

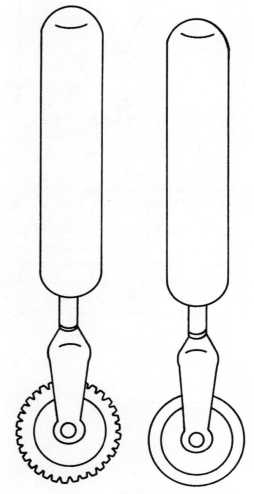

Fig. 4

Cutting Tools. Toothed cutting wheel (left) perforates wallpaper, so it can be torn along a straight line. Smooth cutting wheel (right) scores the paper prior to tearing.

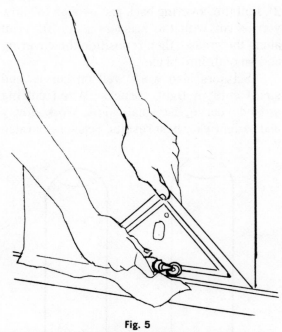

Fig. 5

Cutting Tools. Roll a cutting wheel back and forth along a straightedge to cut wallpaper.

be used to start a hole in the middle of a strip where it fits over a switch or electrical receptacle. Pull the material away from the object, so it forms a little pyramid. Cut off the apex. This gives you a hole to expand as necessary. Do not use scissors for removing selvage, be-

cause they do not cut in as straight a line as a razor blade guided by a straightedge.

Cutting Wheels

Cutting wheels work best when cutting straight lines on wallpapers and other fragile coverings. Although these tools are not essential, cutting wheels reduce the possibility of tearing or stretching wallpapers.

There are two types of cutting wheels— toothed and knife-edge. The toothed wheels perforate the paper with a series of small holes along the edge you are planning to cut. The knife-edge wheel scores the paper, making it easier to tear (Fig. 4). Cutting wheels can be purchased for a few dollars at paint and hardware stores. They are also included in wallcovering kits.

To cut wallpaper with a cutting wheel, crease the paper along the ceiling, baseboard, and window or door trim with a taping knife. Then use a straightedge as a guide while rolling the wheel back and forth along the crease (Fig. 5). Press hard. After several passes, peel the extra covering away. Smooth cut with a smoothing brush or seam roller, and you are finished.

See *Tools*.

DADO

The wall space between baseboard and a *chair rail*. When covering this area, use a material that is washable and withstands heavy abuse from chairs and accidental scuffing by shoes.

See *Choosing Wallcoverings*.

DOCUMENTARY

This term describes wallcovering *patterns* based on authentic sources, usually dating back to colonial times. Although not authentic antiques, these patterns represent what was used in colonial or provincial homes. Documentaries are excellent as backgrounds for fine antique furniture. These designs often come in hand-printed patterns of earth tones such as light blue, green, ocher, and red. When choosing a documentary pattern, remember that simple patterns focus more attention on your furniture.

See *Colors*.

DOUBLE-CUTTING

A commonly used method of producing an invisible *seam* on *vinyl wallcoverings*. Because vinyls do not stick to themselves, making *lapped seams* impossible, this seam is used.

To make a double-cut seam, hang the second strip so it laps the first by ¼ to ½ inch. Center the edge of a straightedge along the hump created by the double thickness of vinyl. Cut down the straightedge with a razor blade or sharp utility knife (Fig. 1). Be careful not to tear or stretch the covering. Make sure to cut through both layers of material. When the cut is completed, peel the excess edge off the top layer of vinyl. Recut where necessary. Then lift the edge of the top layer of vinyl and peel the excess from the bottom edge of the vinyl (Fig. 2). Press the edges together on the wall and finish by rolling seams and wiping with a damp sponge.

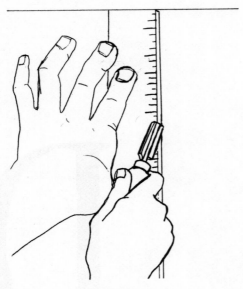

Fig. 1

Double-Cutting. The first step in double-cutting is centering a straightedge on a lapped joint and cutting through both layers of covering with a razor cutter.

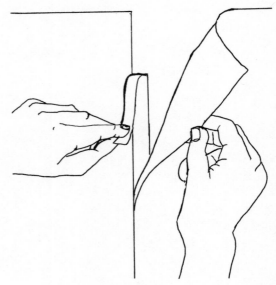

Fig. 2

Double-Cutting. When making a double-cut seam, it is necessary to peel away excess material.

DROP CLOTHS

Used on floors and over furniture when hanging wallcoverings. Use an absorbent material on floors. Plastic can be used, but be careful not to track adhesive onto uncovered areas. Plastic works fine over furniture.

See *Drop Cloths* in Part 1.

EMBOSSING

Embossed wallcoverings have raised patterns that give the covering a rich textured feel. The material is also usually covered with an ink-printed design.

Embossed wallcoverings are hung just like their smooth counterparts, except for one important difference. Seams should not be rolled with a seam roller. Rolling flattens the embossing and produces an alley along the seam. Instead, use a sponge to press the seams together.

ESTIMATING QUANTITY OF MATERIAL

In addition to deciding on *colors, patterns*, and *materials* when *choosing wallcoverings* for a job, you also need to estimate how much of the covering is needed to complete the job with a minimum of wasted material. To insure success, you must remember that an estimation of how much material you need is only as accurate as your measurements.

Knowing the exact size of the area you want to cover insures that you buy enough material of the same *color run* to do the job. If the store does not have enough of the material in one lot number and cannot order it (the pattern has been discontinued, for example), you can switch to a pattern for which the store can provide the amount of material that you need.

Estimating the amount of covering you need for a job is as simple as estimating the quantity of paint you would need to paint the room. It may be easier, because coverings go on at a uniform rate. Ten square feet of wallcovering covers 10 square feet, unless you make a mistake and have to dispose of part of the material.

To estimate the amount of wallcovering you need, measure the perimeter of the room at the baseboards. Then measure the wall height from baseboard to ceiling. Multiply the perimeter measurement by the wall height,

Table
Estimating Quantity of Material. Wallcovering Estimating Chart.

Perimeter of room in feet	Number of single rolls for walls of this height (in feet)						Number of feet of border	Single rolls for ceiling
	8	9	10	11	12	13		
28	8	8	10	11	12	13	33	2
30	8	8	10	11	12	13	33	2
32	8	8	10	12	13	14	36	3
34	8	10	10	13	14	15	39	4
36	8	10	10	14	15	16	39	4
38	10	10	12	14	16	17	42	4
40	10	10	12	15	16	18	45	4
42	10	12	12	16	17	19	45	4
44	10	12	14	17	18	20	48	5
46	12	12	14	17	19	20	51	6
48	12	12	14	18	20	21	51	6
50	12	14	14	19	20	22	54	6
52	12	14	16	20	21	23	57	7
54	14	14	16	20	22	24	57	7
56	14	14	16	21	23	25	60	8
58	14	16	18	22	24	26	63	8
60	14	16	18	22	24	26	63	8
62	14	16	20	23	25	27	66	9
64	16	18	20	24	26	28	69	9
66	16	18	20	25	27	29	69	10
68	16	18	20	25	28	30	72	10
70	16	20	20	26	28	31	75	11
72	18	20	20	27	29	32	75	12
74	18	20	22	28	30	33	78	12
76	18	20	22	28	31	33	81	13
78	18	20	22	29	32	34	81	14
80	20	20	24	30	32	35	84	14
82	20	22	24	31	33	36	87	15
84	20	22	24	31	34	37	90	16
86	20	22	24	32	35	38	90	16
88	20	22	26	33	36	39	93	17
90	20	24	26	33	36	39	96	18

and you have the total square footage of the walls within the room.

Divide the square footage by 30 square feet (the recommended coverage of a *single roll* of wallcovering) to determine how many rolls of material you need. See the table. Many people suggest subtracting a roll of covering for every two windows or doors, but most amateurs tend to underestimate the amount of covering they need. It is better to have extra material than not enough. Besides, unopened packages of material can usually be returned to the store. Scraps can be used to line drawers or for similar household applications.

When estimating the area of stairway walls, you need to measure from the lowest to the highest point on the wall, usually from the base of the staircase to the top of the stairwell. Measure the length of the wall from one end of the stairs to the other. Multiply these two numbers, then divide by two to achieve an estimate for the square footage to be covered. If the walls on both sides of the stairs are to be covered, do not bother dividing by two. Next, figure the area of the headwall (height times width) and add this to your sidewall estimate. Divide the total area by 30 square feet to determine how many rolls of wallcovering you need for the job. Add a roll to the total, because the detailed work of a stairwell may result in one or two mistakes.

To estimate the number of rolls necessary for covering a ceiling, multiply the width by length of the ceiling to get the area. If the ceiling is unobstructed, this figure is divided by 30 to determine the number of rolls you need. Obstructions that jut into the area of the ceiling should not be subtracted from the total. Areas of ceiling that extend beyond the basic measurements should be added to the total before division.

Wall coverings are measured in units called single rolls. A roll may vary in width from 15 to 54 inches, but regardless of the width of a given roll, a single roll contains 36 square feet of coverage. The actual covering rate for a single roll is figured at 30 square feet per roll. The difference between the size of the roll and covering rate is due to the necessary waste of excess covering on the top and bottom of each *strip*, the extra material required to create a *match*, and trimming around the odd shapes you are likely to encounter. Stick with a figure of 30 square feet of coverage to a roll.

When buying a wallcovering, read the label carefully. Some manufacturers sell coverings in double length rolls, sometimes called *bolts*. Two, three, and four-roll bolts are not uncommon, resulting in rolls of covering that contain 72, 108, or 144 square feet. Buying a covering in these longer rolls makes cutting strips a more efficient process. Buy the shortest bolt length possible, and you are more accurate in matching what you need to what you actually buy. In any event, buy extra material, rather than not enough, because you may not be able to match lot numbers or patterns at a later date.

Estimating the time necessary to complete a given wallcovering job is difficult, because people work at a wide range of speeds. An average speed worker can figure on completing a 12 by 16-foot room with few obstructions (windows, doors, bookshelves) in a day. Extensive wall repairs or removal of old coverings could double this time. Set aside more than enough time, so you do not rush the job. If you find that you can only work in short spells, go ahead. Coverings, unlike paint, do not leave lap marks. You can hang a strip of wallcovering right next to one that has been up several days. It is a good practice to stop at natural breaks such as corners, windows, and doors.

See *Choosing Wallcoverings*.

GROUND

The term used for the background color on which a wallcovering *pattern* is printed or embossed.

H

HANGABILITY

The term used to describe the ease with which different types of wallcoverings can be hung. The term includes such factors as pattern *match*, pasting, *trimming*, and washability—all important considerations, especially for amateur hangers. You can make a hanging job easier by remembering a few things when *choosing wallcoverings*.

First, consider the weight of the material you want to apply. Flocks, foils, and other delicate coverings are difficult to hang, because wrinkles and tears seem to pop up out of nowhere. Medium-weight coverings are generally the easiest for beginners to hang, because the weight of these materials reduces tearing and stretching during handling. Be aware, however, that papers and unbacked vinyls may stretch during handling. Selecting a cloth-backed covering reduces the chance of stretching. Heavy-weight materials such as cloth-backed vinyl are more difficult to hang than the medium-weight coverings (mainly because trimming is tricky), but they are still easier to hang than the fragile materials.

Coverings that come with their shelving intact are more difficult to hang than *pretrimmed coverings*. No matter how careful you are, trimming by hand cannot match machine-trimmed coverings for straightness. If you must trim selvage off coverings, make certain that your cuts are straight, or gaps along the seams result.

Whenever possible, choose a prepasted covering. Not only do you eliminate the pasting step of hanging a wallcovering, but these coverings generally come pretrimmed as well.

When selecting a pattern, consider whether it is a straight, drop, or random pattern. Random patterns are easiest to hang, because you do not have to worry about matching the pattern from one strip to the next.

Straight patterns, those that run across the full width of each strip, are also relatively easy to hang. Drop patterns, or those that extend beyond the edge of the strip, are the most difficult to hang. For your first attempt at hanging wallcoverings, choose the easier patterns. As your hanging skills increase, move up to the more difficult patterns.

Roll width also has a bearing on the hangability of a covering. As a rule, the narrower the strip, the easier the wallcovering is to hang. An added advantage is that narrow rolls often reduce the amount of waste when working around obstructions. On the other hand, wide rolls require less aligning of seams, making the job go quicker.

HANGING WALLCOVERINGS

After you have selected a wallcovering, thoroughly prepared the walls, and decided on an *order of hanging*, it is time to begin the job of hanging the covering. Although cutting, pasting, positioning, and *trimming* wallcoverings may seem like a complicated procedure, it is not, as long as you do each step in sequence and do not try to hurry the job.

Once you have established a starting point, it is time to make a plumb line. No house has exactly vertical walls; yet you want the covering to hang on the true vertical. Thus, the first *strip* of covering you hang is lined up on a plumb line. To make this line, tack a string to the wall at the point where the edge of your first strip of covering is to fall (Fig. 1). Tie a *plumb bob* or other heavy object to the string so it hangs freely near the baseboard. Chalk the string, then hold it to the wall at the baseboard and pull the string an inch or so away from the wall. Allow the string to snap against the wall. A faint chalk mark remains, marking true vertical. This, then, is the line along which the edge of the first strip of covering is hung.

Unless you use a *prepasted covering* or a ready-mixed liquid adhesive, you need to mix a batch of paste. The dry pastes need to be mixed and allowed to set for at least 30 minutes before use. By mixing it now, you can move on to the next step, cutting the strips to length, while the paste is curing.

Cutting the strips involves a little thought, especially when hanging coverings with drop matches. Measure the distance between ceiling and floor. This gives you the length of coverage for each strip. Hold the end of a roll of covering (with a couple of inches of excess) against the ceiling and wall corner to determine which part of the pattern you want

Fig. 1

Hanging Wallcoverings. A plumb line will make sure that wallcovering strips are hung on a true vertical.

to fall on the crack. Make a pencil mark at this point and lay the roll out on the floor or a pasting table. Measure from this point the length of the distance between ceiling and baseboard, add a couple of inches of extra material for trimming, and cut off the strip.

Unroll another length of covering beside the first strip. Determine which kind of *match* you have. A straight-across match means that you can cut all the strips based on the first strip, because the pattern runs across the wall. A drop match requires moving the second strip up and down beside the first until a match is achieved. With a drop match you may find 6 to 12 inches of wasted paper at the top of the strip. You may be able to eliminate this waste by switching to another roll and matching it to the first strip. Once you have determined

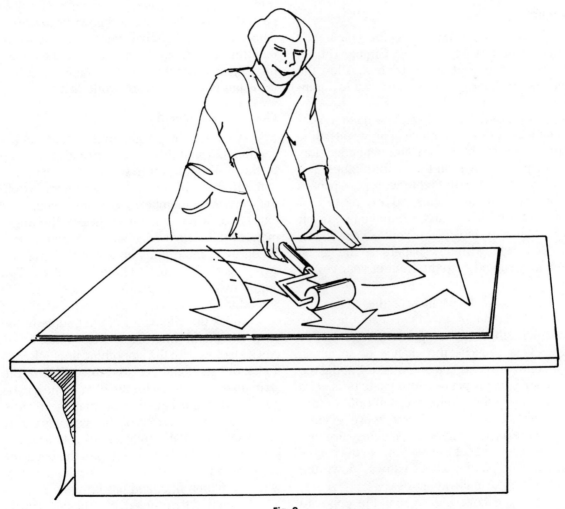

Fig. 2
Hanging Wallcoverings. A pasting table will make spreading paste on the back of coverings an efficient process.

which roll produces a second strip with the least waste, cut it even with the first strip. The extra covering required for the match can be trimmed off the top of the strip, as long as you leave a few inches for trimming once the strip is on the wall. Continue cutting strips in this manner until all the strips necessary to cover one wall are cut. Keep them in order and move on to pasting.

Pasting

Pasting is already done for you if you bought a prepasted covering. Simply roll up the strip and place it in a water box. Allow the material to absorb water and relax a few minutes, and it is ready to hang.

On unpasted coverings, you need a pasting table. A 2 by 8-foot piece of plywood is fine (Fig. 2). A paste brush or roller is needed. Lay the strip face down on the pasting table. You may want to cover the table with newspapers or brown wrapping paper, so any paste that slops onto the table can be removed before it has a chance to damage the front of your covering. Be careful with newspapers, as the ink on them may rub off onto the front of your covering.

Hang ¼ to ½ an inch of the strip's top beyond the end of the table and the same amount of the strip's edge over the table's edge. This reduces the chance of splashing paste onto the pasting table. Starting at the top of the strip, apply paste with a paste brush or a clean paint roller. Rollers usually do a more thorough job and apply paste more evenly. Spread the paste on liberally, making sure that the entire surface of the section of covering is coated. Stop pasting about halfway down the strip and about halfway across.

Shift the covering so that the opposite edge hangs over. Beginning at the top of the strip, work down to a point that corresponds with the previously pasted side. The top half of your covering should now be pasted. Fold the top edge of the paper back, pasted side to pasted side, so the pattern side is out. Do not press into place or crease, because the covering finish may crack.

Repeat the pasting procedure for the bottom half of the strip, overhanging edges and folding back the covering when thoroughly pasted. This procedure is known as *booking*. Allow this piece of covering to cure about 10 minutes. Curing allows all parts of the covering to gain a nearly uniform dampness so the covering is easy to work while hanging.

Checking Alignment

When the strip has cured, unfold the top section. Grasp it by the corners and move it up to the wall. Position it so that the mark you made to indicate the ceiling/wall joint lays in the corner (remember you have a couple of extra inches for trimming). Check the alignment of the strip's edge and your plumb line. When everything lines up correctly, give the covering a gentle pat to hold it in place. You might make a few gentle brushes with the smoothing brush, but do not overdo it.

Check the alignment of the middle of the strip and plumb line. Give the top half a few quick strokes with the smoothing brush. Reach under the strip and peel the lower half of the strip down. Align it with the plumb line as you go. Position the covering so that the excess material on the bottom of the strip lays over the baseboard. Pat into place. Check for wrinkles. If wrinkles are present, pull the covering away from the wall up to the wrinkle, realign with the plumb line, and pat into place.

If you find that the edge of the covering is straying from the plumb line, you can pull the covering loose and reposition it. Adhesives stay loose for quite a while, and the covering can be pulled free of the wall several times without damage. Work patiently and carefully until you are satisfied with the way the strip hangs on the wall.

Brush the strip securely onto the wall. Begin at the top and middle of the strip and make brushing movements from the center of the strip to the edge, working well up into the ceiling joint. Move down the strip and repeat the middle to edge strokes so that they overlap (Fig. 3). Make sure to work all the air out from under the covering, or bubbles form. When you reach the bottom, return to the top and make successive vertical strokes from the top to the bottom of the strip.

Trimming

Trim the excess covering at the ceiling and baseboard. There are several ways to do this, depending on the material with which you are working. With papers and other fragile materials, the best method is to run a *cutting wheel* along the crack several times and then tear the extra material loose. On heavier coverings like vinyl, score the joint with the back of a pair of scissors or a taping knife. Pull the covering away from the wall just enough to work your scissors in and cut along the scored mark. Some coverings can be cut with a razor blade or utility knife. Score the material with the back edge of a taping knife, then follow the line with the knife. Change blades frequently, because dull blades do more tearing and stretching than cutting. Foils and other fine coverings have to be cut in place. Score the material with the back of a taping knife, then use the working edge of the blade as a straightedge to guide your utility knife as you cut the material.

When the covering has been trimmed,

press it back into place. Work it deep into the corner with hard strokes of the smoothing brush. You may have to push the covering into the corner by tapping the material with the bristles of the brush.

The procedure for hanging the second strip is similar to the first. After pasting, position the covering at the ceiling. Check the match of the two strips along the seam. Make sure that the two edges butt securely. If you do not have a solid butt, try sliding the covering over by placing your palms flat on the second strip and pushing it toward the first. Use gentle

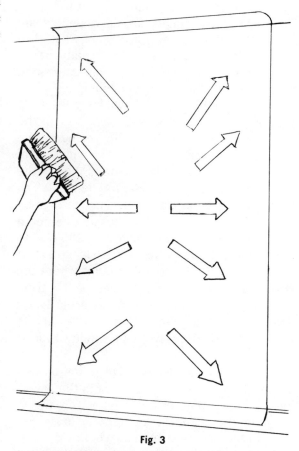

Fig. 3

Hanging Wallcoverings. Brush from the middle of a strip to the edges when smoothing material onto a wall.

firm pressure, so you do not overlap the first strip. Never pull the edge of the second strip in an attempt to line it up with the first.

If you cannot get the two strips to come together, properly peel the second strip from the wall and try again. Do not get discouraged.

Double-Hung Windows

Now that you can hang coverings on flat uninterrupted surfaces, how are you going to handle that window to which you have come? It is not really difficult, as long as you wait until the strip is in position and is overhanging the window before you attempt to cut it to shape. The methods for hanging around casement and double-hung windows vary somewhat, because a double-hung window usually has a molding. Casement windows require working the paper into the window opening.

On double-hung windows, hang the strip that overlaps the edge of the window in the usual way. Position the wallcovering at the ceiling and along the edge of the previous strip, so it forms the regular seam. Smooth the wallcovering into place past the window. Tap the covering as far into the corner formed by window molding and wall as possible. Smooth the covering below the window all the way to the baseboard. Check the seam to make sure it is true. Now locate the exact point where the covering covers the top corner of the trim. With a pair of scissors, snip carefully on diagonal to this point. This allows you to smooth the covering above the window against the trim.

Snip a similar diagonal cut to the bottom corner of the window trim. Smooth the covering along the edge of the window into place, working the material as tight as possible. Smooth the covering into place below the bottom section of trim. If the window has a sill that makes the contours of the trim a little awk-

Fig. 4

Hanging Wallcoverings. Trim excess material from the strip with scissors, cutting wheel, or razor cutter.

ward, cut the covering with scissors as you come to each irregularity, so the covering is allowed to lay flat on the wall. Trim the excess covering now hanging over the trim with a cutting wheel, scissors, or utility knife (Fig. 4).

Hang the next strip. You can use a short scrap of covering as long as there is enough material on the ends for trimming, so the patterns match the edge of the previous strip. The strip does not reach beyond the far side of the window in most cases. Paste and position a short strip above and below the window, trimming as you go (Fig. 5).

The last strip around the window is hung similar to the first, except that you smooth the covering above the window into place down to the corner of the window molding. Make a snip at the top corner to relieve the pressure on the material, then position the strip along the side of the window and smooth into place. Make a snip or two to relieve the pressure on the covering when you reach the bottom corner. Return to the top corner, alter the diagonal cut if necessary, and smooth the covering into

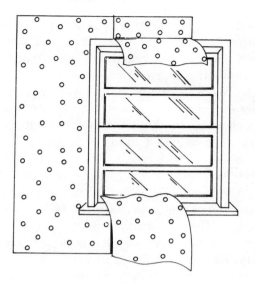

Fig. 5

Hanging Wallcoverings. Short strips above and below double-hung windows do not need to be cut from a roll. They can be salvaged from scraps as long as the patterns match.

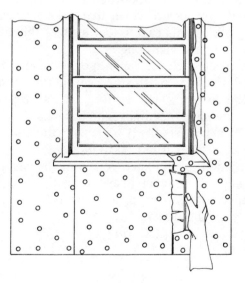

Fig. 6

Hanging Wallcoverings. On the last piece of covering hung around a double-hung window, make cuts at the corners of window trim to release pressure and smooth the covering into place. Come back and finish trimming.

place. Work it well into the wall and trim joints. Return to the bottom corner and cut it so that it fits. Smooth the remainder of the strip into place and trim (Fig. 6).

Casement Windows

On casement windows, hang the first strip to cross the window by aligning it at ceiling and seam. The covering hangs suspended over the window opening. Make a horizontal scissors cut at the center of the suspended piece to within an inch of the edge of the window opening's side. Make a vertical cut from the end of the horizontal cut to within an inch of the top corner. Keep the vertical cut as parallel to the edge of the window opening as possible. The light shining through the window should tip you off as to the location of the window opening's edge. Complete the cut with a 45-degree angle cut into the very corner of the opening (Fig. 7). Make a similar series of cuts down to the bottom corner.

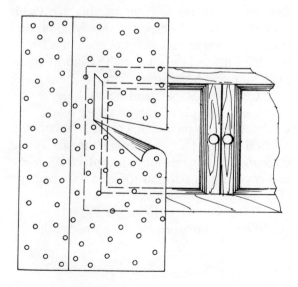

Fig. 7

Hanging Wallcoverings. The first strip of covering over a casement window is smoothed into place and then trimmed.

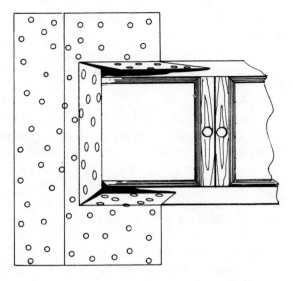

Fig. 8

Hanging Wallcoverings. Finish the first side of the casement window by smoothing a piece of covering onto the side of the opening.

Work the top and bottom flaps of covering into the opening, smoothing them flat against the sides of the opening and tapping them well into the corner formed by the window and opening. Trim as necessary. Smooth the 1-inch overhang around the edge of the window opening's side and brush into place.

Cut a piece of covering as long as the opening is tall, plus 2 inches on each end. Try to match the pattern of this piece to that of the section of strip that laps around the side of the opening. Smooth this piece into place, allowing the covering to overlap top and bottom flaps (Fig. 8).

Hang a short strip above the window so that it bends down around the corner at the top of the opening. Trim and repeat for the bottom strip. The strip that moves beyond the far edge of the window is handled in the same manner as the one that started the window.

Working around doors involves the same set of maneuvers as was used on the double-hung window. Work the covering into place before trimming it to fit.

Rolling Seams

After the first few strips are hung on a wall, you have to perform the task of rolling seams. This job should be performed when the paste is no longer wet, but is not completely dry. Because conditions in the room affect the drying time, no specific guidelines are possible. If the paste is forced out of the seam, it is still too wet. When the covering is still damp, but no paste is forced out with rolling, the time is right. Although you may have some difficulty judging the exact time when a seam should be rolled, you soon discover that the seam ready for rolling trails two to four strips behind the one you have just hung.

Keep a clean, damp sponge handy. You need it to wipe paste smears from the surface of the covering. Do not forget to wipe paste from moldings, ceilings, and baseboards. The water in paste is likely to damage the finish of these surfaces if left on too long.

Additionally, keep your tools as clean as possible to prevent mucking up the front of your covering. When papered walls have dried, apply a conditioner.

See *Ceilings, Corners, Cove Ceilings* and *Slanting Walls*.

LAPPED SEAMS

Seams made by overlapping the edge of one strip of covering with ¼ to ½ of an inch of the following strip's edge. Although this is the easiest seam to make, it is not used much because of the obvious bulge it leaves on the wall. It should be considered when working with a covering that still has its selvage intact.

To make a lapped seam, leave the selvage on one edge of the covering. Trim the edge of the next strip, so it matches the pattern from the previous strip. If you choose to use a lapped seam, begin hanging the wallcovering at the window with dominant light. This way shadows produced by the seam are less noticeable.

Lapped seams are frequently used in corners where the walls are not exactly vertical. By running the covering around the corner and then making a lapped seam with a varying lap from top to bottom, you are able to return the leading edge of the last strip to vertical.

Vinyl wallcoverings cannot be lapped, because these materials do not adhere to themselves and quickly peel. Instead, seams in vinyl coverings are made by *double-cutting*.

See *Butt Joint, Seams,* and *Wire Edge.*

LINING PAPER

An inexpensive unpatterned paper that is often used to hide the imperfections of walls prior to the application of certain coverings.

Although lining paper is not usually used under regular coverings, except where walls are in extremely bad shape, it benefits the appearance of materials such as grass cloth, rice paper, or foil coverings. Grass cloth and rice paper have a bad habit of separating from the wall when they become moist. A layer of lining paper under these materials absorbs the excess moisture and prevents peeling. Foil coverings, because of their reflecting surface, tend to magnify imperfections in the wall's surface. You can reduce this problem by apply-

Lining Paper. Lining paper should be hung under fragile papers or over walls in bad shape. Notice that lining paper can be hung horizontally below and above windows.

ing a lining paper under the foil. Lining papers also form a surface from which coverings can be easily removed at a later date.

Lining paper is hung just like regular patterned paper, except that it does not need to be matched because there are no patterns. Lining paper also requires less precise trimming. When hanging lining paper, use the same adhesive you plan to use on the finish covering. This creates a strong bond between the top covering, lining paper, and the wall. When hanging *prepasted coverings*, consult your salesman for suggestions about a compatible adhesive for the lining paper.

When hanging lining paper, hang as many vertical strips as possible. Ignore the gaps above windows and doors. When all vertical strips are in place, go back and hang strips in the open spaces. Because lining papers are unpatterned, you can hang them horizontally if necessary. See the illustration. Leave a ¼ to ½-inch space between lining paper and ceiling, baseboard, window, and door frame trim. This allowance leaves room for the top wallcovering to bind itself directly to the wall, which reduces the chance of peeling. You should use *butt joints* for the seams between pieces of lining paper. Leave ⅛ inch of space between strips. Allow the lining paper to dry thoroughly before hanging regular coverings.

See *Butt Joints* and *Prepasted Coverings.*

M

MATCH

All wallcoverings are designed to match at the edges. There are three types of matches: straight across, drop, and random. See the illustration. Before you cut any covering, unroll two rolls of the material and tack the loose end of one to the wall. Hold a section of the second roll alongside the first as if it were hung. By shifting the second roll up and down, you can determine the point at which the pattern crosses gracefully from one strip to the next. If you are unable to discover a point at which the two strips match, you have a random or plain match.

Although most random designs are not matched in the strictest sense of the word, some manufacturers recommend that alternate strips be reversed, or hung upside down, to reduce the chances of variations in shade or texture becoming evident. Straight match patterns contain a design that runs across all strips of covering on the horizontal. The design is identical, repeating itself as it moves across the wall. With this type of pattern, your only worry is hanging the first strip perfectly vertical so that the pattern does not angle across the wall.

Drop patterns are designs in which the matching point on one edge of the strip is different than the matching point on the opposite edge. Normally the edge of the strip cuts a major element of the design in half. You must cut the next strip, so the pattern continues smoothly into the next strip. You soon discover that the pattern runs on a diagonal instead of a horizontal line.

Another important consideration is getting the correct alignment of the patterns at the ceiling and wall corner. Because the ceiling corner is more visible than the baseboard of a room, it is essential that the point where the pattern is cut off by the ceiling be aesthetically

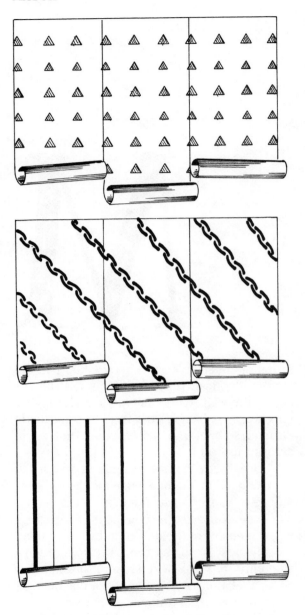

perfectly perpendicular, the misalignment is hardly noticed. If you hung the first strip so that a major element of the pattern was cut in half by the ceiling, you may discover farther down the wall that the ceiling is now cutting away only one-third of the pattern. This accents the less than horizontal nature of the ceiling more than if the unpatterned part of the covering was falling in the corner.

See *Choosing Wallcoverings* and *Repeat*.

MATERIALS

Wallcoverings come in many materials. Anything that can be glued to a wall can be considered a wallcovering. Most commercially available wallcoverings fall into one of the following categories.

Fabrics

Fabric or cloth wallcoverings come untreated, laminated to paper, or in a self-adhesive material. Fabric wallcoverings are usually hung over *lining paper*. These materials add an extra measure of richness to bedrooms, dining rooms, and living rooms. Fragile and easily soiled, these materials can be cleaned with dry-cleaning fluids or powders.

More durable fabrics such as burlap or grass cloth can be used in rooms where a rustic look is desired. Because the natural fibers in these materials tend to swell when wet, they should be hung over a moisture-absorbing lining paper. Do not wash these materials; instead, sprinkle them with a cleaning powder and vacuum.

Flocks

Flocks or fuzzy coverings come on foil, paper, or cloth backings. When hung over lining paper, these materials add plushness to dining rooms and living rooms. Flocks are easily damaged by wear and tear and cleaning.

Match. The three common pattern matches: straight (top), drop (center), and random (bottom).

pleasing. As a general rule, try to get the part of the pattern with the least design to end at the ceiling corner. This way if the ceiling is not

Foils

Foils or shiny metallic coverings come laminated to paper or cloth. They may cause an unattractive glare in rooms with a lot of direct sunlight. The reflective surface of these materials magnifies the imperfections in walls, so they should be hung over lining paper. These coverings can be cleaned. Be careful, though, as tears and wrinkles are next to impossible to mend.

Paper

Paper coverings are the most common and easiest to hang of the wallcoverings. They come untreated, vinyl-coated, and cloth-backed. The latter types of papers can withstand medium wear and are useful in dining rooms, hallways, and bedrooms. Untreated and cloth-backed papers may be stained with grease or dirt; however, there are many *conditioners* that may be applied to these materials to reduce their susceptibility to damage. There are also many powders, putties, and liquids available for *cleaning wallcoverings*. Avoid washing with detergent and water, as the ink patterns may run.

Vinyl

Vinyls are plastic coverings that come with a paper or cloth backing. Vinyl coverings are slightly more difficult to hang than papers. These are the toughest wallcoverings, and their water resistance makes them useful for bathrooms, kitchens, and playrooms. Vinyl coverings can be scrubbed with soap and water.

See *Choosing Wallcoverings* and *Hangability*.

MATTE FINISH

A finish applied to walls and ceilings that is dull.

MURALS

Wallcoverings in which a single subject, usually a landscape or map, is printed across several strips. When hung on large unbroken walls, murals can bring the outdoors inside and add atmosphere to living rooms, dens, and recreational areas. Murals are available in most of the standard wallcovering materials. They differ from regular coverings in that they are precut to strips varying in length from 10 to 15 feet. Murals should be hung on smooth walls to prevent bumps from destroying the effect of the pattern. Using a *lining paper* under murals is a good idea on walls in marginal condition.

Before buying a mural, measure the wall or walls on which the design is to appear. Take this measurement with you when you visit the wallcovering store. The salesman can suggest designs specially suited to the size of the area to be covered and *companion wallcoverings* for the remainder of the room.

You must get the design centered horizontally and vertically on the wall. The package usually tells you how wide and tall each design is. You can use this to decide a general location for the design.

To decide horizontal placement, you must first figure out how many strips fit on the wall. To do this, divide the width of the wall by the width of a strip. The result is the number of strips that is necessary to cover the area. On walls that require an odd number of strips, the first, or center, strip of the design is centered on the wall (Fig. 1). Measure half the width of the strip away from the center of the wall and make a plumb line. Hang the first strip so that one edge falls on the plumb line and covers the center section of the wall. On walls that take an even number of strips, make the plumb line at the middle of the wall. Hang the first two strips so that they butt along this line (Fig. 2).

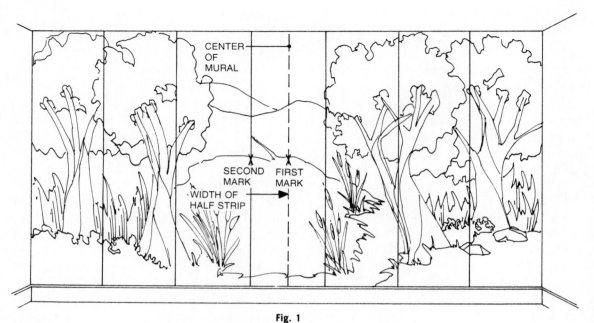

Fig. 1

Murals. When an odd number of strips is required to cover a wall, the first strip should be centered on the wall.

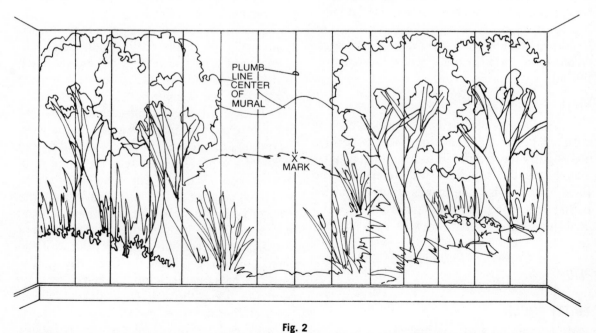

Fig. 2

Murals. When an even number of strips is needed to cover a wall, the first two strips should butt at the center of the wall.

To position the mural vertically, unroll the strip with the highest point of the design. Move it up and down the wall until it is where you want it. Mark the point where this strip meets the ceiling and the baseboard. Lay this strip on a flat surface and unroll the strip that is hung next to it. Match the patterns and transfer the ceiling and baseboard marks to the second strip. Continue until all the strips are marked in this manner. Next, trim each strip so about 6 inches of excess material remain. The strips are now the proper size for hanging.

Although different manufacturers suggest varying sequences for hanging murals, they are generally hung half a wall at a time. Begin with the center strip and work out to a corner. Then return to the center strip and work in the opposite direction to that corner. Trim up the ceiling and baseboard ends of each strip as you go. Trim the ends of the mural at the wall corners, roll the seams, and step back and enjoy.

See *Hanging Wallcoverings, Order of Hanging,* and *Trimming.*

NEW WALLS

New walls seem at first glance to be perfect surfaces for wallcoverings. Preparing new walls for a wallcovering is easier than stripping coverings from old walls, but new walls have a few characteristics that foil even the best covering job. The two most common problems are hot spots and coverings that cannot be peeled from new walls unless properly treated before the covering is applied.

A newly plastered wall should be allowed to cure before covering. This allows the *alkali* present in the plaster to be neutralized. Alkali burns through coverings, especially paper, and causes discoloration if left unsealed. You discover where any alkali hot spots are while *sizing* the wall. Sizing compounds contain a chemical that turns red, purple, or pink when it contacts alkali.

If you discover hot spots on your wall, buy a 28 percent acetic acid solution from your paint dealer. Mix this with water at a ratio of 1 part acid to 2 parts water. Wear rubber gloves while sponging this solution on the hot spots. The stains gradually disappear. When they have vanished completely, the alkali has been neutralized. Allow the spot to dry, then size before hanging wallcoverings.

Because both unpainted plaster and drywall have a lot of *tooth*, they firmly grip coverings applied directly to them. This is fine when applying the covering, but what about when you want to remove the covering for the first time? You find that the covering and the wall are bonded so tight that you damage the wall when pulling the covering loose. To prevent this problem, paint the wall with an interior primer. The primer acts as a lubricating layer between wall and covering, while still providing ample tooth. Latex primers are more resistant to alkali and somewhat reduce hot spots. When the primer has dried, apply sizing. This material provides more tooth in addition to enhancing covering removal later.

ORDER OF HANGING

The order in which you hang wallcoverings is dependent on the *match* of the pattern you have chosen and the shape of the room.

Most people assume that you begin hanging at the edge of the largest open wall—next to a door, window, or corner—and then continue around the room until the covering meets. This method works for random or plain *patterns*. When you have chosen to hang a matching pattern, a pattern that extends from one strip to the next, placement of each strip is important. Without prior thought and planning, you are liable to end up with a mismatched seam in a very conspicuous place. Avoiding this predicament is relatively easy if you plan the placement of your first strip carefully and decide where the last strip and a possible mismatching may occur.

The easiest way to insure success is to decide where the predominant feature of a room is and where the least conspicuous place

is. The idea is to have your pattern centered in the most conspicuous area, with any mismatches occurring in an unnoticeable section of the room (Fig. 1).

In most rooms the conspicuous areas are large unbroken walls, fireplaces, or the areas around picture windows. To center a pattern on a wall, measure the wall and divide by the width of a single strip of covering. This tells you the number of full strips necessary to cover that wall. If the number is even, you want to mark a plumb line in the center of the wall. Butt the first two strips on this line, then work toward each corner. If the number of strips is even, the first strip should be centered over the middle of the wall (Figs. 2 and 3).

If the distance between the last strip hung and the wall is less than 6 inches, it is best to shift the first strip so that the space is more than 6 inches. The reason is that strips less than 6 inches wide are difficult to cut and handle. If the space left for the last strip is

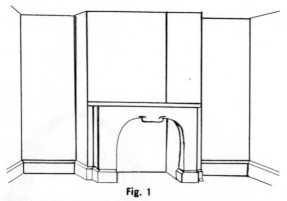

Fig. 1

Order of Hanging. Begin hanging at the least noticeable corner in a room so any mismatch on the last strip is out of view.

more than 6 inches on both ends of the wall, the first strip has been positioned properly.

When starting over the fireplace, the first strip is usually centered so that the pattern flows naturally off the fireplace and onto the wall. As a general rule, corners near a fireplace and facing away from the door of the room are the least conspicuous places in the room. Hang strips on both sides of the first strip until you have worked over both corners nearest the fireplace. Hang strips in order around the room so that the last strip you hang is positioned in the corner facing away from the door. This way mismatches are hidden from view.

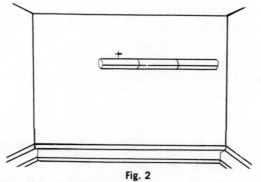

Fig. 2

Order of Hanging. On walls that take an odd number of strips, the center strip should be centered on the wall's center mark.

238

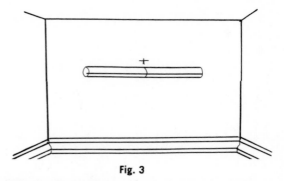

Fig. 3

Order of Hanging. On walls that take an even number of strips, the two center strips should butt at the center of the wall.

When starting between two windows, mark the center point between the openings. Center a strip on this mark and see how much space is left between the edges of the strip and the window. If less than 6 inches, you should hang two strips with their seam at this centerline. If more than 6 inches, you can hang the first strip centered on the mark and still work easily around the windows.

When starting at a picture window, mark the center point of the window on the wall. Center a strip on this mark. Measure to determine if the last strip overhangs the window by more than 6 inches. If so, hang the first strip centered on the mark. If not, position the first two strips so they butt at the center mark.

If the room contains a built-in bookcase or other obstruction that stretches from floor to ceiling, plan to end the covering job at the ends of this feature. Start the job on the opposite side of the room and work around to it. When you position the last strips, the patterns end at a natural break and no mismatch occurs.

If there is no other choice, you can end the job at the edge of a door or window. Although the pattern will probably mismatch, the short amount of seam present in these locations will keep the irregularity at a minimum.

See *Hanging Wallcoverings*.

P

PAINTED WALLS

If you are planning on hanging a wallcovering over a painted wall that is in good shape—no cracks, holes, or rough spots—consider yourself lucky. A painted wall is the easiest surface to work with.

If the wall has been painted with a flat wall paint, you need only wash the wall to remove grease and dirt. Apply *sizing* before hanging a covering. If the wall is painted with a glossy or semigloss paint, you need to cut the gloss with a deglosser or detergent. This can be accomplished when you wash the wall—a necessary step regardless of the type of paint on your walls. When washing walls, wipe up spills on woodwork immediately to prevent staining. After the walls have dried, paint the trim, if that is part of the redecoration scheme, apply a sizing, and then hang your wallcovering.

On painted walls that are in bad shape, you need to scrape off loose paint and patch holes and cracks with a *spackling compound*. If repairs are not extensive, spot prime the wall before sizing. If repairs cover a large percentage of the wall, prime the entire wall before sizing. On extremely rough walls, you may want to hang a *lining paper* prior to hanging the regular wallcovering.

Calcimine or *casein* coatings must be washed completely off walls before hanging wallcoverings. No paste sticks to these materials. Additionally, *strippable wallcoverings* should not be applied directly to latex wall paints, as these paints are liable to peel off with the covering when it is stripped.

PAINTING OVER WALLCOVERINGS

Painting over wallcoverings is not generally considered the best method of converting a covered wall to a painted one. Instead, most manufacturers advocate a complete stripping of the covering. Painting over the old covering may be your only choice. A good example is a covering that was hung on unprimed drywall. Because the wallcovering adhesive is stuck directly to the drywall's paper surface, any attempt to loosen it with water, steam, or chemicals ruins the surface. You can feel relatively secure about painting over a covering in this situation if you remember a few things. The covering has to be stuck tight to the wall, it must be smooth (no embossed, flocked, or textured coverings), and it must be clean and grease-free.

Loose or torn sections of covering should be glued back into place. If the paper is embossed or flocked, you have no choice but to strip it or to hang another covering over it. The texture of rough-surfaced coverings shows through even the thickest of paints. If the old covering is a vinyl or metal foil, neither paint nor another covering sticks to it. It must be removed. Fortunately, foil and vinyl coverings are more easily stripped than paper coverings.

Latex paints generally work best over wallcoverings. Make sure that the water in these paints does not loosen the covering or make the ink pattern bleed through. Test a small section of paint on an inobtrusive section of the covering. Wait a few days to make sure that the covering is not affected. If the ink bleeds through, the entire surface of the covering has to be sealed with *shellac* before topcoating. This consideration may make you decide on a new covering instead of a paint job. It is better to discover these problems before plunging headlong into the job.

Oil-base and alkyd paints are not recommended for painting over wallcoverings, because they may trap moisture behind the covering. The result is a surface that bubbles, peels, or cracks.

As a rule, it takes at least two coats of paint to thoroughly cover the pattern of the wallcovering. Use a primer for the first coat and a topcoating for the second. Darker color paints hide the patterns more effectively than white paints.

See *Removing Wallcoverings* and *Steaming Loose Wallcoverings*.

PAPER REMOVERS

Chemicals that help water penetrate old wallpapers and lift them for removal. Although removing paper by sponging water mixed with a paper remover onto a wall is slower than *steaming loose wallcoverings*, it is less expensive. Be careful that the surface beneath the paper is not damaged by the moisture. Plaster can generally withstand the moisture unlike unprimed drywall and some woods (veneer or particle board).

See *Removing Wallcoverings*.

PASTE

The paste you choose for a specific covering depends on the weight and type of material of which the covering is made. *Prepasted wallcoverings* eliminate the need to select an adhesive. Consult the manufacturer's recommendation or your salesman when selecting a paste for a nonpasted covering.

Pastes come in two basic forms—a powder which is added to water or ready-mixed. To use a ready-mixed paste, simply pour the material into a paste bucket or roller tray before application. Powders should be mixed at least 30 minutes before application, so they can cure. Sift the powder slowly into the water. Mix vigorously to eliminate lumps. A wire whisk or egg beater works well for this job, but try to avoid stirring up too many bubbles in the paste. The paste is the correct consistency when it sticks to your hands without dripping. Paste strengtheners can be added to regular pastes to add the extra adhesion necessary for heavier coverings.

When hanging vinyls, use only the pastes recommended for these nonporous coverings. Because vinyl does not breathe, regular pastes do not dry adequately and are subject to mildew.

Extra powder or ready-mixed paste can be stored in airtight containers for future use. See *Cellulose Paste* and *Wheat Paste*.

PASTE BRUSHES

Wooden-handled tools with synthetic or natural bristles that are used to spread paste on the backing of wallcoverings. Most paste brushes are 6 to 8 inches wide and inexpensive. Synthetic bristles are easier to clean than natural bristles. You do not need a paste brush when hanging *prepasted wallcoverings*. Instead, you need a water box for soaking the covering prior to application.

Many professional paperhangers use a clean paint roller instead of a paste brush to apply paste. The roller is quicker and does a more thorough job of spreading the paste. Choose a short, waterproof nap for the roller. See *Hanging Wallcoverings* and *Tools*.

PATTERNS

There are hundreds of wallcovering patterns to choose from, and your choice depends on your personal preference. Random or straight matched patterns are less complicated to hang than matched patterns. Additionally, coverings with small design elements stand out less than those with big, bold features. Choose a simple, easy-to-hang pattern for your first attempt. Move up to the more complicated and delicate patterns when you have gained a little experience.

Another consideration when choosing a pattern is how true the vertical and horizontal

characteristics of your walls are. If your walls are several inches out of true due to settling of your house, certain patterns work better than others. For example, on walls not square vertically, you should not hang vertical patterns. The design may fade from full width to nothing along corners, windows, and doors. This accents the wall's defect. It is better to hang a horizontal pattern that is less likely to show the misalignment. Rooms that are not square horizontally, along the ceiling or floor, should be covered with vertical designs. Random patterns are best for rooms that suffer both vertical and horizontal misalignment.

See *Choosing Wallcoverings* and *Match*.

PLUMB BOB

A weight suspended on a string. When hung next to a wall, it reveals true vertical. A plumb bob is used to align the first strip of wallcovering on a wall, so it is perpendicular to horizontal.

You can use a seam roller or a cutting wheel for a plumb bob. The weight should be tied to a string that holds chalk dust. A commercial plumb bob in which the string can be coated with chalk by winding the string into the housing of the bob works fine. Be careful not to get too much of a dark chalk on the wall, or you may smudge the surface of the covering.

To make a plumb line, tack the end of a plumb bob's string near the ceiling at the point where the edge of the first strip is to hang. Allow the bob to swing to a rest several inches above the baseboard. Pull the string taut without altering its lateral position and press against the wall. Pull the string an inch or so away from the wall. Allow it to snap against the wall. Remove the string and plumb bob, and hang your first strip using this vertical line as a guide.

PREPASTED COVERINGS

Prepasted wallcoverings have gained popularity in recent years because they eliminate the need to mix and apply a paste to the wallcovering prior to hanging. Not all types of wallcoverings come prepasted.

When you buy a prepasted wallcovering, you need to purchase a water box or tray to make hanging as easy as possible. A water box is a long narrow trough in which each strip of a covering is soaked prior to hanging. The tray should be positioned at the bottom of the wall where you plan to hang a strip. See the illustration.

To use a prepasted covering, cut individual strips to length. Make sure that patterns *match* at the ceiling and along *seams*. Then roll the covering into a tube beginning at the bottom of the strip, so the pattern side is facing in. The prepasted side is exposed. Fill the tray one-half to two-thirds full of tepid water. Place the roll of covering into the tray, so it is totally covered by water. Allow the covering to soak and relax for the time recommended on the package. When the covering has soaked the required time, grasp it at the corners and pull it from the box. It should unroll as you draw the top of the strip up the wall. Work the covering

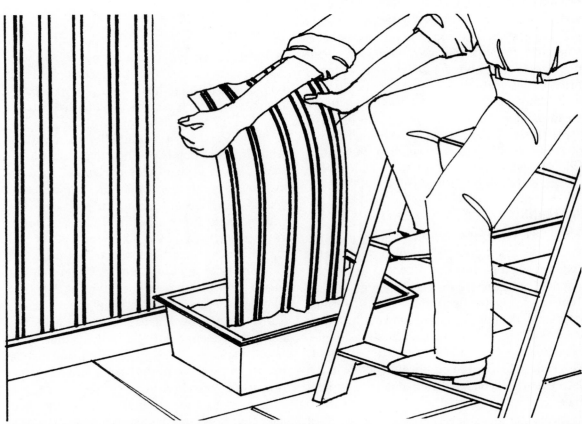

Prepasted Coverings. When hanging prepasted wallcoverings, position a water box next to the wall directly beneath where the strip is to be hung.

onto the wall in the same manner as a covering that you have pasted yourself. When the strip is in position and has been brushed smooth, check the surface for paste. Sponge off excess paste as necessary. Seams should be rolled after the covering has been on the wall for 15 to 20 minutes.

PRETRIMMED WALLCOVERINGS

Pretrimmed means that the selvage, or extra material along the edges of the roll, was cut off at the factory. Usually personnel in wallcovering stores trim the selvage on untrimmed coverings. The mechanical cutters they use produce a straighter line than you can achieve by hand. This makes your seams look better.

PREVIOUSLY COVERED WALLS

Hanging a new layer of wallcovering over an already-covered wall is tricky and should be attempted only when the wall beneath the original covering is too fragile to strip. Despite this warning, coverings can be hung over in-place coverings if the bottom covering is adhered firmly to the wall.

As a general rule, most professionals do not advise hanging more than three layers of covering on a wall before stripping. The reason is that the excess weight of the top coverings can peel all the coverings from the wall. This deterioration is likely to be speeded up by the newly applied paste dissolving previous layers of paste.

If you decide to hang a new covering over an old covering, inspect the wall carefully to make sure that the old covering is stuck firmly in place. Daub a little glue under loose edges and tears and press back into place. Large tears and wrinkles should be torn loose and the edges feathered with coarse sandpaper. Apply a thin coating of vinyl *spackling compound* to the edges to help make them smooth. Make sure the entire covering is free of grease and dirt, or adhesion is affected.

If you are covering a slick material such as a vinyl, degloss the surface by sanding or washing with a solution of detergent, water, and deglosser. This provides a *tooth* for the next layer of adhesive. Under no circumstances should vinyl be hung over wallpaper. The vinyl is considerably stronger than the paper. As the vinyl dries and shrinks, it curls the paper right off the wall. Never apply a new covering over a *strippable wallcovering*, or the same problem occurs. Applying a covering over flocked materials produces a bumpy surface. Fortunately, most vinyls, flocks, and foils can be stripped more easily than wallpapers.

See *Painting over Wallcoverings* and *Removing Wallcoverings*.

R

RAILROADING

A term used by paperhangers to describe strips of wallcovering hung horizontally instead of vertically. Railroading is seldom used with covers that have a printed design; however, lining paper and textured covers such as grass cloth or burlap are often railroaded over and under long windows.

REMOVING WALLCOVERINGS

Because new wallcoverings look nicer and hang better on flat clean walls, it is advisable to strip old wallcoverings from the walls before applying new ones. The methods used for stripping depend on the type of covering. Coverings like some vinyl wallcoverings are no problem to remove, while others may require renting a wallcovering steamer.

Strippable wallcoverings, usually vinyl or vinyl-coated cloth and papers, can be removed without wetting. To see if the material on your wall is strippable, work a corner loose with a putty knife. Gently pull the corner so that it doubles back on itself. While peeling, keep the flap as close to the wall as possible. Pulling it away from the wall may cause the covering to tear, leaving an uneven edge. If the covering is strippable, it peels easily and leaves a fuzzy or rough residue. This material acts as a good backing for the next layer of covering. If this dry stripping method does not work, you need to wet the covering to loosen the adhesive prior to stripping.

On waterproof coatings—vinyls, foils, and vinyl-coated fabrics or cloth—you need to break through the surface in several places to allow water, steam, or paper-removing chemicals to penetrate to the adhesive. You can puncture the covering by sanding with coarse sandpaper, wire brushing it enough to raise a nap, or by making frequent slices in the covering with a wallcovering scraper. Make shallow

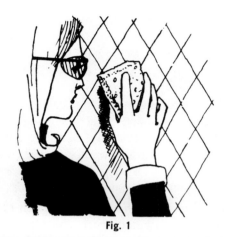

Fig. 1

Removing Wallcoverings. Wallcoverings need to be soaked with a sponge prior to stripping (courtesy Hyde Tools).

cuts just deep enough to penetrate the covering. Then soak the area with a large sponge wet with warm water, detergent, and paper remover. Move the sponge in circular motions (Fig. 1).

Allow the covering to stand for 10 minutes while the moisture soaks in. Make cuts in the next strip while waiting. Come back and resoak the covering before giving the next strip its first soaking. Return to the first strip and work a putty knife or taping knife into the slits. Gently scrape the covering away from the wall (Fig. 2). The covering should peel like a label peels from a glass jar soaked in water. If it does not, resoak and let stand for a few more minutes. When the covering is sufficiently loose, grasp it with your fingers and strip by pulling it back upon itself. Do not pull the material away from the wall or it is likely to tear, leaving ragged edges. When a strip has been totally removed, wash the wall to remove excess paste. Some really stubborn coverings do not strip with this method. For these, you need to steam the surface. Steam penetrates deeper than water, and the extra heat speeds up the loosening process.

A steamer consists of an electrical heating unit with a water hose and perforated plate attached. Steamers can be rented at wallcovering or rental stores. Fill the steamer with boiling water and plug it in. When steam begins to billow out of the plate, hold the plate against the covering. Begin at a top corner and hold the plate in place until moisture collects around the edges, then lift and move to an adjacent area. On nonporous materials like vinyl, you have to break the surface to insure penetration.

When a strip has been steamed loose, work the material off with a taping knife or scraper. Peel the material carefully to insure complete removal. Steaming generally works faster than soaking, especially on coverings that have a strong adhesive.

On porous papers and fragile coverings, wiping with a sponge wet with water and a remover solution penetrates to the adhesive without the need for cutting or roughing up the surface. Peel carefully, because these materials get mushy when wet.

Never let water or paper remover stand on baseboards or trim, because the chemicals and moisture stain the woodwork. Be espe-

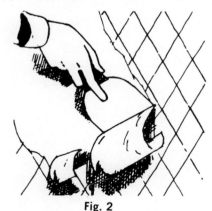

Fig. 2

Removing Wallcoverings. Work a taping knife under wet wallcovering to peel it from the wall (courtesy Hyde Tools).

cially careful when working on drywall not to damage the paper layer on this material.

See *Scrapers, Wallcovering* and *Steaming Loose Wallcoverings*.

REPEAT

The term used to describe the vertical distance between identical points in a wallcovering design. There is no repeat on coverings with a random or straight across match. On drop matches, the repeat varies from 6 inches to a foot and usually measures one-half the height of the design pattern.

ROLLERS, PAINT

A clean paint roller with waterproof nap can be used to spread *paste, sizing,* and *conditioner* on wallcoverings. Choose a short clean nap for your roller when working with wallcoverings.

When sizing a wall, you need to cut in around corners and trim work with a paintbrush before rolling the wall. A roller can also be used to spread paste on strips of wallcovering. Work out of a roller tray, do not spread the paste too thin, and follow the regular procedure of *booking* each strip. The process is the same as if you were using a *paste brush*.

Conditioners can be applied much faster with a roller than a paintbrush. You need to cut in around corners, trim, and workwork before rolling.

See *Hanging Wallcoverings*.

S

SCRAPERS, WALLCOVERING

A wallcovering scraper resembles the hooked scraper used on the exterior of your house for scraping paint, except that the blade is straight. The scraper is used to cut a covering, so moisture intrudes behind the covering and loosens the adhesive. The scraper can also be used to peel a covering while dry. See the illustration.

When slashing a covering to induce moisture intrusion, hold the entire length of the blade against the wall. Slice the covering with gentle pressure. Do not cut too deep, but make sure you penetrate the covering.

To dry strip with the scraper, get a section of the covering loose. Pull it back upon itself as if your are peeling the covering. If you can remove the covering in this way, do as much as you can. When the covering does not budge anymore, work the scraper, with the blade flat against the wall and the handle about 30 to 45 degrees off the wall, between the covering and wall. Work carefully when prying the covering from the wall to prevent damaging the wall. The best scrapers are designed so that you can change blades frequently.

See *Removing Wallcoverings*.

SEAM

The point where two strips of wallcovering join. It can also be the place where the wallcovering meets the ceiling, baseboard, or other woodwork. There are four types of seams used for joining strips of wallcovering: butt joints, lapped seams, wire edge, and double-cut seams. See the illustration.

Butted

Butted joints are by far the most popular and best looking type of seam. The popularity of the butt joint is because lapped or wire edge seams cast shadows and are therefore notice-

Scrapers, Wallcovering. Wallcovering scrapers have replaceable blades that help make wallcovering removal easy (courtesy Hyde Tools).

able on large flat walls. Butted seams are made so that the adjacent edges of trimmed wallcoverings are worked firmly together to form an almost invisible seam.

Double-Cut

Double-cut seams are commonly used on vinyl wallcoverings. The end result is a seam that resembles the butt joint used with the majority of wallcoverings.

Lapped

Lapped seams are not very popular on flat surfaces. They are useful for working coverings around corners and can be used effectively with coverings that have not been trimmed.

Wire Edge

Wire edges are a type of lapped seam. They are most often used with coverings that have their selvages trimmed at home.

See *Butt Joint, Double-Cutting, Lapped Seams,* and *Wire Edge.*

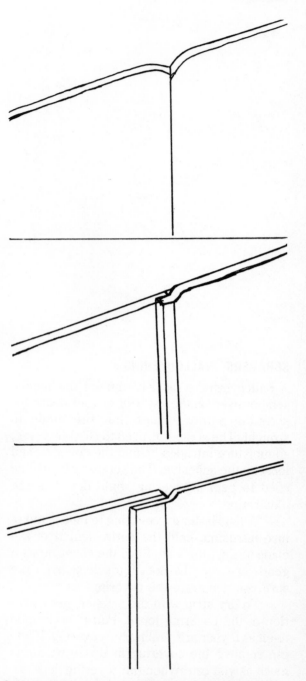

Seam. The three most common types of wallcovering seams: butted (top), wire edge (center), and lapped (bottom).

SEAM ROLLERS

Inexpensive tools designed to press a seam firmly into place and reduce the chances of peeling. See the illustration. Seam rollers should not be used on flocked or embossed papers or on foils, because the rolling mars their surfaces. Instead, the seams of these coverings should be pressed into place with your fingers and a damp sponge.

A seam roller is used on seams after the adhesive begins to dry. Move the roller along the seam from top to bottom, or vice versa, with short, quick rolling movements. If the paste oozes out of the seam during rolling, the covering has not been allowed enough time to dry. Stop rolling, wipe any paste smears from the surface of the covering, and return to another part of the hanging job until the covering has dried enough so that paste does not exit the seam when rolled. Depending on the conditions in your room, 10 to 30 minutes will elapse before seams are ready to roll. Do not forget to

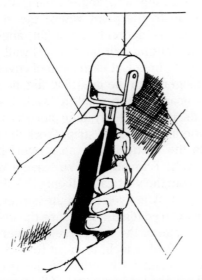

Seam Rollers. Seam rollers are used to press wallcovering seams tightly against the wall (courtesy Hyde Tools).

roll along ceiling and baseboard edges as a precaution against adhesion failures.

SINGLE ROLL

The designation used by wallcovering manufacturers to specify a standard amount of covering. Thirty-six square feet is the usual area of a single roll of covering; however, most manufacturers recommend figuring on getting only 30 square feet of coverage from a single roll. The 6 square feet of waste is a result of matching patterns and trimming.

Although manufacturers have agreed on a standard unit of measurement for a single roll of wallcovering, they do not make all rolls the same width. If you buy a covering that is 18 inches wide, a single roll measures 24 feet in length. A 36-inch-wide covering measures only 13 feet in length. Many manufacturers reduce their handling and shipping costs by selling coverings in bolts. Make sure you know how much coverage to expect from the material you are buying before leaving the store. The salesman will help you convert the size of the area to be covered into single roll measurements.

See *Estimating Quantity of Material*.

SIZING

An inexpensive gluelike substance that is applied to walls and ceilings before hanging wallcoverings. Sizing has several functions. It seals the surfaces against alkali, makes stripping the covering easier, provides tooth for the wallcovering paste, and allows the covering to slide into place more easily than on untreated surfaces. Sizing is available as a powder, gelatin, paste, or liquid. The type you use is largely a matter of personal preference, although you should make sure the sizing is compatible with the paste you plan to use.

Use a roller or brush to apply sizing. Because the sizing will be covered by the wallcovering, its appearance is of little importance. Covering the entire surface is essential. Before applying sizing, scrape all loose paint from the wall, patch holes and cracks with a spackling compound, sand smooth, seal patches, remove switch plates, and protect woodwork and floors agains spatters. On absorbent walls or walls with a rough surface, you may want to apply a sizing that is mixed a little thicker than the recommendations on the package. You can apply two thin coats. Sizing dries so quickly that by the time you finish the first coat, you can start right on the second.

Sizing contains a chemical that turns purple, red or pink in the presence of alkali. Alkali areas are known as hot spots by paperhangers, and they must be sealed or neutralized before hanging the covering. To cure minor hot spots, simply brush on a patch of shellac or sealer over the discolored section. For extensive alkali problems, buy a solution of 28 percent acetic acid. Mix 1 part acetic acid to 2 parts water. Bathe the hot spot with a sponge dipped in this solution. When the discoloration disappears, allow for drying and apply a fresh coat of sizing.

There are also glue and resin sealers that work like sizing as a base for wallcoverings. These materials have the advantage of providing a tooth on glossy or semigloss surfaces without sanding or deglossing. They also form a more water-resistant barrier that prevents damage to walls. These materials are more expensive than sizing and cover less area.

See *New Walls* and *Painted Walls*.

SLANTING WALLS

Many garrets and rooms with dormers have walls that slant. Although these areas may appear difficult to cover, they can be handled effectively by working with shorter strips of covering. Additionally, choosing a random or plain pattern such as small flowers or a woven fabric makes the job easier. Plus, the design does not look awkward when hung around angled corners. Another common practice that takes some of the trouble out of slanted walls is painting the angled wall the same color as the ceiling clear down to the knee wall. Hang a covering on the knee wall only. If you do not have a knee wall, the slanted portion is considered part of the wall area. Hang it accordingly.

When figuring the area of slanting walls, measure the area of each surface (height times width). Add the areas together to get an estimate of the area to be covered. Add an extra roll of material as a precaution against mistakes and waste.

When hanging a covering on slanting walls, it is usually best to cover the inside corners first. Leave outside corners for last. When hanging a covering cn a vertical wall into which a slanting wall angles, hang strips of covering up to the point where the slanting wall begins its descent. Treat the angle between the slanting wall and vertical wall as if it was a ceiling line. Cut each strip of covering 2 inches longer than the greatest distance from the baseboard to the slanting wall. Use the edge of the most recently hung piece as a guide for positioning each new strip. Work the material onto the vertical wall, so it overlaps the slanted wall. Trim so that you leave a ½-inch overlap from the vertical wall onto the slanting wall (Fig. 1). When you reach the corner, cut a strip the desired length. Measure the distance from the edge of the last piece of covering to the corner. Add ½ inch, then cut to size. Hang this piece against the edge of the previous piece. Work the leading edges of the new piece well into the corners of the slanted wall, knee

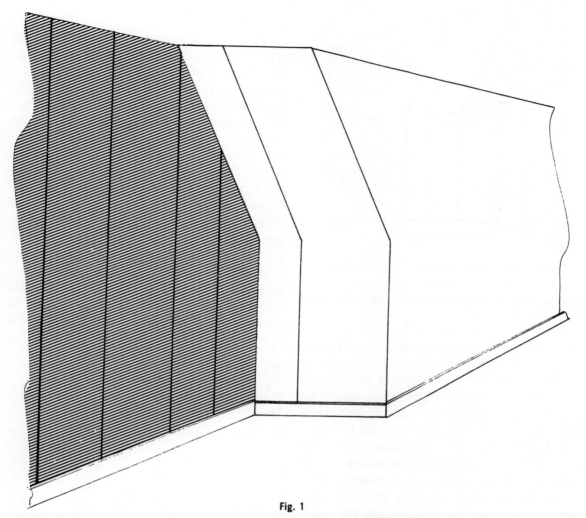

Fig. 1

Slanting Walls. When hanging a covering on a slanting wall, the last strip of material on the vertical wall should overlap the slanting wall.

wall, and baseboard. Cutting a slit through the overlap to the deepest corner allows the material to lie flat.

When you have hung the covering around this inside corner, tackle the slanting wall. On a wall that stretches from the ceiling to floor, this procedure follows the normal method of hanging strips on vertical walls. Be aware

when cutting strips to length that a slanted wall is longer than a vertical wall.

On slanted walls that intersect a knee wall, cover the slanted wall first, then the knee wall (Fig. 2). Measure out from the corner the width of one strip along the intersection of the slanting wall and knee wall. Position a plumb line here and snap a line on the knee wall.

251

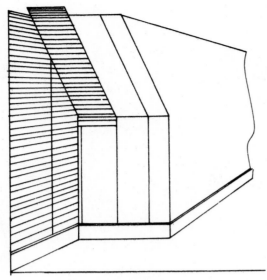

Fig. 2

Slanting Walls. Hang strips on slanted wall first, then tackle the knee wall.

corner and are caught up with the material on the slanted wall.

On outside corners, notice a triangular area of vertical wall between the ceiling and the slanted wall. Save this area until you have hung all the regular strips on this wall (Fig. 3). From the edge of the knee wall, measure out a distance equal to the width of a covering strip. Snap a plumb line from ceiling to baseboard at this distance. The edge of the first vertical strip is aligned on the plumb line. It covers the overlap around the corner of the knee wall and extends to the ceiling, leaving an open uncovered triangle of wall. Ignore the triangle until you have hung the remainder of the wall.

When you come back to the triangle, try to cover it with one piece if at all possible. If not, measure the dimensions of the largest possible piece you can fit. Leave excess at the top, so the piece can be trimmed in the normal way at the ceiling corner. The angled edge (bottom) of

Using the same measurements, snap a line on the slanting wall. Cut the first strip 3 to 4 inches longer than the height of the slanting wall. The placement of this piece should be guided by the plumb line, but make sure it butts into the corner enough to cover the overlap from the vertical wall. Smooth this first piece into place and trim at the ceiling. At the knee wall/slanting wall corner, allow the strip to lap ½ inch onto the knee wall. Continue hanging strips in this manner until you reach the next corner. Work all the way through the corner, leaving a ½-inch overlap. Return to the knee wall.

Hanging covering on the knee wall follows the same procedure as hanging it on vertical walls, except that you should trim the top of each strip so it butts the slanted wall exactly, without overlap. Leave an inch or two of excess at the bottom for trimming the baseboard joint. Work until you turn the next

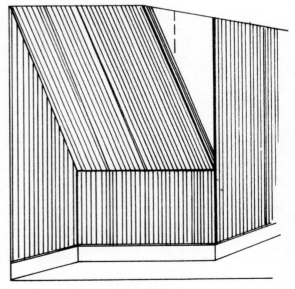

Fig. 3

Slanting Walls. The triangle on outside corners of slanting walls should be saved for covering until last.

the triangular piece should follow the angle of the slanted wall's edge as closely as possible. Make sure to cover the material overlapping the corner.

Cut a small triangular piece to fit in the remaining section of the uncovered wall. Smooth into place and trim at the ceiling. Roll the seams. Return to where you left off hanging the vertical wall strips and continue the job.

When working with a slanted wall bordered on both ends by inside corners, work the covering off the vertical wall and onto one end of the slanting wall. Leave a ½-inch overlap onto the slanted wall and then the knee wall. Leave a ½-inch overlap onto the next vertical wall. Make a plumb line from the highest point of the slanting wall to the baseboard. Use this line as a guide to hang full-sized vertical strips away from the slanting wall. Come back and fit pieces into the triangular area. Work from the plumb line into the deepest corner of the wall.

See *Corners* and *Hanging Wallcoverings*.

SMOOTHING BRUSHES

Used to force wallcoverings onto a wall once the covering has been properly positioned. Standard smoothing brushes have 12-inch-long handles and stiff natural or synthetic bristles. Short (¾-inch) bristle smoothing brushes are used on heavy coverings such as vinyl. Longer (up to 2-inch) bristle smoothing brushes are used for medium-weight and fragile coverings. Keep the brush clean at all times to prevent smearing paste over the surface of your covering.

SPONGING SEAMS

On foils, flocked, embossed, or other fragile coverings, rolling the seams can damage the covering's finish. Use a sponge to press seams tight against the wall.

Sponging Seams. Use your fingers and a sponge to smooth the seams in fragile wallcoverings.

After the covering has dried slightly, press the edges together with your fingers and a damp sponge. See the illustration. If paste oozes out of the seam, the covering has not dried enough. Leave the seam alone for 15 to 20 minutes, then try again. When you have finished pressing the seam, make another check for adhesive on the covering's surface. Wipe paste smears off the covering before they dry.

STAIN-RESISTANT WALLCOVERINGS

Coverings with an exterior coating of vinyl or plastic. These impervious materials allow you to wipe up stains before they damage the wallcovering. Stain-resistant wallcoverings are especially useful in bathrooms, kitchens, and playrooms where the battle against dirt and grease is constant.

See *Cleaning Wallcoverings* and *Vinyl Wallcoverings*.

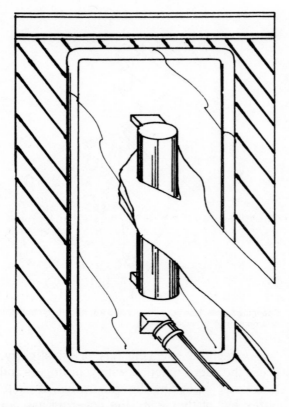

Steaming Loose Wallcoverings. A steamer removes stubborn wallcoverings effectively.

STEAMING LOOSE WALLCOVERINGS

Steamers are electric heating units that turn water into steam. The steam is then used to loosen stubborn coverings prior to peeling. Steamers tend to work quicker and more effectively than wetting down walls with a sponge. These units can be rented from wallcovering or rental stores.

To use a steamer, fill the water reservoir with boiling water. Plug in and turn on the unit. When steam billows out of the perforated plate, place the plate against the wallcovering at one of the top corners of a strip. See the illustration. When water begins to condense around the edges of the plate, move to an adjacent area. Work loosened wallcovering free with a taping knife.

Puncture vinyl-coated wallcoverings so that the moisture can work its way beneath the impervious surface. Roughen the surface with coarse sandpaper, wire brush, or make slits in the covering with a wallcovering scraper.

Be careful when using a steamer on drywall or wood walls. On drywall the steam may damage the paper covering the wall if it is allowed to moisten the surface too much. On wood the moisture may cause the grain in the wood's surface to swell, producing an unpleasant roughness.

See *Removing Wallcoverings.*

STRAIGHTEDGE

A tool with a perfectly true edge that is used to guide razor cutters or utility knives when trimming wallcoverings. See the illustration. Most straightedges are ruled and have a metal edge that resists nicking by cutting tools. Straightedges are especially useful when trimming off selvage or cutting the edges of strips that must butt exactly along ceiling lines or into corners.

STRIP

The term used by paperhangers to describe a length of covering cut from a roll to fit the height of a wall.

STRIPPABLE WALLCOVERINGS

Materials that can be removed from a wall without wetting, steaming, or scraping. They are usually vinyl, plastic, or fabric coverings that leave a fuzzy backing on the wall when peeled free. The backing accepts new wallcovering adhesives.

Do not be tempted to hang a new wallcovering over a strippable one. The adhesive hold-

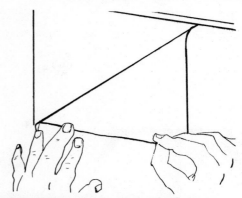

Strippable Wallcoverings. When peeling strippable wallcoverings, begin at one corner and keep the covering folded back on itself to prevent tearing. In most cases wetting is not necessary for removing strippable wallcoverings.

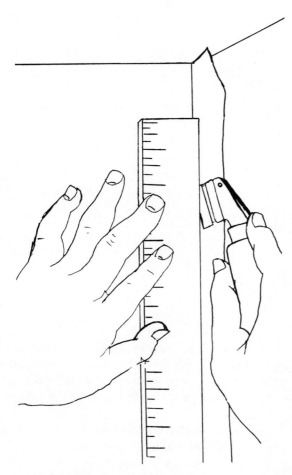

Straightedge. Metal straightedges come in handy for trimming coverings.

ing the strippable wallcovering may be loosened by the moisture from the new wallcovering, resulting in peeling and bubbling problems. Take the extra time to strip these coverings before hanging a new wallcovering.

To strip these coverings, work a fingernail under the top corner of the covering and pull down. Keep the loose flap of covering as close as possible to the wall and pull with steady, firm pressure. This doubling back reduces the possibility of ripping or tearing the covering—a common problem when the covering is pulled out instead of down the wall. See the illustration.

See *Removing Wallcoverings*.

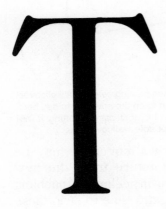

TAPING KNIFE

Although not essential for a wallcovering job, a taping knife can be used as a guide for trimming along ceilings, baseboards, and woodwork. Choose one with a 6-inch flexible blade. See the illustration. It is especially useful for trimming features such as the irregular ends of the apron at the bottom of windowsills. Taping knives also come in handy for scraping wallcoverings from walls and for repairing holes and cracks in walls prior to hanging a wallcovering.

TEARS

Small tears and rips in wallcoverings are easy to repair. For small triangular tears, work the loose flap away from the wall, apply a glue or adhesive to the wall with an artist's brush, and pat the flap back into place. If the flap was crumpled, you may want to roll it with a seam roller to mash it as flat as possible.

On larger damage, where the original tear does not work as its own patch, you have to apply a patch made from an extra piece of the wallcovering. There are two methods for doing this—the torn-patch method and the double-cut method.

The torn-patch method works best with paper coverings that have patterns with small irregular designs and damage that is less than an inch or two across. Select a piece of covering that matches the pattern. You can position the patch over the damage and mark the place where the damage is on the surface of the patch as an aid to tearing. Tear around the mark, leaving at least an inch of overhang on all sides (Fig. 1). Use a tearing motion that produces a feathered edge tapering back from the surface of the covering to the backing. These type of patches should not be made larger than 3 inches wide.

Check the patch for pattern match by holding it to the wall. The patch may not match perfectly, but it is less noticeable than the

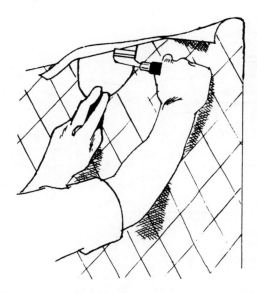

Taping Knife. A taping knife comes in handy as a straightedge when trimming wallcoverings (courtesy Hyde Tools).

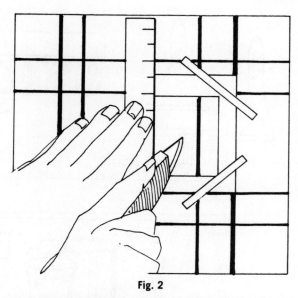

Fig. 2

Tears. To repair a covering using the double-cutting method, tape a piece of covering over the tear and cut to size.

previous flaw. Coat the back of the patch with adhesive or glue, making sure edges are saturated. Position the top of the patch and pat into place. Lower the remainder of the patch into place, adjusting for best fit. When satisfied, pat

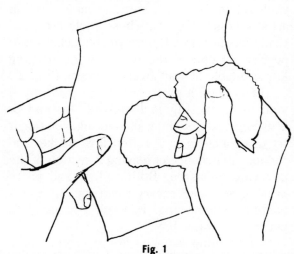

Fig. 1

Tears. To repair small areas of damage on a wallcovering, tear a patch from extra covering and paste into place.

firmly into place. Finish by pressing with a damp sponge.

The double-cut method is useful on vinyl, fabric, foil, and flock that do not respond well to the torn-patch method. Select a piece of extra covering large enough to cover the tear with at least an inch of excess on all sides. Tape the patch into place, so it matches the pattern of your wallcovering. Using a straightedge as a guide, on straight line patterns, cut through both layers of material (Fig. 2). Make sure to use a sharp razor blade cutter as a dull blade will stretch and tear the material, preventing an exact fit. Try to make cuts along the edges of the patterns to make the patch less noticeable. On other than straight patterns, follow the curves of the design as closely as possible.

When the patch has been cut, pull it off. Remove the border. Use a putty knife or other scraper to work the material around the tear off the wall. Check your patch for fit within this hole. If it does not fit, trim as necessary or tape

Fig. 1

Tools. Common wallcovering tools.

a new piece over the hole and recut. Apply adhesive to the wall in the hole. Work the top of the patch into the hole, align the remainder of the patch in place, then pat smooth. Press with a clean damp sponge and check for excess paste or glue exuding from edges of the patch. Recheck in a few minutes to make sure the patch's corners are secure.

See *Bubbles*.

TOOLS

The most common tools required for hanging wallcoverings are drop cloths, stepladders, sponges, taping knives, plumb bobs, straightedges, scissors, paint rollers, 10-quart buckets (two are needed when hanging unpasted coverings), and razor blade or utility knives with plenty of spare blades.

Tools that have specialized uses for hang-

ing wallcoverings include the seam roller, paste brush, water box, smoothing brush, wallcovering scraper, cutting wheel, and an artist's brush (Fig. 1). These tools are relatively inexpensive. Before you buy, check into purchasing one of the wallcovering hanging kits available at wallcovering stores (Fig. 2).

You need a paste brush and pail only if your wallcovering is unpasted. Instead of brushing paste on the wallcovering, you might try using a clean paint roller. It is quicker and reduces the chance of leaving a section of the covering unpasted. Both rollers and paste brushes are unnecessary when you buy a prepasted wallcovering. Instead, you need to purchase a water box.

Smoothing brushes are essential for a good covering job. There are two types—those for use with vinyls and those for more fragile

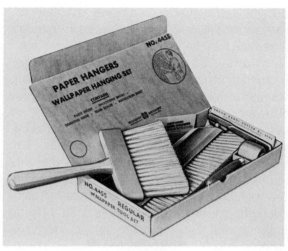

Fig. 2

Tools. Wallcovering kits can be purchased at wallcovering stores. They contain the necessary equipment for doing a professional job (courtesy Wright Bernet).

coverings. The vinyl brush has short stiff bristles. The brush for fragile coverings has longer limper bristles. Smoothing brushes should be at least 12 inches long.

A seam roller is necessary for pressing seams into place. Seam rollers are wood or plastic rollers mounted on short handles. You may be able to eliminate this tool by using your fingers and a sponge to press seams into place (the sponge and finger method is the only alternative when hanging flocked, embossed, or foil coverings). Seam rollers are cheap, so do not bypass them unless absolutely necessary.

A utility knife or razor blade knife is used for cutting wallcovering strips and for trimming, once the strip is in place on the wall. Cutting wheels are used to score ceiling, baseboard, and trim corners. Cutting wheels are not essential for hanging wallcoverings, but on fragile coverings they are the only way to prevent tearing the material.

Scissors should be sharp and as long as possible when used for trimming coverings

along ceiling and baseboard corners. Small scissors are useful in tight corners and around fancy trim work.

As with painting tools, buy the best quality merchandise you can afford. Clean them immediately after each use, and they last through many hanging jobs.

TRIM AND WOODWORK

Trim and woodwork should be painted before hanging a wallcovering. Choose a glossy or semigloss enamel (or a varnish over natural trim), and you can wipe up paste smears easily. Additionally, if you decide to paint woodwork after the covering is in place, the likelihood of damaging the covering with paint drips is increased.

If you are planning to cover only selected walls in a room, paint the other walls and the ceiling prior to beginning the hanging job. On the ceiling, this prevents the possibility of dripping paint onto the newly covered walls. On walls, this allows a cleaner line between the covering and the paint in corners where they meet.

The color you choose for trim depends on personal preference, but as a general rule you should choose one of the lighter, background colors in your pattern. This way trim work seems to blend into the total style of the room. Choosing one of the bolder colors in the pattern for the trim makes the trim stand out. Trim finished in this manner often competes with the wallcovering's pattern.

See *Colors* and *Cornice*.

TRIMMING

There are three basic methods of trimming excess material from a wallcovering strip after it has been smoothed into place on a wall. They are creasing and cutting with scissors, rolling

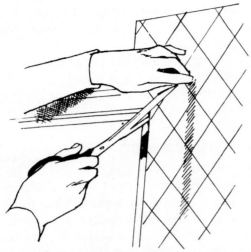

Trimming. After a strip has been positioned, you can use scissors to trim the covering at corners (courtesy Hyde Tools).

with a cutting wheel, and slicing with a razor or utility knife. The method of trimming is determined by the type of material you are hanging. Heavy materials like vinyl and fabric require the use of scissors. Medium-weight materials like coated papers and foils can be trimmed with a razor blade or utility knife. Fragile papers, which may tear under even the sharpest knife, require the services of a cutting wheel.

When using scissors for trimming, smooth the covering into place and work it well into corners. Use the back of the scissors or a blunt edge of a taping knife to score the covering along the corner. Pull the material away just enough to cut with the scissors. Trim the excess off by cutting along the scored line. Smooth the covering back into place and press firmly with a sponge or seam roller.

To use a razor blade or utility knife, work the covering into the corner. Position a guide, such as a straightedge or the blade of your taping knife, along the covering side of the corner. Cut along the corner with the blade,

using the straightedge as a guide. Use smooth, cutting strokes and change blades frequently to reduce the chances of tearing the covering.

Cutting wheels come in two varieties—toothed and smooth. Smooth-bladed cutting wheels score the material more than cut it, allowing you to tear away excess. Toothed cutting wheels poke tiny holes in the material, weakening it and allowing a clean tear. The advantage of using a cutting wheel is that this method of trimming produces a feathered edge that is less noticeable than the clean cut produced by trimming with a blade. Use a taping knife or other straightedge as a guide when trimming with a cutting wheel. Use short vigorous strokes, bearing down hard enough to weaken the material. Go back and tear off excess material. Then smooth the edge onto the wall with a smoothing brush.

Around window and door trim, all three tools have their place during trimming. Wheels are restricted to the long straight cuts, such as along door trim and down the sides of windows. For extremely complicated maneuvering, a combination of scissors and razor blade works the best.

To trim complicated corners, position the strip on the wall so that it laps over the trim. Use scissors to snip diagonal cuts in the covering to the corners of the trim. See the illustration. These cuts allow you to further smooth the covering against the trim. When the covering is as tight as possible against the trim, place a straightedge guide against the corner formed by wall and woodwork. Trim off excess covering with a knife or cutting wheel. In extremely short sections that are impossible to get a guide into, cut the covering freehand. Use the bottom of the "V" formed by the material in the corner as a guide. You may find that scoring the material with the back of your scissors first gives you a more definite line to follow.

VINYL WALLCOVERINGS

Flexible plastic materials that stand up to scrubbing and wear. Because of this resistance to moisture and abuse, vinyls are popular in kitchens, bathrooms, and other heavy wear and tear areas.

Vinyls are available in cloth, fabric, and paper-backed compositions or in all-vinyl materials. Vinyls are slightly more difficult to hang than conventional papers, but many have the added feature of being strippable, thereby making removal easier.

Vinyls require extra-strength adhesives.

Make sure you get the correct paste when purchasing a vinyl material. Vinyls do not stick to themselves, as papers do, so you also need to buy a vinyl-to-vinyl adhesive for areas where lapping is necessary.

Although vinyls are impossible to cut with wheel cutters, you can use the trimming techniques described earlier for scissors and razor knives with excellent results. Vinyls should be hung with butted joint or double-cut seams.

See *Choosing Wallcoverings, Hanging Wallcoverings* and *Materials*.

WALLCOVERINGS

The variety of materials—from foils and plastics to fabrics and papers—that can be hung on walls. Because any material that can be pasted to a wall is considered a wallcovering, the term wallpaper is being used more often to describe those materials made of paper.

Wallcoverings are available in a variety of patterns, colors, and materials. Hanging a wallcovering is often no more difficult than painting a room. These materials add special interest to walls and ceilings, and a wallcovering job may be serviceable long after painted areas need repainting.

WALLPAPER

A subgroup of the broad class of wallcoverings. Wallpaper, as its name implies, is made from paper. Papers can be coated with fabrics, flocks, or vinyl to produce pleasing combinations. Wallpaper is the easiest material to hang.

WALLS, PATCHING

Walls to be covered with a wallcovering should be as smooth and clean as walls to be painted. Patch all cracks and holes with a vinyl spackling. If you choose to use patching plaster, the plaster must cure and then be sealed with shellac to prevent any discoloration of the covering.

Sand all rough spots smooth, because even the slightest imperfection raises a bump in wallcoverings. Raised areas are especially noticeable on glossy surfaced wallcoverings such as vinyl or foils. If the walls are covered by a maze of cracks and imperfections, you may want to forego the spackling and apply a lining paper prior to hanging the regular covering.

If you plan to hang pictures or other decorations in their original holes after hanging a new covering, try sticking a toothpick in the hole. When you hang the strip that covers the hole, remove the toothpick, smooth down the covering, and replace the toothpick, puncturing the covering. This takes the guesswork out of locating the holes after the hanging job is completed.

WHEAT PASTE

A fibrous adhesive made from wheat. It is used primarily on wallpapers and other fragile coverings. When buying a wheat paste, make sure it contains an antimold agent. Consider adding a paste strengthener to help the paste keep the covering on the wall.

WIRE EDGE

A seam where one strip of covering barely overlaps another. It is used with coverings that have a tendency to shrink during drying. The seam is also used effectively with covers that have had their selvages hand-trimmed.

To make a wire edge, the edge of the most recent strip should be positioned to overlap the previous strip 1/16 inch or less. When the strip is in position, roll the seam with an edge roller. Although wire edges are noticeable, they do not stand out as much as conventionally lapped seams.

The How-To-Do-It Encyclopedia of Painting and Wallcovering

by Bob Percival

Here's an incredibly complete sourcebook that covers all types of interior and exterior paints and wallcoverings: the materials used, application procedures, even problem situations *and* practical solutions. Never before have homeowners and do-it-yourselfers had access to such thorough, easy-to-follow information on every facet of painting and wallcovering! You'll find step-by-step instructions (supported by plenty of detailed illustrations) for planning, completing, and clean-up of every conceivable home painting and wallcovering job — all arranged alphabetically and cross-referenced so you can find exactly the information you need when you need it!

You'll find more than 300 entries in all — from acoustic paint to varnish, applicators to wax removal, choosing wallcoverings to sizing, paper removers to trimming. Armed with this hands-on do-it-yourself manual, you'll be able to confidently tackle any type of painting or wallcovering project and get professional-quality results, even if you're a complete novice.

The book is divided into two sections: painting and wallcovering. Separate headings cover definitions of the products used in painting, application techniques, tips on comparing materials and application methods that give the best looking and longest-lasting coatings for different surfaces, what to look for in tools and equipment, how to prepare surfaces for painting, how to apply all kinds of coatings, and practical cleanup methods. The section on wallcoverings describes materials and application techniques, advice on choosing wallpaper styles, hints on tools, and how-to's for avoiding common mistakes (like mismatched patterns, or applying wallcoverings to brand new walls).

There's lots of information on paint styling, maintenance, repairing interior and exterior walls, spray painting, and even figuring your own estimate for a job when hiring out work to a professional painter or paperhanger. Crammed with hundreds of time- and money-saving tips, this outstanding manual deserves a prominent place on every do-it-yourselfer's and home handyman's bookshelf.

Bob Percival has a BA degree in Journalism and Environmental Studies and an MA in Journalism. He worked as a professional painter for five years, painting everything from oil storage tanks and barns to home interiors and exteriors.